E-Z

For Article

MW00322951

Contracts & Sales

With Selected Provisions from Articles 7 and 5

And Other Relevant UCC Provisions

BY:

Jack S. Ezon, Esq.

and

Jeffrey S. Dweck, Esq.

Law Rules Publishing Corporation
Old Tappan, NJ 07675

(800) 371-1271

QUALITY CONTROL EDITOR

Daniel A. Serouya

PRINTED IN CANADA

Library of Congress Catalog Number: 95-79293

ISBN 1-887426-29-9

LAW RULES PUBLISHING CORPORATION
184 Central Avenue
Old Tappan, NJ 07675 - 2234
(800)371-1271

To Mom and Dad
For dedicating themselves to
their children, family, and community
and for their love and support in
everyone of my endeavors.

SUMMARY TABLE OF CONTENTS

USING E-Z RULES FOR CONTRACTS AND SALES

Welcome to E-Z Rules, a new way of presenting federal rules and laws, designed to put the "ease" into *legalese*!

E-Z Rules translates the confusing statutory language of the UCC into plain and simple English. E-Z Rules are designed to give you quick access to important information you often need, without the unnecessary strain of dissecting long, monotonous, statutory texts. And remember, E-Z Rules does this WITHOUT EXCLUDING ANY KEY POINTS OF THE ACTUAL RULE OR STATUTE!

E-Z Rules is easy to use. It has been carefully tailored to meet the needs of both the law student and today's active law firm. In order to take full advantage of the E-Z Rules system, it would be beneficial to review some of its features:

* The rules are **boldly** titled for quick spotting.

* E-Z Rules is laid out so that the entire substance of a rule or statute could be grasped in a single glance.

* All rules follow the format of the Uniform Commercial Code. Where the actual subsection of the rule is used, it is enclosed between parenthesis "( )." <u>All other numbers and letters are produced by E-Z Rules</u> and should, therefore, not be cited to when discussing a rule.

For Example, in §2-711 there are three sections, referred to in E-Z Rules as (1) - (3). These are actual sections used in the U.C.C. and may be called, for example, "subsection (1)" Under subsection (2) there are two subsections, (a) - (b). Since these are surrounded by parentheses, these two may be reference by their names (ex: "§2-711(2)(a)"). Under §2-711(2), however, there consists items labeled "1.", "a.", and so forth. Since these are not enclosed in parenthesis, they are not the letters used by the Uniform Commercial Code.

* All rules follow the Uniform Commercial Code. In order to make the substance more comprehensive, "E-Z Rules bullets" have been added in addition to the official sub-sections found in the actual code. Sub-section letters or numbers surrounded by parentheses "( )" are official sub-sections. All others are E-Z Rule bullet headings.

* Key words and phrases are emphasized with either **bold**, *italic*, or <u>underline</u>. Some words begin with Capital Letters in order to emphasise them. This not only helps in making the rules easier to understand, but has been proven to help the user focus in on pivotal words or phrases, which may otherwise go unnoticed. In addition, certain words have been abbreviated in order to facilitate quick referencing and easier reading.

Note: E-Z Rules are not a substitute for the actual text of the UCC, and should not be quoted or cited to. E-Z Rules is meant to be used as a quick reference and guide to understanding Article 2 of the UCC, and cannot completely replace it. In addition, the "overview" for each section of the "Roadmap to Article 2" is not meant to be a comprehensive teaching tool. It is merely meant to remind the reader of certain key points.

TABLE OF ABBREVIATIONS:

BIOC ..... Buyer In The Ordinary Course
BOL ...... Bill of Lading
CIF .... Cost, Insurance, Freight
C&F ...... Cost & Freight
DOT ...... Document of Title
GFP .... Good Faith Purchaser
HDIC ..... Holder in Due Course
HDN ...... Holder By Due Negotiation
FAS .... Freight Along Side
FOB .... Freight on Board
L/C .... Letter of Credit
PMSI. ..... Purchase Money Security Interest
S/I .... Security Interest

THE E-Z RULES ROADMAP

One of the most beneficial features of the E-Z Rules is its built-in **Roadmap to Article 2.** This section consists of an overview of the key topics of Article 2 and the relevant statutes alongside. The "roadmap" places all sections needed for a given topic at your fingertips, each with a brief overview. Please note that the overview appears in a different typeface than the text of the rule. Also note that where only a portion of a rule is included in the overview, its title is not bolded.

> THE ROADMAP WILL BE MOST BENEFICIAL TO READERS WHO ARE LOOKING TO ANALYZE PROBLEMS. By using the roadmap as a checklist, it will help the reader breakdown a problem and "attack" it in a comprehensive and organized fashion in accordance with the rules.
>
> Studying the Roadmap will also help the reader get an overall picture of the relevant law, and help with grasping the concepts behind Article 2.

The use of the roadmap is one of the most beneficial tools of the E-Z rules, and we strongly recommend it.

ROADMAP TO ARTICLE 2
CONTRACTS AND SALES

IV. The Buyer
A. The Buyer's Obligations: (p.85)
1. **§2-301; §2-309:** Accept Goods
2. **§2-507; §2-511:** Make Payment
3. **§2-603**: Duties upon Rejection

B. The Buyer's Rights (p.89)
1. **§2-513:** Right to Inspect Goods before Acceptance (p.90)
2. **§2-602:** Right to Reject Goods (p.91)
3. **§2-608:** Right to Revoke Goods (p.92)
4. **§2-717:** Buyer's Right to Set-off (p.93)
5. **§2-716:** Buyer's Right to Receive Goods (p.93)

C. Buyer's Remedies: (p.95)
1. Buyer's Remedy Upon Repudiation (p.95)
    a) **§2-609; §2-610; §2-611:** Repudiation (p.95)
    b) Buyer's Remedies Upon Repudiation (§2-610)
        1. Await Performance
        2. Suspend Performance
        3. Resort to Remedies in **§2-711:** (p.102)
            A. Either:
                1) **§2-712**: Cover (p.103)
                2) **§2-713:** Sue Seller for Damages (p.104)
            C. Remedies if Seller Does Not Deliver
                1) **§2-502**: Recover Identified Goods
                2) **§2-716**: Specific Performance; Replevin (p.106)

2. Buyer's Remedies Upon Breach of Warranty: (p.107)
    A) Types of Warranties (p.107)
        1) **§2-312:** Warranty of Title (p.109)
        2) Warranty of Quality
            a. **§2-313:** Express Warranties (p.109)
            b. Implied Warranties
                - **§2-314:** Merchantability (p.110)
                - **§2-315:** Fitness (p.111)
    B) **§2-316:** Disclaiming Warranties (p.112)
    C) Breach of Warranty (p.116)

I. *USING AND UNDERSTANDING ARTICLE 2*

A. *THE UCC:*

- The Uniform Commercial Code ("UCC") governs many commercial transactions throughout the United States.

- What makes the UCC so powerful and important is the fact that every state has adopted at least some portions of it. Many states, however, make minor changes to the original UCC provisions, and it is therefore imperative to check the applicable jurisdiction's version of the UCC.

- The UCC is divided up into 11 "Articles," each dealing with a variety of commercial law issues such as Secured Lending, Checks, Banking, Commercial Paper, Shipping, Letters of Credit, Contracts, and Sales.

- Article 2 of the UCC deals with CONTRACTS FOR THE SALE OF GOODS, which is the main focus of this book. Other provisions of the UCC, however, often come into play when dealing with Article 2 issues. Those most relevant are portions of Article 7, dealing with Carriers and Warehouseman, and Article 5, dealing with Letters of Credit. The sections included in this book are those portions which relate to Article 2 transactions.

B. *USING ARTICLE 2*

- Article 2 of the UCC applies only to transactions (contracts) dealing with the **SALE OF GOODS**.

- Thus, in order to use the rules of Article 2, one must first determine whether we are dealing with GOODS purchased in a SALE transaction (ex: A contract to sell Real Estate does not fall within the scope of Article 2 (they are not goods); Contracts to repair goods are also not governed by Article 2 (there is no sale)). Either other state statutes or state common law governs such contracts).

- It is therefore imperative to ask 3 questions before attempting to apply Article 2 to a particular set of circumstances:
  - Is there a transaction of Sale? (§2-106)
  - Does the Sale involve Goods? (§2-105)
  - Is there a valid contract?

- Once all of these criteria have been filled, one may proceed to study the case in light of Article 2's provisions.

A. **GOODS**: Whether or not the subject of the contract is the Sale of Goods must be determined:

§2-105(1) "Goods":

"**Goods**" are all things which are *movable at the time they are identified to a contract.*

a) The Following are "Goods":
  1. Unborn young animals
  2. Growing crops
  3. Other identified things attached to realty (as described in §2-107: "Goods to be Severed From Realty")

b) The Following are NOT "Goods":
  1. Money in which the price of the contract is to be paid
  2. Investment Securities (see Article 8)
  3. Things in Action

§2-107(1): Goods Severed By Seller:

a. The following is considered a Contract for the Sale of Goods (and therefore governed by Article 2) so long as the material being sold is to be *severed* (i.e. removed) from the Realty (on which they are sold) by the Seller:

1. A contract for the sale of Natural Resources (including minerals, oil and gas) to be removed from the realty

or 2. A contract for the sale of a Structure (or its materials) to be removed from the realty

b. Until such "goods" are severed from the Realty a puported sale of such material is:
    1. Effective as a *Contract to Sell*
    2. Not effective as a *Transfer of Interest*

§2-107(2): Goods Severed By Buyer or Seller:

a. The following will be considered a Contract for the Sale of Goods if the material is to be severed by the <u>Buyer</u> or the <u>Seller</u>:
    1. A contract to sell <u>Growing Crops</u> (apart from the land)
    2. A contract to sell <u>Timber</u> to be cut
    3. Other things attached to realty and capable of severance without material harm to the property (but not described in 2-107(1))

b. Such contracts are deemed Contracts for the Sale of Goods even though the "goods" form part of the Realty at the time the contract was made (therefore, the parties can effect a present sale *before* severance (by identifying the actual goods sold under the contract)).

B. **SALES TRANSACTION**: The transaction involved must be a "Sale."

§2-106(1) Contract for Sale:

a. <u>Limitation to Present and Future Sales of Goods</u>: In this Article (unless the context otherwise requires) the terms *"contract"* and *"agreement"* are limited to those relating to the <u>present or future sale of goods</u>.

b. **"Contract for Sale"** - includes both:
    1. A <u>Present Sale</u> of goods
    and 2. A contract to sell goods at a <u>Future Time</u>.

c. **"Sale"** - a sale consists of the <u>passing of title</u> from the Seller to the Buyer for a price (as per §2-401).

d. **"Present Sale"** - a sale which is accomplished by the making of the contact.

C. **EXISTENCE OF A CONTRACT**: The next section discusses in detail whether, according to Article 2, a contract has been created.

C. *THE STATUTE OF FRAUDS:*

OVERVIEW

- The Statute of Frauds requires that certain contracts be recorded in writing in order to be enforced. These include:
    1. Marriage contracts
    2. Real Estate contracts
    3. Contracts appointing Executors
    4. Contracts appointing Guarantors or Sureties
    5. Contracts which are impossible to be completed within 1 year
    6. **Contracts for the Sale of Goods over $500**

- The Statute of Frauds has been implemented to prevent fraud. By reducing an agreement to writing, the terms of such contracts cannot be easily altered or forgotten. As one can see, the 7 types of contracts requiring that the Statute of Frauds be fulfilled are expected to last long periods of time or relate to large amounts of money.

- The UCC restates the Statute of Frauds. Section 2-201 requires a contract for the sale of goods > $500 to be in writing. However, according to the UCC, a contract violating the SOF (i.e. it is not in writing) may still be enforceable if the Seller *delivers* the goods and the Buyer *accepts* them.

- Contracts enforceable because performance has begun:
    - *Accepted Goods:* An oral contract will be enforced if the Buyer has already accepted the goods; however, the contract will only be enforceable to the extent goods were accepted (ex: if the oral contract called for Seller to deliver 800 pounds of sugar at $1.00 a pound, the enforceable portion of the oral contract will only be up to the quantity that the Buyer accepted. Any other outstanding quantity (promised in the oral agreement) will not enforceable (§2-201(3)(c))).
    - *Special Goods*: An oral contract to make specially manufactured goods (valued more than $500) will only be enforceable if the Seller either (§2-201(3)(a)):
        - Substantially began manufacturing the goods
        - or Made substantial commitments to manufacture the goods (ex: purchased $10,000 of cotton to produce special shirts)

- **Fulfilling the Statute of Frauds**:
    - A formal written contract is not necessary to fulfill the SOF. A memorandum reflecting the creation of a contract is sufficient:
        - <u>Non-Merchants</u> - if one of the parties is not a *Merchant* (as per §2-104), a written memorandum from a party will qualify as a writing if (§2-201(2)):
            - It indicates that a contract was created
            and - It specifies the *quantity*
            and - It is signed (as per §1-201(39)) by the adverse party.

        - <u>Between Merchants</u> -
            - If the transaction is between two merchants, a written letter of confirmation of the contract is sufficient to fulfill the SOF.
            - The confirmation will bind the parties unless the one receiving the confirmation objects to it within <u>10 days</u> after receiving it.

    - <u>Modifications</u>: Modifications of a contract must be in writing if the contract would have had to be in writing (i.e. the contract value after the modification is over $500). (See "MODIFICATIONS").

---

§2-201: Formal Requirements of a Contract:

(1) <u>**Statute of Frauds**</u>:
   a. A Contract for the Sale of Goods for ≥ **$500** must be in **writing** to be enforceable by way of action or defense (except as otherwise provided in this section).
   b. <u>The Writing Requirement</u>:
      1. The writing need only indicate that a contract for sale has been made between the parties.
      2. The writing must be <u>signed</u> by the party against whom enforcement is sought (or his authorized agent or broker (ex: if Seller is suing Buyer, Buyer's signature must be on the writing)).
      3. A writing is not insufficient if it omits or incorrectly states an agreed upon term.
   c. The Contract will not be enforceable under §2-201(1) beyond the quantity of goods shown in such writing.

(2) **Contract Between Merchants:**
  a. <u>Merchant's Confirmation</u>: A Merchant may satisfy the requirements of writing (§2-201(1)) by sending the other Merchant party a confirmation of the contract.
  b. <u>Notice of Objection</u>: The confirmation will be an effective writing unless the party receiving the confirmation gives the sender a *written notice of objection* within <u>10 Days</u> after it received the confirmation.
  c. If the party receiving the confirmation does not properly object to it, it will be effective if:
      1. The writing is in confirmation of the contract
   and 2. It is also sufficient to hold the sender responsible
   and 3. It is sent within a *reasonable time* after the contract was created
   and 4. The party receiving the confirmation has reason to know its contents

(3) A contract which does not satisfy the writing requirements in §2-201(1) (but is valid in all other respects), will still be enforceable if:

   (a) <u>The Goods Are To Be Specially Manufactured</u>:
       1. The goods are to be specially manufactured for the Buyer
    and 2. The goods are not suitable for sale to others in the *Ordinary Course of the Seller's Business*
    and 3. The Seller has either substantially begun their manufacture or made commitments to obtain them:
           a. *Before* any notice of repudiation was received
        and b. Under circumstances which reasonably indicate that the goods are for the Buyer

   or (b) <u>An Admission Is Made</u>
       1. If the party against whom enforcement is sought admits (in his pleadings, testimony, or otherwise in court) that a contract for sale was made, the writing requirement will be satisfied.
       2. The contract is only enforceable (under this provision) up to the quantity of goods admitted.

   or (c) <u>The Goods Under The Contract Have Been Accepted</u>
       1. Payment has been made and accepted
    or 2. Goods have been received and accepted (as per §2-606)

§2-104(1): "Merchant":

A person is considered a "Merchant" if he is *either:*

  a) <u>Dealer</u>: A person who *deals* with goods of the kind

or b) <u>Expert</u>: A person who *either:*

     1) Holds himself out as having <u>*knowledge or skill*</u> peculiar to the type of goods involved in the transaction

    or 2) Employs an Agent, Broker, or other Intermediary who holds himself out as having such *knowledge* or *skill*

II. *THE SALES CONTRACT*

In order to determine whether Article 2 applies to a transaction, one must determine whether a <u>Contract</u> exists.

A. <u>Basic Elements of a Contract</u>

OVERVIEW ⸻⸻⸻⸻⸻⸻

- According to the UCC, a contract need not be formed with any special formality; rather it may be formed in any manner *"sufficient to show agreement"* between the parties (§2-204(1)). This includes conduct of the parties.
- A contract requires the *Mutual Assent* of the parties.
- A contract is usually created when an **"Offeror"** makes an *offer* to an **"Offeree"**; Once the Offeree *accepts* the offer a contract will be formed if there is sufficient *consideration* exchanged by each party.
- Since the Offer and Acceptance are the most basic and initial elements of a contract's formation, it is critical to determine whether an offer has been made and if acceptance has occurred. It is therefore imperative to understand when an offer or acceptance becomes effective:
  - **Offer:** effective when <u>RECEIVED</u>
  - **Acceptance:** effective when <u>SENT</u>
  - **Revocation of Offer/Counteroffer:** effective when <u>RECEIVED</u>

§2-204: **Formation of a Contract:**

(1) **Creation of Contract:** A Contract for the Sale of Goods may be created by:

    a. The conduct of *both* parties (which recognizes the existence of such a contract)

  or b. Any other manner sufficient to show agreement (written, oral or otherwise (subject to Statute of Frauds (§2-201))).

(2) **Time of Creation Not Certain:** An agreement sufficient to constitute a contract for sale may be found even though the exact moment the contract was created is undetermined.

(3) **Open Terms:**

    A contract will not fail for *indefiniteness* if one or more terms are left open, if:

      a. The parties have intended to make a contract

  and b. There is a reasonably certain basis for giving an appropriate remedy

B. *THE OFFER*

OVERVIEW

- **"Offer"** - an offer is an expression which a *reasonable person* would interpret as a present willingness to enter into a bargain.
- <u>Requirements</u>: in order to be a valid offer, two requirements must be present
    1. **INTENT** -
        - The offeror (i.e. the person making the offer) must intend to be inviting acceptance (as per §2-206(1)).
        - <u>Test</u>: the test is whether a reasonable person would construe the "offeror's" expressions as constituting an offer. The offeror's actual intent is therefore not determinative.
        - Often, situations arise when the "offeror" is merely inviting someone to make an *offer*. The following are some examples illustrating how *intent* plays a role in determining whether an offer has been made:
            - <u>Business Letters</u> - for a business letter to be considered an offer, the language must be that which a *reasonable business person* would use in making an offer to buy or sell someone a *definite amount* of property.
            - <u>Advertisements</u> - advertisements are usually considered *invitations to make an offer*; a very misleading ad, however, may be enforced as an offer.
            - <u>Prizes</u> - prizes are usually considered offers, which invite acceptance through performance.
            - <u>Bids</u> - whether a bid is an offer is very questionable. Most courts consider bids binding offers only if they induce reliance.
            - <u>Orders</u> - an order to buy goods is considered an offer (§2-206(2)).

    and 2. **DEFINITENESS** -
        - The terms of the offer must be certain. They cannot be *"illusory"* (ex: I'll buy sugar from you if you want; The "offeror" is not making a definite offer; he is simply informing the Seller that he'll buy sugar from him if the Seller wants him to. The Offeror did not commit to any price or quantity).

- The offer must be definite enough for the offeree to accept.
- The offeror must make some commitment.
- An offer will be deemed *illusory* if the missing terms cannot be filled with the UCC's "gap-filling" provisions (SEE "GAP-FILLING PROVISIONS") (§2-204(3)).
- The more terms left open, the less likely a court will conclude that a binding agreement has been created (§2-204 official comment).

- **Quantity**:
    - Commitment to buy or sell a certain quantity of goods is the most crucial element of a true offer.
    - Quantity is the only element absolutely required since it is virtually impossible to infer what it should be.
    - Output and Requirement Contracts: (§2-306)
        - Output and Requirement contracts are not considered illusory since the parties are, in essence, binding themselves to buying or selling a *good faith quantity*.
            - **Output Contracts** - output contracts bind the Buyer to purchase whatever the Seller produces in *good faith*.
            - **Requirement Contract** - Requirement contracts require the Seller to sell the Buyer whatever quantity of goods the Buyer requires.

- **Price**:
    - If the parties set price at a future market price the contract will be valid (ex: I'll sell you apples for whatever price John Smith is selling his apples for on April 6).
        - Even if a party has the power to fix the price himself the contract is not considered illusory since the UCC's good faith requirement (§1-203) restricts such price within the bounds of good faith (§2-305(2)).
        - If the price is fixed in bad faith, or never fixed at all, the other party has the option of:
            - Canceling the contract
            - or ■ Taking the goods at a *reasonable price* (to be measured at the time and place of delivery)

18

- **No Price**: even if the contract is absent of a price, it is considered illusory under the UCC. The UCC's gap-filling provisions will once again save the contract, and bind the parties to a *reasonable price* (to be measured at the time and place of delivery).

- The Firm Offer:
  - A Firm Offer is an irrevocable offer. It is often known as an *"Option Agreement"* since it assures the other party that it has the option to buy or sell something (usually at a set price).
  - No consideration is needed to enforce a Firm Offer; nevertheless, firm offers are usually made for consideration (ex: for $100, Mark promises to sell Lee 10 lbs of cotton at $1.00 a pound if Mark decides to buy the cotton within the next three months)
  - Requirements to enforce a Firm Offer (§2-205):
    - Offer must be made by a **Merchant**
    - and ▪ In writing
    - and ▪ Signed
    - and ▪ Specifically state that the "option" will be held open (or that it is a "firm offer")
  - The UCC will not enforce a Firm Offer which lasts longer than 3 months.
  - If a time frame for the firm offer is not specified, it shall remain open for a *reasonable amount of time* (but not more than 3 months)

---

§2-206: Offer and Acceptance in Formation of Contract:

(1) Unless otherwise <u>unambiguously</u> indicated by the language or circumstances:

   (a) **An Offer to Make a Contract:**
     1. An offer to make a contract is considered to be *inviting* acceptance.
     2. <u>Mode of Acceptance</u>: Acceptance to such an offer may be made *in any manner and by any medium* reasonable under the circumstances.

(b) **An Order or Other Offer to Buy Goods for Prompt Shipment:**
1. An order or offer to buy goods for prompt or current shipment is considered to be *inviting* acceptance.
2. <u>Mode of Acceptance</u>: Acceptance to such an offer may be made either by:
   a. A prompt promise to ship
   or b. Prompt or Current Shipment (of conforming or non-conforming goods)
3. <u>Shipment of Non-Conforming Goods</u>: The shipment of non-conforming goods does not constitute acceptance of the Buyer's offer if the Seller *seasonably* notifies the Buyer that the shipment was offered only as an "accommodation" to the Buyer.

(2) <u>Reasonable Time of Acceptance</u>: An offeror who is not notified of acceptance within a *reasonable time* may treat the offer as having lapsed before acceptance even if the beginning of the offeree's performance was a reasonable mode of acceptance.

§2-205: Firm Offers:

1. **"Firm Offer"** - an offer which:
   a. Is made by a <u>Merchant</u>
   and b. Is evidenced by a <u>Signed</u> Writing
   and c. By its terms, gives assurance that the offer will be held open

2. A Firm Offer is <u>not revocable</u> for lack of consideration.

3. **Effectiveness of Firm Offer:**
   a. The period of time in which a Firm Offer is irrevocable is either:
      1. For the time stated in the Firm Offer
      2. For a *reasonable time*, if no time is stated
   b. The period of irrevocability may not exceed <u>3 Months</u>

4. <u>Firm Offer on Offeree's Form</u>: Any terms of assurance in a Firm Offer which is made on a form supplied by the <u>offeree</u> must be separately signed by the offeror.

§2-305: Open Price Term

(1) **Price Unsettled:**
>   i) If the parties intend, they can conclude a contract for sale even if they have not yet settled on a price (subject to §2-305(4) below).
>
>   ii) The price of the contract shall be a *reasonable price* <u>at the time for delivery</u> if:
>> (a) Nothing is said about the price
>>
>> or (b) The price is left to be agreed upon by the parties, and they fail to agree
>>
>> or (c) The price is to be fixed in terms of some agreed market which has not been set or recorded (or other standard as set or recorded by a third person or agency (ex: setting the price of cotton at $5.00 over the COMEX price on the date of delivery)) (see §2-305(3) below for the effects of not fixing price).

(2) A **"price to be fixed by the Seller/Buyer"** - means a price fixed by him in <u>Good Faith.</u>

(3) **Fault of a Party**:
>   If the price of a contract is left to be fixed (other than by agreement of the parties), and that price fails to be fixed due to the fault of one party, the other party may:
>> 1. Treat the contract as canceled
>>
>> or 2. Fix a reasonable price on his own

(4) **Failure of Contract**:
>   a) There will be <u>no contract</u> if the parties intend not to be bound unless the price is fixed or agreed upon, and it is not.
>
>   b) <u>Consequences If Contract Fails Due to Absence of Price</u>:
>> 1. <u>Buyer's Obligations</u> - the Buyer must:
>>> a. Return any goods already received
>>>
>>> or b. If the Buyer is unable to return the goods she must Pay the Seller the *reasonable value* of the goods <u>at the time of delivery</u>
>>
>> 2. <u>Seller's Obligations</u> - The Seller must return any portion of the price paid on account.

§2-306: **Output, Requirements, and Exclusive Dealings Contracts**

(1) **Output & Requirement Contracts:**
  a. Terms Measuring Quantity:
    1. **"Output Term"** - a term which measures the quantity of the contract by the Seller's output (ie "Total Production" contract).
    2. **"Requirement Term"** - a term which measures the quantity of the contract by the requirements of the Buyer (ie "Total Needs" contract).
  b. Good Faith Requirement:
    1. "Output" and "Requirement" terms refer to actual output and requirements that occur in <u>Good Faith</u>.
    2. Estimates - if an estimate of output or requirement is included in the agreement, no quantity *unreasonably disproportionate* to the estimate may be:
        a) Tendered by the Seller
      or b) Demanded by the Buyer
    3. In absence of a stated estimate, no quantity which is more than any *normal or comparable* prior output or requirement may be:
        a) Tendered by the Seller
      or b) Demanded by the Buyer

(2) **Exclusive Dealings** - *"Best Efforts Test"*:
  A lawful agreement by either a Seller or Buyer for Exclusive Dealing (in the kind of goods concerned) creates the following obligations (unless otherwise agreed):
    a) <u>Exclusive Right to Sell</u>: Obligation by the Seller to use its <u>*Best Efforts*</u> to supply the goods
    b) <u>Exclusive Right to Buy</u>: Obligation by Buyer to use its <u>*Best Efforts*</u> to promote the sale of such goods

C. *ACCEPTANCE*

OVERVIEW ─────────────────────────────

- Common law recognizes Acceptance to be effective upon *dispatch* only if the offeree accepts in the same or a similar manner as the offeror sent his offer; The UCC allows the Offeree to accept in any *reasonable manner* (§2-206(1)).
- **Methods of Acceptance:**
    - Express Acceptance: Acceptance may be in any manner and by any medium *"reasonable under the circumstances"* (§2-206(1)(a)).
    - Acceptance by Beginning Performance - A party may accept an offer by beginning performance if it notifies the offeror of its intention to accept the offer (§2-206(2)).
    - Acceptance by Shipping Goods - An offer to ship (i.e. an order to buy goods) may be accepted by
        1. Actually shipping the merchandise
        or 2. Promising to ship
    - Shipping Non-Conforming Goods - The UCC recognizes this as (§2-206(1)(b)):
        - Acceptance of the Buyer's offer
        and - A Breach of contract
    - Shipping Non-Conforming Goods With Notice -
        - If the Seller sends goods and notifies the Buyer that they are *substitutes*, the UCC will recognize the shipment as a **counteroffer** (§2-206(1)(b)).
        - The Buyer is under no obligation to "accept" such a counteroffer, but if he does a contract is created.
        - Exact Time of Acceptance: Since many business contracts entail a series of correspondence between the parties, it is often difficult to determine exactly at what point an offer was created. The UCC, therefore, does not require that the exact moment of acceptance be known in order to enforce a contract.

- **Counteroffers**:
  - **Common Law: "Mirror Image Rule"**:
    - Under the common law, only a *"mirror image"* of the offer could act as a valid acceptance. If the offeree "accepted" the offer with any other terms, he will be deemed to have made a *counteroffer*.
  - **"Counteroffer"** -
    - A counteroffer is considered a *rejection* of the offer.
    - Since it is a rejection of the offer, the original offeree's *power of acceptance* is also terminated.
    - In order for a contract to be formed, the original offeror must accept the counteroffer.

(ex: Seller offers to sell Buyer 30 pounds of sugar at $1.00 a pound, to be delivered on January 1. Under common law rules, Buyer may only accept Seller's offer if he accepts all of Seller's terms. If Buyer attempts to accept by saying "I accept to buy sugar at $1.00 a pound, but sugar must be shipped in bags, by December 31" a contract will not be created; rather, Buyer will have made a counteroffer; Buyer is now considered the offeror and Seller the offeree; Seller must now accept Buyer's "counteroffer" in order for a contract to be created).

  - **UCC Rule: Battle of the Forms** -
    - According to the UCC, a contract will be formed even if the offeree accepts an offer with *Additional* or *Different* terms (ex: if the example above, a contract will have been created even though Buyer accepted stating that he wanted the sugar placed in bags) (§2-207(1)).
    - **Exception** - The offeree may opt out of §2-207(1) by expressly stating that a contract will only be formed if the offeror expressly accepts the terms of the counteroffer. (§2-207(1)).
    - "Battle of the Forms": *Additional and Conflicting Terms:* - The UCC attempts to harmonize the additional and conflicting terms of the offer and acceptance (§2-207(2)) (see "TERMS OF CONTRACT" for more detail (§2-207(2)).
    - **Special Note on §2-207**: This notoriously intractable section has been subjected to numerous interpretations, lucidly summarized by Judge Posner in Northrop Indus. v. Litronics Indust. 29 F.3d 1173 (7th Cir. 1994).

§2-206: Offer and Acceptance in Formation of Contract:

(1) Unless otherwise <u>unambiguously</u> indicated by the language or circumstances:

    (a) **An Offer to Make a Contract:**
       1. An offer to make a contract is considered to be *inviting* acceptance.
       2. <u>Mode of Acceptance</u>: Acceptance to such an offer may be made *in any manner and by any medium* reasonable under the circumstances.

    (b) **An Order or Other Offer to Buy Goods for Prompt Shipment:**
       1. An order or offer to buy goods for prompt or current shipment is considered to be *inviting* acceptance.
       2. <u>Mode of Acceptance</u>: Acceptance to such an offer may be made either by:
          a. A prompt promise to ship
       or b. Prompt or Current Shipment (of conforming or non-conforming goods)
       3. <u>Shipment of Non-Conforming Goods</u>: The shipment of non-conforming goods does not constitute acceptance of the Buyer's offer if the Seller *seasonably* notifies the Buyer that the shipment was offered only as an "accommodation" to the Buyer.

(2) <u>Reasonable Time of Acceptance</u>: An offeror who is not notified of acceptance within a *reasonable time* may treat the offer as having lapsed before acceptance even if the beginning of the offeree's performance was a reasonable mode of acceptance.

§2-207: **Additional Terms in Acceptance or Confirmation** (Counteroffer):

(1) **Acceptance With Different Terms**:
- a) The following operates as an acceptance even if it states <u>additional</u> or <u>different</u> terms from the offer if it is made as a:
  - 1. Definite and seasonable expression of acceptance which is sent within a reasonable time
  - or 2. Written Confirmation which is sent within a reasonable time
- b) If Acceptance is expressly made conditional to the offeror's acceptance of the offeree's additional or different terms, then it is considered a counteroffer (and not an acceptance).

(2) **Additional Terms:**
- i) <u>Between Non-Merchants</u>: Additional terms shall be construed as *proposed additions* to the contract.
- ii) <u>Between Merchants</u>: Additional terms shall become part of the contract *unless:*
  - (a) The Offer expressly limits acceptance to the terms of the offer
  - or (b) The additional terms materially alter the offer
  - or (c) Notification of objection to the additional terms has already been given (or is given within a reasonable time after notice of the additional terms is received)

(3) **Contracts Implied By Conduct**:
- a. <u>Conduct</u> by both parties which recognizes the existence of a contract is sufficient to establish a contract for sale (even though the writings of the parties do not otherwise establish one).
- b. <u>Terms of Contracts Implied from Conduct</u>: The terms of such a contract (implied by the parties' conduct) shall be:
  - 1. Those terms on which the writings of the parties agree
  - and 2. Any supplementary terms incorporated under any other provision of this Act

D. *CONSIDERATION:*

OVERVIEW

- Common law used to require contracts to be *"sealed"* in order to be enforceable. The seal was meant to formalize the contract process in order to prevent fraud.

- Today the UCC and most jurisdictions do not rely on a such a seal to create a valid contract. Rather, *consideration* is sufficient to make a contract enforceable (§2-203).

- In order for a contract to be valid, each party must exchange promises in return for promises or actions. Such consideration may be:
    - Something which is a gain to the promissor
  or - Something which is a loss, forbearance or detriment to the promisee
  or - Something which induces the promise

- When dealing with the Sale of Goods, consideration usually involves:
    - The Buyer's promise to pay for the goods in exchange for the Seller's promise to ship them
  and - The Seller's promise to ship the goods in exchange for the Buyer's promise to pay for them
- **"Bargained For" Consideration:**
    - Consideration must be *"bargained for"* when creating a contract. Thus, consideration must be a present or future promise to perform (if it was already done, it would not be bargained for).
    - PAST CONSIDERATION IS NO CONSIDERATION since it is not "bargained for" (ex: The following is an invalid contract: "I sell Isaac my watch in return for the services he performed for me last week," since Isaac performed before the contract was made).

- **Sufficiency of Consideration:** It is rare for a court to check into the "adequacy" of consideration. Only in rare cases of fraud or unconscionability will a court look into whether the consideration was enough to exchange for the other party's promise.

§2-203: Seals Inoperative:

The common law rules relating to <u>Sealed Instruments</u> do not apply to:
  1. A writing evidencing a contract for sale
  or 2. An offer to buy or sell goods

E. TERMS OF THE CONTRACT:

1) Gap Filling Provisions

OVERVIEW ─────────────────────────────

- The UCC recognizes the fact that business people usually do business without the constant guidance of a lawyer. In doing so, many business people use preprinted order forms, invoices and confirmation forms in the course of a sales transaction.

- Since business people deal with each other so frequently, they often only write down crucial terms (ex: send me 10 lbs of sugar). There may be many contractual terms which they do not discuss, yet assume apply, either from their past dealings or the general practice in the trade.

- To alleviate the problems that arise in the course of such business, the UCC features several "gap-filling" provisions and other mechanisms to "complete" the contracts created by business people in their daily transactions.

- Basically, Article 2 is a list of many "default" provisions which would be "added" should any contract neglect to deal with (or improperly deal with) certain essential terms.

- Almost every section of Article 2 can be bypassed with specific clauses in the parties' contract saying that they have agreed otherwise; it is therefore very important to know the UCC when drafting contracts so that one may be aware of the options available and the issues that arise with respect to the particular clauses included.

- **Examples Gap Filling Provisions:**

  - **Price**: If the parties have never reached a decision as to the price of the goods, it shall be a *reasonable price* at the time and place of delivery (§2-305(1)).

  - **Payment**: Sales are presumed to be Cash on Delivery ("COD"), and thus, payment is due upon delivery of the goods or documents (unless the parties arrange credit terms) (§2-310).

- **Delivery**:
    - *Place:* If the contract is silent about delivery, delivery shall take place at the Seller's place of business (the Buyer must pick it up) (§2-308).
    - *Time:* If the contract does not mention a delivery date, delivery should be made within a *reasonable time* after the contract is made (§2-309(1)).

- **Risk of Loss**:
  If the contract calls for the Seller to deliver the goods, but does not specify whether Risk of Loss should pass when they arrive at the Carrier or when they reach the Buyer's place, Risk of Loss shall pass when they reach the Carrier (§2-509).

- **Duration**: If the contract does not state when it will end, termination shall occur after (§2-309(3)):
    - A *reasonable time*
  or - Upon *reasonable advance notice* to the other party

- **Quantity**: Quantity is one thing which the UCC will not "fill" into the contract.

---

§2-204(3) Open Terms:

A contract will not fail for *indefiniteness* if one or more terms are left open, if:

    a. The parties have intended to make a contract

and b. There is a reasonably certain basis for giving an appropriate remedy

2) *Battle of the Forms*

OVERVIEW

- <u>Battle of the Forms</u>: *Additional and Conflicting Terms:* The UCC attempts to harmonize the additional and conflicting terms of the offer and acceptance (The UCC allows such an acceptance since most business people make offers and acceptances on preprinted forms which contain certain terms on them (ex: a purchase order form). In order to facilitate the creation of a contract between such parties, the UCC handles such additional and conflicting terms separately).
    - **Additional Terms:** If the offeree accepts an offer with new terms (ex: In the example above, Buyer wants sugar shipped in bags), such new terms may become part of the contract, depending upon the parties involved.
        - <u>Non-Merchants</u> - if one of the parties is not a Merchant, any new terms are considered *Proposals* (§2-207(2)). These "proposals" will become part of the contract only if:
            - The parties expressly agree to modify the contract to add them in.
            - or ■ The parties' course of performance implies that they have been accepted.

        - <u>Between Merchants</u> - if both parties are Merchants the additional terms will *automatically* become part of the contract, *unless*:
            - **Original Offeror Objects:** If the original offeror objects to the new terms in the "acceptance" they will not automatically become part of the contract. The original offeror must object to such terms as follows:
                - <u>Advanced Objection</u>: The offeror must specifically state (in his offer) that additional terms may not be contained in an acceptance (§2-207(2)(a)).
                - or ■ <u>Subsequent Objection</u>: The offeror must object to the new terms within a *reasonable time* after the are received (§2-207(2)(c)).
            - **Terms Materially Altering Contract**: Any additional terms of the acceptance which materially alter the original terms of the offer will not automatically become part of the contract (§2-207(2)(b)).

■ **Conflicting Terms:** The UCC is not very clear as to terms of the offer and acceptance that conflict (ex: Seller offered to ship sugar on January 1; Buyer "accepted," requiring shipment on December 31). As the comments indicate, courts have ruled on this matter in three basic manners:
  ■ No contract created
  ■ The UCC considers conflicting terms as if they are "missing terms", and the UCC Gap-filler provisions determine what such terms shall be.
  ■ Conflicting terms will prevail if they do not materially alter the original offer
  ■ If such express, written modes of acceptance cannot be harmonized to construe the creation of a contract, a contract can still be made if the parties begin performance (as per §2-207(3)). In such a situation, the UCC's gap-filling provisions will prevail.
  ■ **Important Note:** §2-207, which discusses the "Battle of the Forms," has been subject to many different interpretations. Although many courts follow the interpretations described above, some courts differ.

---

§2-207: Additional Terms in Acceptance or Confirmation (Counteroffer):

(1) **Acceptance With Different Terms**:
  a) The following operates as an acceptance even if it states <u>additional</u> or <u>different</u> terms from the offer if it is made as a:
    1. Definite and seasonable expression of acceptance which is sent within a reasonable time
  or 2. Written Confirmation which is sent within a reasonable time
  b) If Acceptance is expressly made conditional to the offeror's acceptance of the offeree's additional or different terms, then it is considered a counteroffer (and not an acceptance).

(2) **Additional Terms:**

   i) <u>Between Non-Merchants</u>: Additional terms shall be construed as *proposed additions* to the contract.

   ii) <u>Between Merchants</u>: Additional terms shall become part of the contract *unless:*

      (a) The Offer expressly limits acceptance to the terms of the offer

    or (b) The additional terms materially alter the offer

    or (c) Notification of objection to the additional terms has already been given (or is given within a reasonable time after notice of the additional terms is received)

(3) **Contracts Implied By Conduct**:

   a. <u>Conduct</u> by both parties which recognizes the existence of a contract is sufficient to establish a contract for sale (even though the writings of the parties do not otherwise establish one).

   b. <u>Terms of Contracts Implied from Conduct</u>: The terms of such a contract (implied by the parties' conduct) shall be:

    1. Those terms on which the writings of the parties agree

  and 2. Any supplementary terms incorporated under any other provision of this Act

3) *Parol Evidence*

OVERVIEW ─────────────────────────────

- **"Parol Evidence"** refers to information or circumstances not reflected in a contract, which may affect the terms of the contract.
    - Under the common law version of the Parole Evidence Rule, courts would not allow parties to introduce evidence regarding oral agreements made *before* a written contract was signed (rationale: if the parties would go through the trouble of writing up a contract, they should include any agreements or understandings had made before the contract was written).
    - The Parole Evidence Rule comes into effect when the parties put their contract in a writing intended to be a *Final Expression* of their agreement (this is often known as a "Completely Integrated Agreement")(§2-202). In such a case, the following evidence will not be admitted (§2-202):
        - Evidence of Prior Agreements
      or - Evidence of any Contemporaneous Oral Agreements
    - Problems often arise when such writings do not reflect all of the agreements and assumptions made between the parties.

- **UCC Rule:** The UCC limits the use of the Parole Evidence Rule to 3 situations:

    - Evidence Explaining Contractual Terms (§2-202(a)) - normally parol evidence may be used to interpret or explain terms of a contract (§2-202(a) ex: usage of a term in the trade, the course of the parties' dealings, or the course of the parties' performance).

- <u>Evidence of Consistent or Additional Terms</u> (§2-202(b)) -
  - Consistent or Additional terms may be admitted if (§2-202 official comment 3):
    1. The parties <u>did not</u> intend their writing to be the *complete and exclusive* statement of the terms of their agreement (§2-202(b)).
    and 2. The additional/consistent terms are not material enough that they would have *definitely* been included in the writing (ex: A term specifying that sugar should be shipped in 5 pound bags may be considered an additional or consistent term since it is possible that the parties may have "forgotten" to include such a term, but a term saying that the sugar will be sold at $1.00 a pound instead of the regular price of $1.50 would certainly have been included in any writing the parties would have made).

- <u>Evidence of Fraud, Misrepresentation, or Mistake</u> - parol evidence may be used to prove the existence of fraud, misrepresentation or mistake.

2-202: Final Written Expression; Parol or Extrinsic Evidence:

1. <u>Final Written Expression</u>: The following are considered Final Written Expressions of the parties:
   a. Agreed upon terms reflected in a <u>Confirmatory Memorandum</u>
   or b. Terms set forth in a <u>Writing</u> which were intended to be a *Final Expression* of their agreement (on those terms)

2. **Writing Cannot Be Contradicted:** The terms of a Final Written Expression CANNOT be contradicted by evidence of any:
   a. Prior Agreement
   or b. Contemporaneous Oral Agreement

3. **Writing May Be Explained:** A Final Written Expression may, however, be *explained* or *supplemented* by:
   (a) The Course of Dealing or Usage of Trade (§1-205) or by the Course of Performance (§2-208)
   and (b) Evidence of consistent additional terms, *unless* the court finds the writing was intended by both parties as a <u>complete</u> and <u>exclusive</u> statement of all the terms of the agreement

§2-208: **Construction of Contract:**

(1) **When Course of Performance Relevant:** The <u>Course of Performance</u> (accepted or acquiesced in without objection) will be relevant in determining the meaning of the agreement between the parties when:

    a. The contract for sale involves repeated occasions for performance by either party

and b. The non-performing party knows the nature of the other party's performance

and c. The non-performing party had an opportunity to object to the nature of that performance

(2) **Interpretation of Contract:**

    a) When interpreting the terms of a contract, the following factors shall be construed to be <u>consistent</u> with each other *whenever reasonable:*

        1. The Express Terms of the agreement

    and 2. Any Course of Performance

    and 3. Any Course of Dealing

    and 4. Any Usage of Trade

    b) When it is unreasonable to read the above factors consistently, then:

        1. <u>The Express Terms</u> - shall be used to construe the "Course of Performance"

    and 2. <u>The Course of Performance</u> - shall be used to construe both

        a) The "Course of Dealing"

        and b) The "Usage of Trade" (as per §1-205)

(3) The <u>Course of Performance</u> shall be relevant to show the existence of a waiver or modification of any term inconsistent with such Course of Performance (subject to §2-209).

F. *MODIFICATION AND WAIVER:* (§2-209)
OVERVIEW ————————————————————————

A. **Modification**:
- Consideration: Unlike the common law, new consideration is NOT needed to modify a contract if it is modified in good faith (§2-209(1))
- Writing: Modifications must be in writing if the contract itself would be required to be in writing under the SOF (ex: If the contract was for goods over $500 and the modification increases the price of the contract [ex: contract originally for 100 coats at $45.00 each (total $450) was increased to $150 coats at $40 each (total $600)] the modification must be in writing). (§2-209(2)).
- *Good Faith:* Good faith is required in modifying a contract (§1-203). The modification must have a *legitimate commercial reason* (§2-209 official comment 2).

B. **Waiver**:
- Even if a party's attempt to modify a contract proves to be invalid (ex: Statute of Frauds requirement is not fulfilled), a waiver may exist (§2-209(4)).
- A *Waiver* will prevent a party from avoiding the terms of the attempted modification; thus, although the modification itself is not valid, the waiver will allow the parties to proceed as if the modification were valid.
- A Waiver will be deemed to exist if (§2-209(5)):
  - The party attempting to modify the contract *changes its position in reliance* of the modification
  - and The other party did not **retract** the waiver by demanding strict adherence to the original contract.

§2-209: Modification, Rescission and Waiver:

(1) **No Consideration Required for Modification**: A modification of a sales contract does not require consideration to be binding.

(2) **Writing Requirement:**
    a. An agreement cannot be rescinded or modified without a signed writing if the original agreement:
        1) Is in <u>writing</u>
    and 2) Is <u>signed</u>
    and 3) Requires that modifications or rescissions be made with a signed writing
    b. Such a term (requiring a modification or rescission to be in writing) must be <u>separately signed</u> if:
        1) One party is not a Merchant
    and 2) The term is on a form supplied by the party who is a Merchant

(3) **Statute of Frauds Requirement:**
    The requirements of the Statute of Frauds (§2-201) must be satisfied if the modified contract falls under §2-201(1) (i.e. it is or is modified to be a Contract for the Sale of Goods for ≥ $500).

(4) **Creation of Waiver**: Although an attempt to modify or rescind a contract fails (because it is not a signed writing (§2-209(2) or (3) above)), it can operate as a <u>Waiver.</u>

(5) **Retraction of Waiver:**
    a. A party who has made a waiver affecting an *executory portion* of a contract may retract the waiver by giving reasonable notice to the other party that <u>Strict Performance will be required</u> of any term waived.
    b. In order for the retraction of the waiver to be effective, the other party <u>must receive the notification</u> requiring strict performance.
    c. A party will not be able to retract such a waiver if it would be unjust in view of a *material change of position* in reliance on the waiver.

G. *EXCUSES FOR NON-PERFORMANCE:*

OVERVIEW

The following is a list of excuses which a party may use to escape its obligation to perform.

- **Invalid Contract:**
    - No contract - a contract was never actually created
    - Statute of Frauds not fulfilled - a contract for the sale of goods over $500 was never put into writing, and is therefore unenforceable (§2-201(1)).

- **Repudiation:** If a party repudiates, the non-repudiating party may suspend performance (§2-610(c)) or cancel the contract (§2-703(f); §2-711(1)).

- **Impossibility** - When dealing with a Sale of Goods, a contractual obligation will be excused for *impossibility* in the following situations:
    - Unproduced Goods: If a contract specified certain means of producing or obtaining the goods, and such means of obtaining or producing them is no longer available (§2-615).
    - Identified Goods: If Unique or Identified goods are destroyed (§2-613).
    - Goods From an Identified Inventory: If the contract calls for goods from a particular inventory and that inventory is destroyed (ex: The contract calls for Seller to ship Buyer $50 pounds of wheat located in the silo on Grant Avenue; if the silo on Grant Avenue burns down the Seller can avoid the contract even if he has wheat stored in a silo down the road)(§2-613).

- **Commercial Impracticability** (§2-615)
    - Commercial Impracticability will excuse a party from performing under a contract when *unforeseeable circumstances* develop (§2-615).
    - Commercial Impracticability is usually a valid excuse for the **Seller** not to perform.
    - Basic Requirements for Commercial Impracticability to occur:
        1. Performance becomes either:
            - Highly impracticable
            - or Unreasonably expensive
            - or Of little value to the promisee
        - and 2. The impracticability arises without fault
        - and 3. The contract was made with the *basic assumption* that the event/risk would not occur
        - and 4. The problem was unforeseeable
        - and 5. Cost increases were unforeseeable and drastically high.
    - Commercial Impracticability is easier to prove than impossibility since it relies on more of a subjective test (i.e. even though performance is possible, it may be excused if it is unreasonable).

- **Commercial Frustration** (§2-615)
    - Commercial Frustration excuses performance when performance by the promissor (usually the Seller) would deprive the promisee of any benefit.
    - Commercial Frustration is usually a valid excuse for the **Buyer**.
    - Basic Requirements for Commercial Frustration:
        - The event/problem causing the commercial frustration was underlying unforeseeable
        - and The Value of the performance is *Totally* or *Nearly Totally* destroyed
        - and The promisee's benefit was a *basic assumption* of the contract (ex: Seller promises to sell Buyer cabinets to be used in Buyer's new store. If, after the contract is executed, Buyer's store burns down, Buyer will have no use for the cabinets, and will therefore be excused from buying them from the Seller.)
    - Unlike impossibility, the promisee is not prevented from performing; rather, performance is excused because return performance has become worthless to the promisee.

- **Mistake** (§2-615)
  - When the parties make a mistake about a *basic fact* or *assumption* of the contract, it may be avoided.
  - <u>Test</u>: Courts usually look to see if the mistake was *material* by checking to see if the contract would have been made had the truth been known.

- **Unconscionability** (§2-302)
  - According to the UCC a court will refuse to enforce a contract if its terms *"shock the conscience of the court"* (See §2-302 official comment).
  - Business-people using standardized forms with terms strongly in their favor often fall prey to the unconscionability excuse, especially if they are dealing with <u>consumers</u>.

- **Fraud/Misrepresentation** (§2-721)
  - <u>Misrepresentation</u>: If a material misrepresentation of fact *reasonably induces* a party to enter into a contract, that party may avoid the contract.
  - <u>Fraud</u>: If the misrepresentation was made with intent to deceive (*scienter*), courts are more likely to allow a party to avoid the contract and perhaps even award punitive damages.

- **Waiver** (§2-209)
  - A party can be excused from performance if the other party has waived its right to performance due.
  - Waiver usually occurs when a party does not protest the other party's neglect to perform or altering of the terms of performance.

  (ex#1: Buyer never pays for goods shipped and Seller neglects, within a reasonable time after shipment, to notify Buyer that he expects Buyer to pay in full immediately. ex#2: Buyer sends Seller a check for the goods, but the check is 20% less than the contract price. Buyer's letter accompanying the check reads: "Goods not as nice as I thought, I'm reducing price by 20%." If Seller does not demand full payment within a reasonable time, Seller will not be entitled to the remaining 20%.)

- **Economic Duress**
  - A party may avoid a contract if it was made under duress.
  - When dealing with goods, duress can usually be found when a party is induced into entering into a contract by the other party's threats.
  - <u>Requirements of Economic Duress</u> - most courts require the following conditions to be fulfilled in order to be excused from a contract for economic duress:
    1. The Seller threatens not to deliver the goods
    2. The Buyer can't obtain the goods from any other source
    3. Ordinary breach remedies would be inadequate (ex: Buyer's goodwill is in jeopardy)

- **Incapacity** - A party may avoid a contract if he never had the capacity to enter into a contract to begin with. An insane person or an infant (a person under the age of 18) are examples of people who can avoid a contract for incapacity.

---

§2-201(1) Statute of Frauds:

  a. A Contract for the Sale of Goods for ≥ **$500** must be in **writing** to be enforceable by way of action or defense (except as otherwise provided in this section).
  b. The Writing Requirement:
    1. The writing need only indicate that a contract for sale has been made between the parties.
    2. The writing must be <u>signed</u> by the party against whom enforcement is sought (or his authorized agent or broker (ex: if Seller is suing Buyer, Buyer's signature must be on the writing)).
    3. A writing is not insufficient if it omits or incorrectly states an agreed upon term.
  c. The Contract will Not be enforceable under §2-201(1) beyond the quantity of goods shown in such writing.

§2-610(c):Rights of Aggrieved Party upon Anticipatory Repudiation:

The aggrieved party may:
- (a) <u>Await Performance</u> - from the repudiating party, for a *commercially reasonable time*
- or (b) <u>Resort to Breach Remedies</u> (as per §2-703 (for Seller) or §2-711 (for Buyer)) - even if he told the repudiating party that he will wait for performance (subsection (a))
- or (c) <u>Suspend Performance</u> - The aggrieved party may suspend his own performance.
- or d) <u>Identify and Salvage Goods</u> - The Seller may identify goods to a contract or salvage unfinished goods (as per §2-704).

§2-613: Casualty to Identified Goods:

(a) **Total Loss:** A contract may be <u>avoided</u> if:
- 1) The contract requires that the goods be identified when the contract is made
- and 2) <u>All</u> of the identified goods suffer from a casualty
- and 3) The casualty is not the fault of either party
- and 4) *Either*:
  - a) The risk of loss did not yet pass to the Buyer
  - or b) The contract was a "No Arrival, No Sale" contract (as per §2-324 (in a proper case))

(b) **Partial Loss or Deteriorated Goods:**
- 1) The Buyer has the option of <u>avoiding</u> or <u>accepting</u> the contract if:
  - a) The contract requires that the goods be identified when the contract is made
  - and b) *Either*:
    - 1. <u>Some</u> of the identified goods suffer from a casualty
    - or 2. The goods have deteriorated so much that they do not conform to the contract
  - and c) The casualty is not the fault of either party
  - and d) *Either*:
    - 1. The risk of loss did not yet pass to the Buyer
    - or 2. The contract was a "No Arrival, No Sale" contract (as per §2-324)

- 2) <u>Accepting Goods at a Discount</u>:
  - a) The Buyer may accept the goods and receive a discount for the deterioration or deficiency in the goods.
  - b) If the Buyer receives such a discount he will not have any other rights against the Seller.

§2-615: Excuse by Failure of Presupposed Conditions: ("Commercial Impracticability")

(a) Delay In Delivery/Non-Delivery:
The Seller is not considered to have breached its contract if he delays delivery or fails to deliver goods (in whole or in part) if:
   1. The Seller had complied with (b) and (c) below
and 2. The agreed upon manner of performance has become *impracticable*, either by
   - a. The occurrence a certain event, if the contract was made with the basic assumption that such an event would not occur
   - or b. Good Faith compliance with any foreign or domestic governmental regulation or order (whether or not it later proves to be invalid)

(b) Diminished Number of Goods:
   1. Allocation of Goods: If the causes in (a) (above) affect only part of the Seller's capacity to perform (by reducing the amount of goods he has to ship) the Seller must allocate production and delivery of the goods among all of his customers.
   2. Guidelines for Allocation: The Seller must allocate the goods according to these guidelines (in any manner which is fair and reasonable):
      - a) The Seller does not have to allocate the goods only to customers with outstanding orders.
      - b) The Seller may allocate goods to "regular customers," even though they do not have outstanding orders for goods.
      - c) The Seller may allocate goods for his own requirements or for future manufacture.

(c) Notice to the Buyer:
   1. The Seller must *seasonably* notify the Buyer of the delay or non-delivery.
   2. If the Seller will be allocating goods (as per (b) above), he must *seasonably* notify the Buyer of the estimated quantity he will be shipping.

d) This Section is subject to §2-614 and to any "greater" obligation which the Seller may assume.

§2-614: Substituted Performance:

(1) **Substitute Delivery:** Substitute Performance must be Tendered and Accepted if:

    a) *Either*:

        1. The agreed berthing, loading or unloading facilities fail

    or 2. An agreed type of Carrier becomes unavailable

    or 3. The agreed upon manner of delivery otherwise becomes commercially impracticable

  and b) A *commercially reasonable substitute* is available

  and c) Neither party is at fault

(2) **Substitute Payment:**

    a) *Before Delivery Begins*:

      The Seller may Withhold or Stop Delivery if:

        1) The Agreed upon means or manner of payment fails (due to foreign or domestic governmental regulations)

      and 2) The Buyer does not provide a *commercially substantial equivalent* manner of payment

    b) *After Delivery Begins*:

      The Buyer's obligation to pay the Seller will be discharged if:

        1) Payment is made in the manner provided for by the governmental regulations

      and 2) Such regulations are not *discriminatory*, *oppressive*, or *predatory*.

§2-302: Unconscionable Contract or Clause:

(1) **Treatment of Unconscionable Contracts or Clauses**: If the court finds (as a matter of law) a contract or any clause of the contract to have been *unconscionable* at the time it was made, the court may:

    a. Refuse to enforce the entire contract

  or b. Refuse to enforce only the unconscionable portions of the contract

  or c. Limit the application of any unconscionable clause to avoid any unconscionable result

(2) **Proving Unconscionability**:
   a. When a contract clause appears unconscionable, or when a party claims it is unconscionable, the parties shall have a reasonable opportunity to present evidence (to aid the court in making its determination).
   b. Evidence presented to the court may include evidence as to:
      1. The <u>commercial setting</u> of the contract
   and 2. The <u>purpose</u> of the contract
   and 3. The <u>intended effect</u> of the contract

§2-209: Modification, Rescission and Waiver:

* * * *

(3) **Statute of Frauds Requirement:**
   The requirements of the Statute of Frauds (§2-201) must be satisfied if the modified contract falls under §2-201(1) (i.e. it is or is modified to be a Contract for the Sale of Goods for ≥ $500).

(4) **Creation of Waiver**: Although an attempt to modify or rescind a contract fails (because it is not a signed writing (§2-209(2) or (3) above)), it can operate as a <u>Waiver.</u>

(5) **Retraction of Waiver:**
   a. A party who has made a waiver affecting an *executory portion* of a contract may retract the waiver by giving reasonable notice to the other party that <u>Strict Performance will be required</u> of any term waived.
   b. In order for the retraction of the waiver to be effective, the other party <u>must receive the notification</u> requiring strict performance.
   c. A party will not be able to retract such a waiver if it would be unjust in view of a *material change of position* in reliance on the waiver.

III. *THE SELLER:*

A. *SELLER'S OBLIGATIONS:*
OVERVIEW —————————————————————

Unless otherwise agreed, the Seller has the following
  obligations:
  1) **Deliver Goods** (§2-301)
    ▪ Seller must ship goods within a <u>Reasonable Time
      for Delivery</u> (§2-309)
    ▪ To determine when *"reasonable time for delivery"*
      occurs, the UCC looks at the following factors:
      ▪ Industry Norm
      ▪ Customary practice between parties (ex: does
        Seller always send Buyer's order overnight?)
      ▪ <u>Terms of Delivery</u> (see "RISK OF LOSS" below):
        ▪ *Destination Contract* - Seller maintains
          risk of loss until the goods arrive at
          their destination (§2-504)
        ▪ *Shipment Contract* - Seller maintains
          risk of loss until the goods are
          delivered to the Carrier (§2-504)
      ▪ Delivery is presumed to be a *Shipment*
        contract unless otherwise specified (§2-504).
      ▪ <u>Seller's Shipping Requirements</u> (§2-504):
        1. Arrange for shipping
        2. Notify the Buyer of the shipment
        3. Send Buyer the appropriate documents
    ▪ **Shipment by Reservation**
      ▪ When goods are shipped under
        "Reservation," the Seller:
        1. Retains a Security Interest in the
          goods
        and 2. Is issued a Negotiable Bill of
          Lading
      ▪ The Negotiable Bill of Lading will be
        transferred to the Buyer through
        banking channels only upon payment
        (Buyer will usually make payment with a "sight
        draft" (See "BILLS OF LADING" below)).
      ▪ Shipping by reservation allows the
        Seller to retain greater rights in the
        goods, should Buyer fail to pay for
        them or become insolvent before
        payment is due.

2) **Transfer the Goods to Buyer** (§2-301) (see "PASSAGE OF
   TITLE AND RISK OF LOSS" below)

3) **The Perfect Tender Rule** (§2-601)
   - Goods must perfectly conform to what was
     contracted for.
   - Tender must be made at a reasonable time
     (§2-503(1)(a)).
   - The Seller has a *right to cure* for imperfect tender
     if the delivery date has not yet passed (i.e.
     Seller shipped the goods early)(§2-508).

4) **Warranties to Seller** (see "WARRANTIES" for more detail):
   - The Seller makes the following warranties:
     - **Warranty of Title:** The Seller promises:
       1. Good Title: That he is transferring good
          title, and is doing so rightfully
          (§2-312(1)(a)).
       2. Free of Claims: The goods are free from
          any claims by the Seller's creditors
          (except for those that the Buyer knows about)
          (2-312(1)(b)).
       3. No Infringements: *Merchant* sellers
          warrant that goods are delivered free of
          the rightful patent or trademark claims
          of a third person (unless Seller delivered goods
          according to the Buyer's specifications) (2-312(3)).

- **Warranty of Quality:** These are warranties regarding the goods themselves and can either be <u>expressed</u> or <u>implied</u>:

  - **<u>Express Warranties:</u>** Any statements that relate to the goods and are part of the basis of the bargain are **express warranties** (2-313(1)(a)).

  - **<u>Implied Warranties</u>:** Some warranties are implied by law, for example:
    - <u>Warranty of Merchantability</u>: The law imposes upon a Merchant Seller a warranty that the goods are of a *"merchantable" quality* (§2-314). (Note that this is in addition to the good faith requirement of §1-203 that even nonmerchants are held to.)

    - <u>Fitness For a Particular Purpose</u> (§2-315): An implied warranty of fitness will be created if:
      1. A Seller has reason to know of the particular use of the goods that the Buyer intends
      and 2. The Seller is aware that the Buyer is relying on the Seller's judgment.

- **Performance Excused:** See "EXCUSES FOR NON-PERFORMANCE" above

---

§2-301: General Obligations of Parties:

1. <u>Obligation of the Seller</u>: **Transfer** and **Deliver** the goods in accordance with the contract.

2. <u>Obligation of the Buyer</u>: **Accept** and **Pay** for the goods in accordance with the contract.

§2-309(1) Implied Reasonable Time:

The time for <u>shipment</u> or <u>delivery</u> (or any other action under a contract) shall be a *"reasonable time"* (unless otherwise agreed upon or provided for in this Article).

§2-504: Shipment by Seller:

1. This Section applies only if:
   - a. The Seller is *required* or *authorized* to send the goods to the Buyer
   - and b. The contract doesn't require the Seller to deliver the goods to a particular destination
   - and c. The parties have not otherwise agreed

2. The Seller must (unless otherwise agreed):
   - (a) <u>Arrange for Goods to be Shipped</u>:
       1. Put the goods in the Carrier's possession
       - and 2. Make a contract for the transportation of the goods in a manner reasonable under the circumstances (considering the type of goods to be shipped (ex: frozen food, fragile glass)).
   - and (b) <u>Send Documents</u>: Obtain and *promptly deliver* or *tender* any documents (in due form) which:
       - i) Buyer may need to obtain possession of the goods (ex: BOL)
       - or ii) Are otherwise required by the agreement
       - or iii) Are otherwise required by Usage of Trade
   - and (c) <u>Promptly notify the Buyer of shipment</u>

3. The following are grounds for Rejection only if <u>*material delay*</u> or <u>*loss*</u> results:
   - a) Failure to make a proper shipping contract (as per §2-504(a))
   - or b) Failure to promptly notify Buyer of the shipment (as per §2-504(c))

§2-601: Buyer's Rights on Improper Delivery:

1. **Remedies For Imperfect Tender:** If the goods or the tender of delivery *in any way* fail to conform to the contract, then Buyer may:
   - (a) Reject the whole shipment
   - or (b) Accept the whole shipment
   - or (c) Accept any "commercial unit," and reject the rest

2. This rule is subject to
   - a) §2-612 (Breach of Installment Contracts)
   - b) Liquidated Remedy Agreements (under §2-718 and §2-719)

§2-503: Manner of Seller's Tender of Delivery:

(1) **Tender of Delivery:**
   i) <u>Requirements for Tender</u>:
      a) The Seller must <u>Put and Hold</u> conforming goods at the Buyer's disposition.
   and b) The Seller must give the Buyer any type of <u>notification</u> *reasonably necessary* to enable the Buyer to take delivery.
  and ii) <u>Manner, Place & Time of Tender</u>:
      Manner, time and place are determined by the agreement and Article 2, and specifically the following:
      (a) **Time for Tender of Delivery:**
         1. Tender must be at a *reasonable hour.*
         2. <u>If Goods</u> - they must be kept available for a sufficient period *reasonably necessary* for Buyer to take possession.
      (b) **Place to Deliver:** The Buyer must furnish a facility *reasonably suited* to receive the goods (unless otherwise agreed).

(2) **Shipment by Seller:** Where shipment is by Seller (as per §2-504), the Seller must tender according to the provisions of §2-504.

(3) **Delivery at a Particular Destination:** If Seller is required to deliver goods to a particular destination, the Seller must:
     a) Comply with §2-503(1)
  and b) Tender documents as per §2-503(4) and (5) (where appropriate)

(4) **Goods In A Bailee's Possession To Be Delivered Without Being Moved:**
    (a) <u>Tendering a Negotiable Document of Title</u> - Seller must *either:*
       1) Tender a Negotiable Document of Title (covering the goods)
    or 2) Have the Bailee acknowledge the Buyer's right to possession of the goods

(b) <u>Tendering a Non-Negotiable Document of Title</u> (or written direction to the Bailee to deliver):

    1) A **Non-Negotiable DOT** or a **Written Direction to the Bailee** is sufficient to tender delivery unless the Buyer *seasonably objects*.

    2) Once the Bailee is notified of the Buyer's rights, the Buyer's rights will be fixed against the Bailee <u>and</u> all third persons.

    3) The <u>Seller</u> bears the risk of:
        a) Loss
      and b) Failure of Bailee to honor the non-negotiable document of title
      and c) Failure of Bailee to obey a written direction

    4) The Seller's risk remains until the Buyer has had a reasonable time to present the document or written direction.

    5) Tender is defeated by the Bailee's refusal to honor the instrument/written direction.

(5) **Contracts Requiring Seller to Deliver Documents:**

  (a) <u>Requirements of Documents</u>:

    1. The Seller must tender each required document.

    2. The documents must be:
        a) The actual documents required by the contract
      and b) In their correct form

    3. <u>Exception</u>: This section shall not apply to Bills of Lading in a set (see §2-323).

  (b) <u>Tendering with Banks</u>:

    1. Tender through customary banking channels is sufficient.

    2. If an accompanying draft is dishonored, the goods are deemed to be either:
        a. Rejected
      or b. Not accepted

§2-505: Seller's Shipment Under Reservation:

(1) Goods Identified By Seller By or Before Shipment:

    (a) <u>Negotiable BOL</u>: If the Seller has identified goods to a contract by or before shipment, then:

        1. The Seller may reserve a Security Interest in the goods by preparing a *Negotiable Bill of Lading* to his order (or otherwise).

    and 2. Making the Negotiable BOL to the order of the <u>Buyer</u> or a <u>Financing Agency</u> will not impair the reservation of the security interest (it only indicates the Seller's expectations of transferability of interest).

    (b) <u>Non-Negotiable BOL</u>: If the Seller has identified goods to a contract by or before delivery, then:

        1. *Unconditional Delivery*: A non-negotiable BOL naming the Seller or his nominee reserves possession of the goods as a security.

        2. *Conditional Delivery* (as per §2-507(2)): The Seller will not reserve himself a Security Interest if he uses a non-negotiable BOL which names the Buyer as the Consignee (even if the Seller retains possession of the BOL).

(2) Seller's Reservation In Violation of Contract:

    If the Seller's reservation of a Security Interest violates the contract of sale:

        a) The contract is considered an improper contract for transportation (as per §2-504).

    but b) The effectiveness of the contract is not impaired regarding:

        1. The rights given to the Buyer by the shipment and identification of the goods to the contract

    and 2. The Seller's powers as a Holder of a Negotiable Document

§2-312: Warranty of Title:

(1) In a contract of sale, the Seller makes the following Warranties (subject to §2-312(2)):

    (a) **Good Title:**
        1. The title conveyed shall be good
      and 2. The transfer is rightful

    (b) **Goods Free of Liens:** The goods are delivered free from Security Interests or other liens (or encumbrances) which the Buyer had no knowledge of at the time the contract was created.

(2) **Modification or Exclusion:** A Warranty of Title may only be modified or excluded by:

    a) Specific language in the contract
    b) Circumstances which give the Buyer reason to know that
        1. The Seller does not claim title in himself
    or 2. The Seller is only purporting to sell the rights which he (or a third person) may have in the goods (ex: Seller sells goods "as is").

(3) **Goods Do Not Infringe Third Party Rights** - *Merchant Only*: The Seller warrants that the goods do not infringe a third party's rights and will be delivered free from the rightful claim of any third person (ex: free from a patent or copyright infringement) if:

    a) The Seller is a *Merchant* regularly dealing in goods of the kind sold
    and b) The infringement does not arise out of the Seller's compliance with the Buyer's instructions (ex: Buyer tells Seller to apply a label which infringes an already existing copyrighted label to its goods).

§2-313 - Express Warranty by Affirmation:

(1) **Express Warranties** by the Seller are created as follows:

    (a) Warranty That Goods Shall Conform to an Affirmation or Promise - Created by *any affirmation of fact or promise:*
        1. Which is made by the Seller to the Buyer
      and 2. Relating to the goods
      and 3. Which becomes a significant part of the basis of the bargain

    (b) Warranty That The Goods Shall Conform to their Description - Created when any description of the goods becomes a significant factor in the basis of the bargain.

(c) <u>Warranty That Goods Shall Conform to Sample or Model</u> - Created when a sample or model becomes a significant factor in the basis of the bargain.

(2) **Substance Over Form**
   a. It is not necessary for Seller to use formal words such as *"warrant"* or *"guarantee"* to create an Express Warranty
   b. The following do not alone create express warranties:
      1. An Affirmation merely of the <u>value</u> of the goods
      or 2. A Statement purporting to be merely the Seller's <u>opinion</u>
      or 3. <u>Compliments or Commendations</u> of the goods (ex:"Sales Puff")

§2-314: Implied Warranty of Merchantability:

(1) **Implied Warranty:**
   a. A Warranty that the goods shall be merchantable is implied in a contract for their sale if:
      1. The Seller is a *Merchant*, selling goods of the kind sold
      and 2. There is no clause excluding or modifying such a warranty (as per §2-316)
   b. The serving of food or drink *for value* (regardless of where it is consumed) is considered a sale for purposes of this section.

(2) **Warranty of Merchantability:** Under the Warranty of Merchantability, the Seller warrants:
   (a) <u>Goods Fit Trade Description</u> - Goods must pass without objection in the trade under the contract description (ex: if in order to be considered Orange Juice, a drink must contain 75% juice from oranges, the contents of an "Orange Juice" container must be 75% juice from oranges).
   and (b) <u>Quality</u> - *Fungible Goods* must be of fair, average quality (within the description of such goods).
   and (c) <u>Fitness</u> - Must be fit for the *ordinary purposes* for which such goods are used (for particular purposes, see §2-315).
   and (d) <u>Uniformity</u> - They must have similar quality and characteristics (within variations permitted by the agreement) within each unit, and among all units involved in the contract.
   and (e) <u>Packaging</u> - The goods must be adequately contained, packaged, and labeled (as the agreement or nature of the product may require (ex: pills to be sold over the counter should be packaged in tamper-proof containers)).
   and (f) <u>Goods Fit Package Description</u> - Must conform to the Promise or Affirmations made on the container or label.

(3) Other implied warranties may arise from the Course of Dealing or Usage of Trade (unless excluded or modified as per §2-316)

§2-315: Implied Warranty of Fitness for a Particular Purpose:

The Seller impliedly promises the Buyer that the goods shall be fit for a particular purpose if:

   a) At the time the contract was created, the Seller had *reason to know* any particular purpose for which Buyer wanted to use the goods

and b) The Buyer relied on the Seller's skill or judgment to select or furnish suitable goods

and c) Such a warranty has not been excluded or modified (as per §2-316)

B. *SELLER'S RIGHTS:*
OVERVIEW

1) **Right to Payment**
   - Seller has the right to payment from Buyer for the goods:
     - Right to payment upon Tender of goods (§2-507)
     - Right to payment upon Buyer's Acceptance of goods (§2-607(**1**))
   - Seller may sue for payment if Buyer does not pay upon Acceptance (§2-709)

2) **Right to Cure** (§2-508(1)) - if non-conforming goods are delivered before the delivery date (if Seller delivered non-conforming goods early, he may fix them and redeliver the goods by the delivery date, so long as he did not make the mistake intentionally).

3) **Rights upon Rejection** (§2-603):
   - Upon rejection, a <u>Merchant</u> Buyer must:
     a. Contact the Seller (to inform him of the rejection and obtain instructions on returning the goods).
     b. Obey any *reasonable* instructions the Seller gives the Buyer with respect to returning or disposing of the goods (although it shall be at the Seller's expense).
     c. If the Seller does not give the Buyer instructions regarding the rejected goods, the Buyer may do the following:
       - Take a **§2-711** Security Interest in the goods
       and - Resell the goods
       and - Give the Seller any profits the Buyer makes above its damages (usually Resale Price - Contract Price) (See "Buyer's REMEDIES" for more detail).

§2-507(1) Buyer's Obligation to Pay Upon Tender

a. <u>Buyer's Obligation</u>: Tender of delivery is a condition to the Buyer's obligation to:
    1. *Accept* the goods
  and 2. *Pay* for the goods (unless otherwise agreed)
b. <u>Seller's Entitlement</u>: Tender entitles the Seller to:
    1. The Buyer's acceptance of the goods
  and 2. Payment (according to the contract)

§2-607(1) Price of Accepted Goods:

The Buyer must pay the *contract price* (i.e. the price of the goods as stated in the contract) for any goods accepted.

§2-709(1), (3): Seller's Action for the Price:

(1) <u>Buyer Fails to Pay</u>: When the Buyer fails to pay the price as it becomes due, the Seller may recover the following (+ any incidental damages under §2-710):
  (a) **Accepted/Destroyed Goods:**
    1. <u>Accepted Goods</u> - The price of the goods
    2. <u>Destroyed Goods</u> - The price of the goods, if:
      a. The goods were conforming goods,
    and b. The goods were destroyed within a commercially reasonable time after risk of loss has passed to the Buyer
  and (b) **Identified Goods:** The price of goods identified to the contract if:
    1. The Seller is unable after *reasonable effort* to resell the goods at a reasonable price
    or 2. The circumstances reasonably indicate that such effort will be unavailing

*   *   *   *

(3) Even if a Seller is not entitled to the price (under §2-709) he may be awarded <u>damages for non-acceptance</u> (under §2-708) if the Buyer:
    a. Wrongfully rejected the goods
  or b. Wrongfully revoked acceptance of the goods
  or c. Has failed to make a payment due
  or d. Has repudiated (as per §2-610)

§2-508: Cure By Seller for Improper Tender or Delivery; Replacement:

(1) **Non-Conforming Goods:** The Seller may seasonably notify the Buyer of his intention to cure, and may then ship conforming goods if:
   - a) Goods are rejected because they are non-conforming
   - b) The time for performance has not expired
   - c) The Seller re-ships conforming goods before the expiration of performance (i.e. before the delivery date)

(2) **Goods Seller Deemed Conforming:** Seller may extend time of delivery and ship conforming goods if:
   - a) The goods are rejected because they are non-conforming
   - and b) The Seller had *reasonable grounds* to believe they would be acceptable (with or without a money allowance)
   - and c) Seller seasonably notifies the Buyer
   - and b) The extension is reasonable

§2-603: Merchant Buyer's Rightful Rejection:

(1) **Buyer's Duties Upon Rejection:**
   - a) After rejection, any <u>Merchant</u> Buyer must follow any *reasonable instruction* received from the Seller, with respect to such goods if:
      - 1. If Seller has no agent or place of business where goods are rejected
      - and 2. After rejection goods are still in the Buyer's possession or control
   - b) Upon rejection, the Buyer must make reasonable efforts to sell the goods for the Seller if:
      - 1. The Seller has no agent or place of business where goods are rejected
      - and 2. After rejection goods are still in the Buyer's possession or control
      - and 3. The Seller left no other *reasonable instructions*
      - and 4. The goods are perishable or threaten to speedily decline in value
   - c) Instructions are not reasonable if, on the Buyer's demand, indemnity for expenses is not forthcoming.
   - d) This subsection is subject to any S/I in the Buyer (as per §2-711(3)).

(2) **Reimbursement to Buyer:**
   When the Buyer sells goods under §2-603(1), he is entitled to
      <u>reimbursement</u> from the Seller (or out of the proceeds of the sale) for:
      a. Reasonable selling expenses
      b. Reasonable expenses incurred in caring for the goods
      c. Selling Commissions, if they are:
          1. Not included in expenses
       and 2. *Either:*
              a) Reasonable in the trade/industry
           or b) A Reasonable Sum (if no industry norm), *not to exceed
              10% of gross proceeds.*

(3) **Buyer's Standard of Good Faith:**
      a) The Buyer is held to a standard of *Good Faith.*
      b) Good Faith conduct will not be considered Acceptance,
         Conversion, or a basis of an action for damages.

C. SELLER'S REMEDIES:

1) Remedy For Insolvent Buyers:

OVERVIEW ────────────────────

- **Remedy for Insolvent Buyers** - If the Buyer is insolvent:
  - *Before Shipment of Goods:* Seller may refuse to perform *unless* (§2-610):
    - Buyer gives adequate assurance of performance (§2-609)
    - or ▪ Buyer promises to pay in cash (C.O.D.) (§2-702(1))
  - *In Transit:* Stop Goods (§2-705)
  - *After Shipment:* Reclamation Rights (§2-702(2)-(3)) (see "RECLAMATION RIGHTS" below)

2) Remedy For Dishonored Check:

OVERVIEW ────────────────────

- **Remedy for Goods Paid for by Dishonored Check** (§2-507):
  - Upon tender, Seller is entitled to payment (§2-507(2)).
  - If payment due to the Seller is not paid, the Buyer will not be allowed to:
    - Sell Goods
    - or ▪ Dispose of Goods
  - Remedy Against Buyer: The Seller will have the right to reclaim goods paid for by a dishonored check (§2-702) if it demands reclamation within a reasonable time after it is notified of the check's dishonor (some states give Seller a 10 day limit) (See "RECLAMATION RIGHTS" below (§2-702)).
  - Remedy Against Bank: If a Bank collected the payment for the Seller (ex: under a Letter of Credit transaction (see "LETTERS OF CREDIT")) the bank will be liable for any dishonored checks if it accepted a *personal check* as payment under the pre-1993 version of §4-211 (the new statute doesn't say this, but the bank may still be liable for breach of ordinary care under §4-202).

§2-507: Effect of Seller's Tender; Delivery on Condition:

(1) **Effect of Tender:**
>   a. <u>Buyer's Obligation</u>: Tender of delivery is a condition to the Buyer's obligation to:
>   >   1. *Accept* the goods
>   >   and 2. *Pay* for the goods (unless otherwise agreed)
>   b. <u>Seller's Entitlement</u>: Tender entitles the Seller to:
>   >   1. The Buyer's acceptance of the goods
>   >   and 2. Payment (according to the contract)

(2) **Conditional Delivery:**
>   The Buyer's rights to *retain* or *dispose of* the goods is conditional upon making payment due to the Seller, if:
>   >   a. <u>Payment is due</u> upon delivery (of goods or documents of title) to the Buyer
>   >   and b. <u>Seller demanded payment</u> upon delivery (of goods or documents of title) to the Buyer

§2-702: Buyer's Insolvency:

(1) **Seller Discovers Buyer's Insolvency Before Delivery:**
>   If the Seller discovers that the Buyer is insolvent, the Seller may:
>   >   a. Refuse to continue delivering unless Buyer promises to
>   >   >   1. Pay Cash on Delivery (C.O.D.)
>   >   >   and 2. Pay for all shipments already delivered under the contract
>   >   and b. Stop delivery (as per §2-705)

(2) **Buyer Receives Goods on Credit While Insolvent:**

>   If the Seller discovers that the Buyer has been receiving goods on credit while he was insolvent, the Seller may <u>Reclaim the goods</u>:
>   *<u>Reclamation Requirements:</u>*
>   >   1. *10 Day Time Limit* - In order to reclaim the goods, the Seller must:
>   >   >   a) Demand payment or reclamation of the goods
>   >   >   b) Make the *Demand* within <u>10 Days</u> after the Buyer receives the goods
>   >   2. *EXCEPTION - Written Misrepresentation of Solvency:*
>   >   10 Day limit does not apply if the Buyer made a <u>Misrepresentation of Solvency</u>:
>   >   >   a) In Writing
>   >   >   and b) Within <u>3 Months</u> before Delivery

3. The Seller may not base a right to reclaim the goods based on the Buyer's *Fraudulent* or *Innocent* misrepresentation of <u>Solvency</u> or <u>Intent to pay</u>, except as provided in this subsection (i.e. it must be in writing, within 3 Months before delivery).

(3) **Limitations on the Seller's Rights to Reclaim:**
  a. The Seller's rights to reclaim are subject to the rights of:
    1. A Buyer In the Ordinary Course (BIOC)
  and 2. Any other Good Faith Purchaser (under §2-403)
  b. <u>Exclusion of Other Remedies</u>: Successful reclamation of goods *excludes* all other remedies (with respect to the reclaimed goods).

§2-705: Seller's Stoppage of Delivery in Transit or Otherwise:

(1) <u>Seller's Right To Stop Delivery</u>:
  a. **Insolvency**: The Seller may stop delivery of goods in the possession of a <u>Carrier</u> or <u>other Bailee</u> when he discovers the Buyer to be insolvent (§2-702).

  b. **Other Situations**: The Seller may stop delivery of carload, truckload, planeload or larger shipments of express or freight when:
    1. The Buyer repudiates
  or 2. If for any other reason the Seller has a right to <u>withhold</u> or <u>reclaim</u> the goods
  or 3. The Buyer fails to make a payment due before delivery; Failure to make a payment includes (official comment 3):
      a. The dishonor of a check on due presentment
      b. The nonacceptance of a draft
      c. The failure to furnish an agreed letter of credit

(2) <u>Seller's Time Limit</u>: The Seller may stop delivery until:
    (a) The Buyer receives the goods (this includes receipt by the Buyer's designated representative, the sub-purchaser, when shipment is made direct to him and the Buyer himself never receives the goods (official comment))
  or (b) A Bailee of the goods (except a Carrier) acknowledges to the Buyer that the goods are being held for the Buyer
  or (c) The Carrier acknowledges that the goods are being held for the Buyer, *either*:
      1. By reshipment (this does not include diversion of a shipment when it is merely an incident to the original contract of transportation or does not change the destination (official comment))
      or 2. As a Warehouseman (this requires a contract of a truly different character from the original shipment, a contract not in extension of transit but as a Warehouseman (official comment))
  or (d) Negotiation to the Buyer of any negotiable document of title covering the goods.

(3) <u>Stopping Delivery</u>:
    (a) **Notice:** To stop delivery the Seller must give the Bailee notice in order to enable him to prevent delivery by *reasonable diligence.*

    (b) **Seller's and Bailee's Responsibilities:** After such notification:
      1. The Bailee must hold and deliver the goods according to the directions of the Seller.
      2. The Seller is liable to the Bailee for any ensuing charges or damages.

    (c) **Bailee to Stop Delivery:** If a negotiable document of title has been issued for goods the Bailee is not obliged to obey a notification to stop delivery until surrender of the document (a Bailee is under no duty to recognize the stop order of a stranger to the Carrier's contract (official comment)).

    (d) **Carrier to Stop Delivery:** A Carrier who has issued a non-negotiable Bill of Lading is not obliged to obey a notification to stop delivery *unless* he is notified by the <u>Consignor</u> (a Bailee is under no duty to recognize the stop order of a stranger to the Carrier's contract (official comment)).

3) Remedies After Shipment

OVERVIEW ──────────────────────────

- **Reclamation Rights** - voiding title to goods received on credit while insolvent (§2-702).
    - Reclamation voids the Buyer's title in the goods and allows the Seller to get his goods back if the Buyer doesn't pay for them.

    - Availability - Reclamation rights are only available if:
        - The sale involved a Credit Transaction (i.e. payment was not due upon delivery with cash (ex: sale was not C.O.D.; A credit transaction would be one where the Buyer had 30 days to pay for the goods ("Net 30")) Cash and C.O.D. sales are covered by §2-507(2)).
      and - *Either:*
        - Buyer is Insolvent
      or - Buyer's Check is Dishonored (ie. insolvency presumed when check is dishonored)

    - Good Faith Purchaser Exception:
        - Once Buyer has *voidable title* under §2-702, the Seller may get the goods back from Judgment Creditors and Buyers, but NOT Good Faith Buyers for Value ("GFP") (§2-403) or Buyers in the Ordinary Course ("BIOC") (§1-201(9))
        - A GFP or a BIOC can take the goods with full title, thereby denying the Seller the ability to reclaim those goods (see §2-403; §1-201(9)).

- It is questionable whether the Seller has rights to proceeds from the Buyer's sale to a GFP or a BIOC.

- **Reclamation is an Exclusive Remedy** - and cannot be used in conjunction with any of the Seller's remedies in §2-703.

- **Procedure:**
  - a) The Seller must demand that Buyer <u>Pay</u> or <u>Return</u> the goods
  - b) The demand must be made within <u>10 Days</u> of Delivery or notice of Dishonor (§2-702)
    - **Exception:** The 10 Day period does not apply if Buyer <u>Misrepresented</u> his solvency *in writing* within <u>3 months</u> before delivery (§2-702(2)) (the statute is not clear whether the misrepresentation had to come from the Buyer directly or whether the misrepresentation could come from a third party such as a credit bureau).

    - **Bankruptcy:** If a Buyer goes Bankrupt, The Federal Bankruptcy Code ("BRC") will govern this procedure. The BRC eliminates the <u>10 Day</u> time limit to demand reclamation from the Buyer.

---

§2-702: Buyer's Insolvency; Reclamation Rights:

(1) **Seller Discovers Buyer's Insolvency Before Delivery:**
If the Seller discovers that the Buyer is insolvent, the Seller may:
a. Refuse to continue delivering unless Buyer promises to
1. Pay Cash on Delivery (C.O.D.)
and 2. Pay for all shipments already delivered under the contract
and b. Stop delivery (as per §2-705)

(2) **Buyer Receives Goods on Credit While Insolvent:**
If the Seller discovers that the Buyer has been receiving goods on credit while he was insolvent, the Seller may <u>Reclaim the goods</u>:
Reclamation Requirements:
1. *10 Day Time Limit* - In order to reclaim the goods, the Seller must:
   a) Demand payment or reclamation of the goods
   b) Make the *Demand* within <u>10 Days</u> after the Buyer receives the goods
2. *EXCEPTION - Written Misrepresentation of Solvency:*
   10 Day limit does not apply if the Buyer made a <u>Misrepresentation of Solvency</u>:
   a) In Writing
   and b) Within <u>3 Months</u> before Delivery

    3. The Seller may not base a right to reclaim the goods based on the Buyer's *Fraudulent* or *Innocent* misrepresentation of <u>Solvency</u> or <u>Intent to pay</u>, except as provided in this subsection (i.e. it must be in writing, within 3 Months before delivery).

(3) Limitations on the Seller's Rights to Reclaim:
    a. The Seller's rights to reclaim are subject to the rights of:
       1. A Buyer In the Ordinary Course (BIOC)
    and 2. Any other Good Faith Purchaser (under §2-403)
    b. <u>Exclusion of Other Remedies</u>: Successful reclamation of goods *excludes* all other remedies (with respect to the reclaimed goods).

4) *Remedy While in Transit:*
OVERVIEW ───────────────────────

- **Right to Stop Goods**
  In-Transit: The Seller will have the right to stop goods already in-transit if (§2-705):
  - ■ The shipment is very large
  - or ■ Buyer wrongfully rejects or revokes acceptance of a prior installment
  - or ■ Buyer fails to make payment due
  - or ■ Buyer breaches in advance (see "ANTICIPATORY REPUDIATION")
  - or ■ Buyer becomes insolvent

---

§2-705: Seller's Stoppage of Delivery in Transit or Otherwise:

(1) <u>Seller's Right To Stop Delivery</u>:
  a. **Insolvency**: The Seller may stop delivery of goods in the possession of a <u>Carrier</u> or <u>other Bailee</u> when he discovers the Buyer to be insolvent (§2-702).

  b. **Other Situations**: The Seller may stop delivery of carload, truckload, planeload or larger shipments of express or freight when:
    1. The Buyer repudiates
    or 2. If for any other reason the Seller has a right to <u>withhold</u> or <u>reclaim</u> the goods
    or 3. The Buyer fails to make a payment due before delivery; Failure to make a payment includes (official comment 3):
      a. The dishonor of a check on due presentment
      b. The nonacceptance of a draft
      c. The failure to furnish an agreed letter of credit

(2) <u>Seller's Time Limit</u>: The Seller may stop delivery until:
- (a) The Buyer receives the goods (this includes receipt by the Buyer's designated representative, the sub-purchaser, when shipment is made direct to him and the Buyer himself never receives the goods (official comment))
- or (b) A Bailee of the goods (except a Carrier) acknowledges to the Buyer that the goods are being held for the Buyer
- or (c) The Carrier acknowledges that the goods are being held for the Buyer, *either*:
  - 1. By reshipment (this does not include diversion of a shipment when it is merely an incident to the original contract of transportation or does not change the destination (official comment))
  - or 2. As a Warehouseman (this requires a contract of a truly different character from the original shipment, a contract not in extension of transit but as a Warehouseman (official comment))
- or (d) Negotiation to the Buyer of any negotiable document of title covering the goods.

(3) <u>Stopping Delivery</u>:
- (a) **Notice:** To stop delivery the Seller must give the Bailee notice in order to enable him to prevent delivery by *reasonable diligence.*

- (b) **Seller's and Bailee's Responsibilities:** After such notification:
  - 1. The Bailee must hold and deliver the goods according to the directions of the Seller.
  - 2. The Seller is liable to the Bailee for any ensuing charges or damages.

- (c) **Bailee to Stop Delivery:** If a negotiable document of title has been issued for goods the Bailee is not obliged to obey a notification to stop delivery until surrender of the document (a Bailee is under no duty to recognize the stop order of a stranger to the Carrier's contract (official comment)).

- (d) **Carrier to Stop Delivery:** A Carrier who has issued a non-negotiable Bill of Lading is not obliged to obey a notification to stop delivery *unless* he is notified by the Consignor (a Bailee is under no duty to recognize the stop order of a stranger to the Carrier's contract (official comment)).

5) *Remedy Before Shipment:*

a) Repudiation:

OVERVIEW ————————————————————————

In order for Seller to resort to its remedies before it ships the goods, the Buyer must have **repudiated** - the main problem is determining when repudiation occurs:

   1) Repudiation can occur if:
   - Substantive Value at Risk: The injured party will be inconvenienced or injured from the value of the *Repudiated Tender* (in comparison to the promised tender)

and - Expression of Non-Compliance: The other party expresses its noncompliance with the contract by *either*:

   1. *Overt Communications:* A party states that he will not perform (§2-609)
   2. *Action:*
      - A party's actions render its performance impossible
      - A party's actions *reasonably indicate rejection* of its obligation
   3. Breacher *Demonstrates* a *Clear Determination not* to perform
   4. *Demands:* The other party demands an increased price to complete performance
   5. *Lack of Security DEMAND:* A party refuses to confirm its promise within 30 Days after being requested to do so (§2-609)
   6. **Neglect:** The other party fails to specify instructions to the Seller or fails to cooperate in accordance with the contract (§2-311)

   2) *"ANTICIPATORY REPUDIATION"* (§2-610) - a party's repudiation of its duties under the contract before they become due. Anticipatory Repudiation allows a party to resort to its repudiation remedies before performance of the contract would actually be due.

3) <u>Seller's Right to Buyer's Assurance of Performance</u>:
- If the Seller has reasonable ground for insecurity that the Buyer will not perform as promised, he may demand that the Buyer assure him that he will perform as promised.

- <u>Procedure</u>:
  - **Written Demand** (§2-609) - A Seller may send a demand to assure that the Buyer will:
    - *Perform* its obligations
    - or ▪ *Conform* with the terms of the contract
  - **Repudiation Occurs If** (§2-609):
    - The Buyer does not assure performance/conformance within <u>30 Days</u> after he receives the demand (§2-609(4))
    - or ▪ The Buyer responds to the demand that he does not intend to perform (§2-609(4)).

---

§2-609: Right to Adequate Assurance of Performance:

(1) **Adequate Assurance:**
   a) A contract for sale creates an obligation in each party to maintain the other party's expectations of due performance.
   b) A party will be excused from performing any contractual obligation if:
   1) The party had *reasonable grounds of insecurity* as to whether the other party will perform according to the contract
   and 2) The party sends a written notice to the other party demanding *adequate assurance* of due performance
   and 3) The other party did not yet respond to the demand
   and 4) It is commercially reasonable to suspend such performance
   and 5) The party did not receive payment (or other return) for the obligations it plans to suspend.

71

   c) <u>Parties</u>:
     1) *"Repudiating Party"* - The party failing to give adequate assurance of performance
     2) *"Aggrieved Party"* - The party demanding assurance of performance

(2) **Standards:** The following terms shall be construed according to *commercial standards* if the contract is <u>between Merchants</u>:
     a) "Reasonable Grounds for Insecurity"
     b) "Adequacy of assurance"

(3) **Installments:** A party is not precluded from demanding adequate assurance of future obligations even if he accepted an improper delivery or payment of earlier obligations.

(4) **Repudiation:** A party who fails to provide *adequate assurance* (under the circumstances of the case) to a justified demand within a reasonable amount of time (no more than <u>30 days</u>) will have repudiated the contract.

§2-610: Anticipatory Repudiation:

1. **"Anticipatory Repudiation"** - Anticipatory Repudiation occurs when:
     a. Either party repudiates the contract (see §2-609)
  and b. The repudiated portion of the contract is not yet due
  and c. The loss of such performance will *substantially impair* the value of the contract

2. **Rights of Aggrieved Party upon Anticipatory Repudiation:** The aggrieved party may:
     (a) <u>Await Performance</u> - from the repudiating party, for a *commercially reasonable time*
  or (b) <u>Resort to Breach Remedies</u> (as per §2-703 (for Seller) or §2-711 (for Buyer)) - even if he told the repudiating party that he will wait for performance (subsection (a))
  or (c) <u>Suspend Performance</u> - The aggrieved party may suspend his own performance.
  or d) <u>Identify and Salvage Goods</u> - The Seller may identify goods to a contract or salvage unfinished goods (as per §2-704).

§2-611: Retraction of Anticipatory Repudiation:

(1) **Time for Retraction:** The repudiating party may retract his repudiation if:
    a) His next performance is still not yet due
and b) The aggrieved party has <u>not</u>:
      1. Canceled the contract
    or 2. Materially changed its position
    or 3. Otherwise indicated that it considers the repudiation final

(2) **Requirements for Retraction:** A valid retraction of repudiation must:
    a) *Clearly indicate* to the aggrieved party that the repudiating party <u>intends to perform</u>
and b) Include any <u>adequate assurance</u> *justifiably* demanded under §2-609

(3) **Effect of Retraction:**
    a) The repudiating party's rights under the contract are reinstated
and b) The aggrieved party is excused for any delay due to the repudiation.

b) Seller's Remedies Upon Repudiation:

OVERVIEW ————————————————

1. Await Performance by the Repudiating Party (§2-610(a))

and 2. Suspend His Own Performance (§2-610(c))

or 3. Resort to §2-703 Remedies (even if Seller told Buyer that he would await performance):

    A. Withhold Delivery (§2-703(a))

    B. Stop Delivery of Goods In Transit (§2-703(b))

- *Regular Shipments* - Regular shipments may be stopped only if Buyer is insolvent.
- *Large Shipments* - Large shipments may be stopped upon repudiation (even if Buyer is solvent)
- Goods Must Be In Transit - Seller cannot stop shipment once (§2-705(2)):
  - The Buyer receives the goods
  - or A Bailee acknowledges that the goods are held for the Buyer
  - or The Carrier acknowledges that the goods are held for the Buyer by Reshipment or as a Warehouseman
    - or A Negotiable Document of Title has been negotiated to the Buyer

    C. Salvage Unfinished Goods (as per §2-704) (§2-703(c)) - Seller must use *"commercially reasonable judgment"* when deciding whether to either:

- Complete production and sell the goods to another Buyer, and sue the original Buyer for the deficiency (Contract Price - Resale Price))
- or Stop production and sell whatever he has (ex: the input products and unfinished goods), and sue Buyer for the deficiency (Contract Price - Resale Price)

D. **Identify Conforming Goods** to resell them (as per §2-704) (§2-703(c)):
- The Seller must designate the specific pieces which would have been sold to the Buyer
- The Seller may then sell goods to another party (as per §2-706) and sue the Buyer for deficiency (**Contract Price - Resale Price**)

E. **Resell and Recover** (as per §2-706) (§2-703(d)):
- Seller must identify goods which would have been given to Buyer (as per §2-704)
- Seller's resale must be made:
  - In *Good Faith*
  - Within a *Commercially Reasonable Time*
  - In a *Commercially Reasonable Manner*
- Seller must notify the Buyer of the time and place of the sale (unless the goods are perishable).
- Seller may sue Buyer for any deficiency in price (**Contract Price - Resale Price**).

F. **Sue Buyer for Damages or Lost Profit** (as per §2-708) (§2-703(e)) (see "LIMITATIONS ON DAMAGES"):
  ▪ Seller may sue Buyer for:

  DIRECT DAMAGES
  + INCIDENTAL DAMAGES
  - EXPENSES SAVED

  ▪ **Incidental Damages** - Seller may recover incidental damages (§2-706) (ex: stop delivery charge, commissions, storage, resale costs).
  ▪ **Expenses Saved** - by not having to tender goods to the Buyer must be deducted.

  ▪ **Direct Damages** are *either*:

    ▪ **Damages for Price:** Market Price - Contract Price (§2-708(1))

  or ▪ **Damages for Price if Resold:** Resale Price - Contract Price (§2-706)

  or ▪ **Lost Profit:** Seller can sue for *Lost Profits* (§2-708(2)) if:
      ▪ Damages for price are *"inadequate"*
      ▪ The Seller is a *"Lost volume Seller"* - he has access to an unlimited supply of such items (and could have made two sales)
      ▪ **Lost Profit = Retail Sale Price - Contract Price**

G. Sue Buyer for Purchase Price; Specific Performance (as per §2-709)(§2-703(e)):

- Suing Buyer for the purchase price is equivalent to Specific Performance
- The Seller must set aside the goods identified as Buyer's
- Seller may not use them since, upon recovery of purchase price, they rightfully belong to Buyer (§2-709(1)).
- If the Seller does end up reselling such identified goods, he must give the proceeds to the Buyer (§2-709(2)).
- <u>Courts usually allow Specific Performance if</u>:
  - Seller could not resell goods (ex: goods specially made for the Buyer)
  - or ▪ Goods were already accepted by the Buyer
  - or ▪ Conforming goods were lost/stolen after Risk of Loss passed to Buyer (see §2-509, and "RISK_OF_LOSS" below)

H. Cancel (§2-703(f)) - Seller may cancel the contract and relieve himself of his obligation.

---

§2-610(a)-(c) Rights of Aggrieved Party upon Anticipatory Repudiation:

The aggrieved party may:

    (a) <u>Await Performance</u> - from the repudiating party, for a *commercially reasonable time*

or (b) <u>Resort to Breach Remedies</u> (as per §2-703 (for Seller) or §2-711 (for Buyer)) - even if he told the repudiating party that he will wait for performance (subsection (a))

or (c) <u>Suspend Performance</u> - The aggrieved party may suspend his own performance.

or d) <u>Identify and Salvage Goods</u> - The Seller may identify goods to a contract or salvage unfinished goods (as per §2-704).

§2-703: Seller's Remedies in General:

1. Seller is entitled to remedies when:
    a. The Buyer wrongfully rejects goods
  or b. The Buyer wrongfully revokes acceptance of goods
  or c. The Buyer repudiates with respect to the whole or a part of the contract
  or d. The Buyer fails to make a payment due on or before delivery;
      Failure to make a payment includes (official comment 3):
        a. The dishonor of a check on due presentment
        b. The nonacceptance of a draft
        c. The failure to furnish an agreed letter of credit

2. The Seller's remedies apply with respect to:
    a. Any goods directly affected
  and b. If the breach is of the whole contract (§2-612), then also with respect to the whole undelivered balance

3. **Remedies Available** - The Seller may:
    (a) Withhold delivery of the goods
  or (b) Stop delivery by any Bailee (as per §2-705)
  or (c) Identify or salvage unfinished or unidentified goods (under §2-704)
  or (d) Resell and recover damages as provided in §2-706
  or (e) Recover damages for non-acceptance (§2-708) or in a proper case the price (§2-709)
  or (f) Cancel the contract

§2-704: Seller's Right to Identify Goods to the Contract Notwithstanding Breach or to Salvage Unfinished Goods:

(1) Rights of Aggrieved Seller under §2-703 may:
    (a) *Conforming Finished Goods:* Identify to the contract goods which have not yet been identified if:
        1. The goods conform to the contract
      and 2. At the time the Seller learned of the breach they are in the Seller's possession or control (the goods are then available for resale under §2-706 (official comment))
    (b) *Unfinished Goods:* Resell goods which have *clearly* been intended for the particular contract (even though those goods are unfinished).

(2) <u>Seller's Remedies Where Goods are Unfinished</u>:
  a. Where the goods are unfinished an aggrieved Seller may *either*:
    1. Complete the manufacture and wholly identify the goods to the contract
    or 2. Cease manufacture and resell them for scrap or salvage value
    or 3. Proceed in any other *reasonable manner*

  b. The Seller must exercise reasonable commercial judgment (the burden is on the Buyer to show otherwise) for the purposes of:
    1. Avoiding loss
    and 2. Effective realization

§2-705: Seller's Stoppage of Delivery in Transit or Otherwise:

(1) <u>Seller's Right To Stop Delivery</u>:
  a. **Insolvency**: The Seller may stop delivery of goods in the possession of a <u>Carrier</u> or <u>other Bailee</u> when he discovers the Buyer to be insolvent (§2-702).

  b. **Other Situations**: The Seller may stop delivery of carload, truckload, planeload or larger shipments of express or freight when:
    1. The Buyer repudiates
    or 2. If for any other reason the Seller has a right to <u>withhold</u> or <u>reclaim</u> the goods
    or 3. The Buyer fails to make a payment due before delivery; Failure to make a payment includes (official comment 3):
      a. The dishonor of a check on due presentment
      b. The nonacceptance of a draft
      c. The failure to furnish an agreed letter of credit

(2) <u>Seller's Time Limit</u>: The Seller may stop delivery until:
- (a) The Buyer receives the goods (this includes receipt by the Buyer's designated representative, the sub-purchaser, when shipment is made direct to him and the Buyer himself never receives the goods (official comment))
- or (b) A Bailee of the goods (except a Carrier) acknowledges to the Buyer that the goods are being held for the Buyer
- or (c) The Carrier acknowledges that the goods are being held for the Buyer, *either*:
  - 1. By reshipment (this does not include diversion of a shipment when it is merely an incident to the original contract of transportation or does not change the destination (official comment))
  - or 2. As a Warehouseman (this requires a contract of a truly different character from the original shipment, a contract not in extension of transit but as a Warehouseman (official comment))
- or (d) Negotiation to the Buyer of any negotiable document of title covering the goods.

(3) <u>Stopping Delivery</u>:
- (a) **Notice:** To stop delivery the Seller must give the Bailee notice in order to enable him to prevent delivery by *reasonable diligence.*

- (b) **Seller's and Bailee's Responsibilities:** After such notification:
  - 1. The Bailee must hold and deliver the goods according to the directions of the Seller.
  - 2. The Seller is liable to the Bailee for any ensuing charges or damages.

- (c) **Bailee to Stop Delivery:** If a negotiable document of title has been issued for goods the Bailee is not obliged to obey a notification to stop delivery until surrender of the document (a Bailee is under no duty to recognize the stop order of a stranger to the Carrier's contract (official comment)).

- (d) **Carrier to Stop Delivery:** A Carrier who has issued a non-negotiable Bill of Lading is not obliged to obey a notification to stop delivery *unless* he is notified by the <u>Consignor</u> (a Bailee is under no duty to recognize the stop order of a stranger to the Carrier's contract (official comment)).

§2-706: Seller's Resale Including Contract For Resale:

(1) <u>Resale By Seller for Buyer's Breach or Insolvency</u>:
    a. Seller's Right: Under the conditions stated in §2-703 (breach or insolvency), the Seller may:
        1. Resell the goods concerned,
       or 2. Resell the undelivered balance of the goods
    b. <u>Seller Damages Recoverable</u>: The Seller may recover:

> **The resale price**
> **- The contract price**
> **+ Any incidental damages** (allowed under §2-710)
> **- Expenses saved in consequence of the Buyer's breach**

    c. <u>Requirements</u>: In order to recover damages, Seller has to resell:
        1. In good faith
     and 2. In a commercially reasonable manner

(2) <u>Method of Resale</u>:
    a. **General Notes**:
        1. Every aspect of the sale including the <u>method</u>, <u>manner</u>, <u>time</u>, <u>place</u> and <u>terms</u> must be *commercially reasonable*.
        2. The resale must be reasonably identified as referring to the broken contract, but it is not necessary for:
           i. The goods to be in existence
         or ii. Any or all of the goods to have been identified to the contract before the breach.
        3. Terms of resale are subject to:
           i. §2-706(3)
         and ii. Agreement otherwise by parties.
    b. **Type of Sale** - Depending on commercial reasonableness, resale may be at:
        1. Public sale (auction)
     or 2. Private sale (ex: solicitation and negotiation conducted either directly or through a broker)
    c. This section includes sale by way of:
        1. One or more contracts to sell
     or 2. Identification to an existing contract of the Seller
    d. **Units of Sale** - Sale may be:
        1. As a unit
     or 2. In parcels
    e. **Time and Place** - Sale may be at any time and place and on any terms.

(3) <u>Private Resale</u> - Where the resale is at private sale the Seller must give the Buyer reasonable notification of his intention to resell (notification of the time and place of this type of sale is not required).

(4) <u>Public Resale</u> - Where the resale is at public sale:
    (a) <u>Type of Goods That Can Be Sold</u>:
        1. Only identified goods can be sold.
        2. Futures Market Exception: Where there is a recognized market for a public sale of futures in goods of the kind.
    (b) <u>Seller's Requirements</u>:
        1. **Place:** The auction must be made at a *usual place or market* for public sale (which prospective bidders may reasonably be expected to attend).
        2. **Notice:**
            a. The Seller must give the Buyer reasonable notice of the time and place so that he may:
                i. Bid
             or ii. Secure the attendance of other bidders
            b. Perishable Goods Exception: In the case of goods *"which are perishable or threaten to decline speedily in value,"* notice is not required.
    (c) <u>Goods Not Present at Sale</u> - If the goods are not to be within the view of those attending the sale:
        1. The notification of sale must <u>state the place</u> where the goods are located
        and 2. The notification must provide for <u>reasonable inspection</u> of the goods by prospective bidders
    (d) The Seller may buy (his own goods) at the sale.

(5) <u>Purchaser's Rights</u>: A purchaser who buys in good faith at a resale takes the goods <u>free of any rights of the original Buyer</u> (even though the Seller fails to comply with one or more of the requirements of this section).

(6) <u>Profits</u>:
    a. The Seller retains profit, if any, made on any resale.
    b. A person in the position of a Seller (as per §2-707) must give any excess (above his "security interest" as defined in §2-711(3)) to the Seller.
    c. A Buyer who has rightfully rejected or justifiably revoked acceptance must also give any "profits" to the Seller (i.e. the difference between the sale price and the Seller's "security interest" in the goods (as defined in §2-711(3)).

§2-707: "Person in the Position of a Seller":

(1) A **"Person In The Position of a Seller"** includes:
    a. An agent who has paid or become responsible for the price of goods on behalf of his principal
  or b. Anyone who otherwise holds a security interest or other right in goods similar to that of a Seller

(2) A person in the position of a Seller may:
    a. Withhold or stop delivery (§2-705)
  and b. Resell (§2-706)
  and c. Recover incidental damages (§2-710)

§2-708: Seller's Damages for Non-acceptance or Repudiation:

(1) <u>Expectation Damages</u>: If the Buyer does not accept or repudiates, the Seller's damages are (subject to 2-708(2) and to §2-723 (proof of market price)):

> **The market price at the time and place for tender**
> - **The unpaid contract price**
> + **Any incidental damages provided in this Article** (§2-710)
> - **Expenses saved in consequence of the Buyer's breach**

(2) <u>Lost Profit</u>: If the measure of damages in subsection (1) is not enough to put the Seller in as good a position as he would have been had the Buyer performed (i.e. the Seller is a "lost volume seller"), then the measure of damages is:

> **The profit** ((including reasonable overhead) which the Seller would have made from full performance by the Buyer)
> + **Any incidental damages provided in this Article** (§2-710)
> + **Due allowance for costs reasonably incurred**
> + **Due credit for payments or proceeds of resale**

§2-709: Action for the Price:

(1) <u>Buyer Fails to Pay</u>: When the Buyer fails to pay the price as it becomes due, the Seller may recover the following (+ any incidental damages under §2-710):

    (a) **Accepted/Destroyed Goods:**

        1. <u>Accepted Goods</u> - The price of the goods

        2. <u>Destroyed Goods</u> - The price of the goods, if:

            a. The goods were conforming goods,

        and b. The goods were destroyed within a commercially reasonable time after risk of loss has passed to the Buyer

    and (b) **Identified Goods:** The price of goods identified to the contract if:

        1. The Seller is unable after *reasonable effort* to resell the goods at a reasonable price

      or 2. The circumstances reasonably indicate that such effort will be unavailing

(2) <u>Seller's Requirements With Respect to Identified Goods</u>:

    a. Seller must hold goods which have been identified to the contract for the Buyer if:

        1. The Seller is suing the Buyer for their price

      and 2. The goods are still in the Seller's control

    b. <u>Resale</u>: If resale becomes possible, the Seller may resell the goods at any time before the judgment (price) is collected.

    c. <u>Buyer's Rights</u>:

        1. The net proceeds of any such resale must be credited to the Buyer.

        2. Payment of the judgment entitles the Buyer to any goods not resold.

(3) Even if a Seller is not entitled to the price (under §2-709) he may be awarded <u>damages for non-acceptance</u> (under §2-708) if the Buyer:

    a. Wrongfully rejected the goods

    or b. Wrongfully revoked acceptance of the goods

    or c. Has failed to make a payment due

    or d. Has repudiated (as per §2-610)

§2-710: Seller's Incidental Damages:

Incidental damages to an aggrieved Seller include any *commercially reasonable* <u>charges</u>, <u>expenses</u> or <u>commissions</u>:

    1. Incurred in stopping delivery

  or 2. Incurred in the transportation, care and custody of goods <u>after</u> the Buyer's breach

  or 3. Incurred in connection with <u>return</u> or <u>resale</u> of the goods

  or 4. Otherwise resulting from the breach

IV. *THE BUYER:*

A. *BUYER'S OBLIGATIONS:*
OVERVIEW———————————————————

1) **Accept Goods** (see also "ACCEPTANCE OF GOODS" below) (§2-301)
   - Buyer must make available reasonably suited facilities to receive goods (§2-503).
   - Buyer must accept goods within a *reasonable time* after delivery (§2-309).
   - To determine how long a "reasonable time" is, one must look to:
     - Industry Norm
     - Customary Practice between parties
   - Buyer has a right to inspect the goods before Acceptance (see "ACCEPTANCE OF GOODS" below).

2) **Make Payment** (§2-301)
   - Payment is conditional upon Seller's performance (to tender and deliver goods) (§2-511) (i.e. the Buyer is not obligated to pay until Seller tenders (unless otherwise agreed)).
   - Buyer must make payment as follows:
     - Delivery of Documents: If the sale involves Documents of Title the Buyer must pay when he receives the documents
     - COD Sale: If the Sale is COD the Buyer must pay when the goods arrive.
   - The Buyer and Seller usually enter into a credit arrangement, where the Seller takes a Security Interest in the goods (known as a Purchase Money Security Interest ("PMSI")) so that the Buyer has time to pay after Seller's tender (ex: the term "Net 30" means that Buyer must pay within 30 days *after* delivery).
   - Payment may be made by any manner in the ordinary course, *unless* (§2-511):
     - Seller demands money ("legal tender" as per §1-201(24))
     and - Seller gives the Buyer additional reasonable time to make such payment
   - **Payment by Letter of Credit** - A Letter of Credit must be *seasonably furnished*; if it is not, the Buyer is considered to have repudiated his obligation to pay (§2-325).

3) **Merchant's Duties Upon Rejection of Goods** (§2-603):
- Upon rejection, a <u>Merchant</u> Buyer must:
  - Contact the Seller (to inform him of the rejection and obtain instructions on returning the goods)
  - If the Seller does not give the Buyer instructions regarding the rejected goods, the Buyer must:
    - Take a **§2-711** Security Interest in the goods
    - Resell them (any profits above the Buyer's damages must go to Seller)
- <u>Buyer may *"Cover"*</u> - buy substitute goods elsewhere (§2-712; §2-713) and charge the Seller for the difference in price (Cover price - Contract price) (See "Buyer's REMEDIES" for more detail).
- <u>Lost Sales</u>: The UCC does not compensate for *"lost sales"* of a Buyer (although §2-708(2) does for Sellers).

- **Performance of Obligations Excused:** (See "EXCUSES")

---

§2-301: General Obligations of Parties:

1. <u>Obligation of the Seller</u>: **Transfer** and **Deliver** the goods in accordance with the contract.

2. <u>Obligation of the Buyer</u>: **Accept** and **Pay** for the goods in accordance with the contract.

§2-511: Tender of Payment:

(1) Tender of Payment is a condition to the Seller's duty to tender and complete any delivery (unless otherwise agreed).

(2) Tender of Payment is sufficient if it is made by any manner in the ordinary course of business, *unless:*
   a) Seller demands money (legal tender)
and b) Seller gives an extension of time *reasonably necessary* for Buyer to comply

(3) Payment by check is *conditional* and is defeated if it is dishonored on due presentment (Subject to §3-802 (Effect of an Instrument on an Obligation)).

§2-512: Payment by Buyer Before Inspection:

(1) **Payment Required Before Inspection:** If a contract requires goods to be paid for before inspection (ex: Seller will tender documents), a non-conformity of the goods will not be an excuse for non-payment, *unless*:

        (a) The non-conformity appears without inspection (i.e. when the goods are delivered, the non-conformities are very obvious)

    or (b) The circumstances would justify an <u>injunction</u> against honoring the Seller's tender of the required documents (as per §5-114)

(2) **Effects of Payment Before Inspection:**

    a. PAYMENT (as per §2-512(1)) DOES NOT CONSTITUTE ACCEPTANCE.

    b. Payment does not impair the Buyer's right to inspect the goods (before accepting them).

    c. Payment does not impair any of the Buyer's remedies.

§2-325: Letter of Credit:

(1) Failure of a Buyer to seasonably provide an agreed Letter of Credit is a breach of the contract for sale.

(2) **L/C as Payment:**

    a) The delivery of a proper L/C to the Seller *suspends* the Buyer's obligation to pay.

    b) If the L/C is dishonored, the Seller may require payment directly from Buyer upon *seasonable notification*.

(3) <u>Definitions</u>:

    a) **"Letter of Credit"** (or "banker's credit") - means (unless otherwise agreed) an irrevocable credit issued by a financing agency of good repute.

    b) **"Confirmed Credit"** - means that the credit carries the direct obligation of a financing agency which does business in the Seller's financial market.

§1-201(24) Money:

"**Money**" is a medium of exchange authorized or adopted by a domestic or foreign government, and includes a Monetary Unit of Account established by either:

    a) An intergovernmental organization

    or b) By agreement between one or more nations

§2-603:Merchant Buyer's Rightful Rejection:

(1) Buyer's Duties Upon Rejection:

a) After rejection, any <u>Merchant</u> Buyer must follow any *reasonable instruction* received from the Seller, with respect to such goods if:

    1. If Seller has no agent or place of business where goods are rejected

    and 2. After rejection goods are still in the Buyer's possession or control

b) Upon rejection, the Buyer must make reasonable efforts to sell the goods for the Seller if:

    1. The Seller has no agent or place of business where goods are rejected

    and 2. After rejection goods are still in the Buyer's possession or control

    and 3. The Seller left no other *reasonable instructions*

    and 4. The goods are perishable or threaten to speedily decline in value

c) Instructions are not reasonable if, on the Buyer's demand, indemnity for expenses is not forthcoming.

d) This subsection is subject to any S/I in the Buyer (as per §2-711(3)).

(2) Reimbursement to Buyer:

When the Buyer sells goods under §2-603(1), he is entitled to <u>reimbursement</u> from the Seller (or out of the proceeds of the sale) for:

    a. Reasonable selling expenses

    b. Reasonable expenses incurred in caring for the goods

    c. Selling Commissions, if they are:

        1. Not included in expenses

        and 2. *Either:*

            a) Reasonable in the trade/industry

            or b) A Reasonable Sum (if no industry norm), *not to exceed 10% of gross proceeds.*

(3) Buyer's Standard of Good Faith:

a) The Buyer is held to a standard of *Good Faith.*

b) Good Faith conduct will not be considered Acceptance, Conversion, or a basis of an action for damages.

B. BUYER'S RIGHTS:
OVERVIEW ─────────────────────────────

- *Consumers:* When the Buyer is a Consumer many states change the laws of Article 2.

  1) **Buyer's Right to Inspect Goods Before Acceptance** (§2-513):
     - Inspection must be made within a reasonable time after receiving the goods (§2-513(1)).
     - Inspection may be made anywhere, unless parties fix a reasonable place (§2-513).
     - Inspection is usually at the Buyer's expense (unless the goods are non-conforming) (§2-513(2)).
     - **Loss of Right to Inspect Before Payment**: The Buyer will forfeit his right to inspect the goods before paying for them when:
          - <u>Payment Against Documents</u>: When payment is made on documents the Buyer must pay for goods before inspecting them (he must pay in order to get the Bill of Lading or Documents of Title) only if the contract *specifically* says that payment shall be made before inspection (ex: "payment to be made on Documents") (§2-513(b)).
          - or <u>Payment C.O.D.</u> - the Seller requires payment COD or on similar terms
          - or <u>Goods in Seller's Possession</u>: If the Seller would have to give up possession for Buyer to inspect the goods, the Buyer must inspect goods *after* payment (and before acceptance/rejection) (§2-507(1)).
- NOTE: **PAYMENT IS NOT ACCEPTANCE**; if payment is made before inspection and the goods are insufficient, the Buyer may reject them and sue the Seller for his money back.

  2) **Buyer's Rights to Reject Goods** - if they are nonconforming (see "PERFECT TENDER RULE: §2-601; see "REJECTION", below).

  3) **Buyer's Right to Revoke Goods** - after acceptance (See "REVOCATION", below).

  4) **Buyer's Right to Set-Off** - for any non-conformity in accepted goods (§2-717).

5) **Buyer's Right to Receive Goods:** Buyer may claim goods (obtain specific performance (§2-604)) if:
      a) The Seller has already identified the goods as the Buyer's
and b) The Buyer pays the full contract price
and c) The contract is an **Installment Contract**
and d) Delivery on the contract has already begun
and c) The Seller became *insolvent* within <u>10 Days</u> after the Buyer received the first installment

---

§2-513: Buyer's Right to Inspect Goods:

(1) **Buyer's Right to Inspection of Goods:**
    a) The Buyer has a right to inspect the goods before payment or acceptance if the goods are:
        1. Tendered
     or 2. Delivered
     or 3. Identified to the contract for sale
    b) The Buyer has a right to inspect the goods:
        1. At any reasonable place and time
     and 2. In any reasonable manner
    c) When the Seller is required or authorized to send the goods to the Buyer, the inspection may be after their arrival.
    d) This subsection may be changed by agreement of the parties, and is subject to §2-513(3).

(2) <u>Expense of Inspection</u>:
    a) Expenses must be borne by the Buyer.
    b) If the goods do not conform and are rejected, the Buyer may recover inspection expenses from Seller.

(3) **No Right to Inspect:**
    i) The Buyer is not entitled to inspect the goods before payment if the contract provides:
        (a) For delivery *"C.O.D."* (or on other similar terms)
     or (b) For payment against DOT's (except where such payment is due only after the goods are to become available for inspection)
    ii) This subsection may be changed by agreement of parties, and is subject to §2-321(3) (dealing with C.I.F. contracts).

(4) Fixed Place/Method of Inspection:
   a) A place or method of inspection fixed by the parties is presumed to be *exclusive*.
   b) Unless otherwise agreed, such an agreement does not:
      1. Postpone identification
   or 2. Change the place for delivery
   or 3. Shift the passing of risk of loss
   c) If compliance with fixed terms becomes impossible -
      Buyer shall have a right to inspect (as per §2-513), unless the fixed place/method was clearly intended as an *indispensable condition*, failure of which avoids the contract.

§2-507: Effect of Seller's Tender; Delivery on Condition:

(1) Effect of Tender:
   a. Buyer's Obligation: Tender of delivery is a condition to the Buyer's obligation to:
      1. *Accept* the goods
   and 2. *Pay* for the goods (unless otherwise agreed)
   b. Seller's Entitlement: Tender entitles the Seller to:
      1. The Buyer's acceptance of the goods
   and 2. Payment (according to the contract)

(2) Conditional Delivery:
   The Buyer's rights to *retain* or *dispose of* the goods is conditional upon making payment due to the Seller, if:
      a. Payment is due upon delivery (of goods or documents of title) to the Buyer
   and b. Seller demanded payment upon delivery (of goods or documents of title) to the Buyer

§2-602: Manner and Effect of Rightful Rejection:

(1) When to Reject:
   a) The Buyer must seasonably notify the Seller that it is rejecting the goods.
   b) Rejection will be ineffective if it is not made within a *reasonable time* after delivery or tender occurs.

(2) **Buyer's Rights and Obligations** (subject to §2-603 and §2-604):
  (a) After rejection, any "exercise of ownership" over the goods (by the Buyer) is considered *wrongful* against the Seller.
 and (b) The Buyer will have an obligation to hold the goods with *reasonable care* for a reasonable time *after* rejection (in order to allow the Seller to remove them) if:
    1. The Buyer has taken physical possession of the goods before he rejected them
   and 2. The Buyer does not have a Security Interest in the goods (as per §2-711(3))
 and (c) The Buyer has no further obligations with regard to rightfully rejected goods (unless he is a Merchant, in which case §2-603 applies).

(3) **Seller's Rights:** The Seller's rights in *wrongfully* rejected goods are governed by §2-703 (Seller's Remedies).

§2-608: Revocation of Acceptance:

(1) **When Buyer May Revoke:** The Buyer may revoke his acceptance if:
  i) A non-conformity *substantially impairs* the value of the goods to the Buyer
 and ii) *Either*:
    (a) He has accepted the goods assuming that the Seller would cure the non-conformity, but the Seller neglected to do so *seasonably*
   or (b) He accepted the goods without knowing of the non-conformity either because:
     1. It was difficult to discover the non-conformity before acceptance
    or 2. The Seller's assurances induced him to accept

(2) **Time of Revocation:**
  a) Revocation of acceptance must occur within a reasonable time:
    1. After the Buyer discovers *or should have discovered* the non-conformity
   and 2. Before there is any *substantial change* in the condition of the goods (which is not caused by their own defects)
  b) Revocation is not effective until the Buyer notifies the Seller of it.

(3) **Effect of Revocation:** A Buyer who properly revokes has the same rights and duties as if he had rejected them.

§2-717: Deduction of Damages from the Price:

a. The Buyer is permitted to deduct all or any part of the resulting damages from any part of the contract price still due if:
   1. The Seller breaches
 and 2. The Buyer gives notice of his intention to deduct all or part of the price

b. There is no formality of notice, and any language which reasonably indicates the Buyer's reason for holding up his payment is enough.

§2-716: Buyer's Right to Specific Performance or Replevin:

(1) <u>Availability</u>: Specific performance may be decreed where:
   a. The goods are *unique* (The test is made in terms of the total situation which characterizes the contract, e.g., output and requirement contracts involving a particular or peculiarly available source or market)
 or b. *In other proper circumstances* (<u>Note</u>: Inability to cover is evidence of "other proper circumstances")

(2) <u>Terms of Specific Performance</u>: The decree for specific performance may specify terms and conditions relating to:
   a. Payment of the price
 or b. Payment of damages
 or c. Other relief as the court may deem just

(3) <u>Replevin</u>: The Buyer has a right of replevin in cases in which:
   a. Goods have been identified to the contract
 and b. *Either:*
     1. Cover is not reasonably available
    or 2. The circumstances reasonably indicate that an effort to cover will be unavailing
    or 3. The goods have been shipped under reservation (i.e. the Seller shipped the goods while retaining a Security Interest in them (as per §2-505)) and the Security Interest in the goods has been satisfied or tendered.

C. *BUYER'S REMEDIES:*

1) *Remedy Upon Repudiation:*

a) Repudiation:

OVERVIEW —————————————————————————

The main problem is determining when repudiation occurs:
a) **Repudiation:** In order for Buyer to resort to its
remedies before goods are shipped, the Seller
must have **repudiated** - the main problem is
determining when repudiation occurs:
- Repudiation can occur if:
  - Substantive Value at Risk: The injured
    party will be inconvenienced or injured
    from the value of the *Repudiated
    Tender* (in comparison to the promised tender)
  - and ▪ Expression of Non-Compliance: The
    other party expresses its
    noncompliance with the contract by
    either:
    1) *Overt Communications:* A party
       states that he will not perform
       (§2-609)
    2) *Action*:
       - A party's actions render its
         performance impossible (ex:
         Seller sells identified goods to
         someone else)
       - A party's actions *reasonably
         indicate rejection* of its
         obligation
       3) Breacher *Demonstrates* a *Clear
       Determination not* to perform
    4) *Demands*: The other party
       demands an increased price to
       complete performance
    5) *Lack of Security DEMAND:* A party
       refuses to confirm its promise
       upon within **30 Days** after
       being requested to do so
       (§2-609).
    6) **Neglect:** The other party fails to
       specify instructions to Seller or fails
       to cooperate in accordance with the
       contract (§2-311)

- **"ANTICIPATORY REPUDIATION"** (§2-610) - a party's repudiation of its duties under the contract before they become due. Anticipatory Repudiation allows a party to resort to its repudiation remedies before performance of the contract would actually be due.
- Buyer's Right to Seller's Assurance of Performance:
  - If the Buyer has reasonable ground for insecurity that the Seller will not perform as promised, he may demand that the Seller assure him that he will perform as promised.
  - Procedure:
    - **Written Demand** (§2-609) - A Buyer may send a demand to assure that the Seller will:
      - *Perform* its obligations
      - or *Conform* with the terms of the contract
  - **Repudiation Occurs If** (§2-609):
    - The Seller does not assure performance/conformance within 30 Days after he receives the demand (§2-609(4))
    - or The Seller responds to the demand that he does not intend to perform (§2-609(4))

§2-609: Right to Adequate Assurance of Performance:

(1) **Adequate Assurance:**
  - a) A contract for sale creates an obligation in each party to maintain the other party's expectations of due performance.
  - b) A party will be excused from performing any contractual obligation if:
    - 1) The party had *reasonable grounds of insecurity* as to whether the other party will perform according to the contract
    - and 2) The party sends a written notice to the other party demanding *adequate assurance* of due performance
    - and 3) The other party did not yet respond to the demand
    - and 4) It is commercially reasonable to suspend performance
    - and 5) The party did not receive payment (or other return) for the obligations it plans to suspend.

c) <u>Parties</u>:
    1) *"Repudiating Party"* - The party failing to give adequate assurance of performance
    2) *"Aggrieved Party"* - The party demanding assurance of performance

(2) **Standards:** The following terms shall be construed according to *commercial standards* if the contract is <u>between Merchants</u>:
    a) "Reasonable Grounds for Insecurity"
    b) "Adequacy of assurance"

(3) **Installments:** A party is not precluded from demanding adequate assurance of future obligations even if he accepted an improper delivery or payment of earlier obligations.

(4) **Repudiation:** A party who fails to provide *adequate assurance* (under the circumstances of the case) to a justified demand within a reasonable amount of time (no more than <u>30 days</u>) will have repudiated the contract.

§2-610: Anticipatory Repudiation:

1. **"Anticipatory Repudiation"** - Anticipatory Repudiation occurs when:
    a. Either party repudiates the contract (see §2-609)
  and b. The repudiated portion of the contract is not yet due
  and c. The loss of such performance will *substantially impair* the value of the contract

2. **Rights of Aggrieved Party upon Anticipatory Repudiation:** The aggrieved party may:
    (a) <u>Await Performance</u> - from the repudiating party, for a *commercially reasonable time*
  or (b) <u>Resort to Breach Remedies</u> (as per §2-703 (for Seller) or §2-711 (for Buyer)) - even if he told the repudiating party that he will wait for performance (subsection (a))
  or (c) <u>Suspend Performance</u> - The aggrieved party may suspend his own performance.
  or d) <u>Identify and Salvage Goods</u> - The Seller may identify goods to a contract or salvage unfinished goods (as per §2-704).

§2-611: Retraction of Anticipatory Repudiation:

(1) **Time for Retraction:** The repudiating party may retract his repudiation if:
    a) His next performance is still not yet due
and b) The aggrieved party has <u>not</u>:
        1. Canceled the contract
      or 2. Materially changed its position
      or 3. Otherwise indicated that it considers the repudiation final

(2) **Requirements for Retraction:** A valid retraction of repudiation must:
    a) *Clearly indicate* to the aggrieved party that the repudiating party <u>intends to perform</u>
and b) Include any <u>adequate assurance</u> *justifiably* demanded under §2-609

(3) **Effect of Retraction:**
    a) The repudiating party's rights under the contract are reinstated
and b) The aggrieved party is excused for any delay due to the repudiation.

b) *Remedies upon Repudiation:*

OVERVIEW ────────────────────

Upon Repudiation, the Buyer obtains rights under **§2-610**, which allows the Buyer to:

      1. <u>Await Performance</u> by the Repudiating Party (§2-610(a))

or   2. <u>Suspend His Own Performance</u> (§2-610(c))

or   3. <u>Resort to §2-711 Remedies</u> (even if Buyer told Seller that he would await performance):

      A. *Either:*

        1. **"Cover"** (as per §2-712) (§2-711((1)(a)):

          ■ A Buyer can *"cover"* by purchasing *substitute* goods, and later suing the Buyer for the difference

        (Cost of Substitutes - Contract Price).

          ■ <u>Buyer's Requirements to Cover</u>: In order to property Cover, the Buyer must:

            1) Purchase a *"commercially reasonable substitute"*

              2) Purchase it within a *"commercially reasonable time"*

          ■ Although the Buyer is not required to cover, he cannot recover *consequential damages* if he does not make a *reasonable attempt* to mitigate (i.e. reduce) his damages by covering.

or 2. **Sue Seller for Damages for Non-Delivery** (as per §2-713) (§2-711(1)(b)):
- Buyer may sue Seller for:

DIRECT DAMAGES
+ INCIDENTAL DAMAGES
- EXPENSES SAVED

- <u>**Incidental and Consequential Damages**</u> (§2-715):
    - Only available if Buyer attempted to *cover* or cover was unreasonable
    - Buyer's inspection costs and other expenses Buyer already incurred in performing under the contract (which Buyer couldn't reasonably prevent)
    - Buyer's storage, reshipping, and costs to find substitutes
- <u>**Expenses Saved**</u> - must be *deducted* from damages
- <u>**Direct Damages**</u> are *either*:
    - a) **Damages for Price:**
      <u>Contract Price</u>
      - <u>Market price</u> (at the time Buyer learned of breach) (§2-713; §2-714)
    - or b) **Cover Damages:** <u>Cover Price</u> - <u>Contract Price</u> - if Buyer covered in *good faith* (as per §2-712)
    - or c) **Breach of Warranty** (§2-714) - (see "WARRANTIES")

and B. <u>If Seller never Delivers</u>, *either*:
1. **Recover Identified Goods** (as per §2-502) (§2-702(2)(a))
or 2. **Obtain Specific Performance / Replevin** (as per §2-716) (§2-702(2)(b))
   - <u>Specific Performance</u> - a rarely available remedy which may be obtained if (§2-716(1) and official comment):
       - Goods are *"Unique"*
       - or Goods are in *Short Supply*
       - or Other damages are *inadequate*

- <u>Replevin</u> may be available if (§2-716(3)):
  - a) <u>The Buyer Cannot Cover</u> because:
    - The Goods are identified to the contract
    - and *Either:*
      - Buyer can't buy a substitute using *reasonable effort*
        - or Circumstances *reasonably indicate* that such efforts to cover would be unavailing.

  - or b) <u>Buyer has Tendered goods Shipped under Reservation</u> if:
    - The Seller shipped goods under reservation
    - and The Buyer has other:
      - Satisfied the security interest in them
        - or Tendered payment
    - and The goods have not been released to the Buyer

---

§2-610(a)-(c) Rights of Aggrieved Party upon Anticipatory Repudiation:

The aggrieved party may:

- (a) <u>Await Performance</u> - from the repudiating party, for a *commercially reasonable time*
- or (b) <u>Resort to Breach Remedies</u> (as per §2-703 (for Seller) or §2-711 (for Buyer)) - even if he told the repudiating party that he will wait for performance (subsection (a))
- or (c) <u>Suspend Performance</u> - The aggrieved party may suspend his own performance.
- or d) <u>Identify and Salvage Goods</u> - The Seller may identify goods to a contract or salvage unfinished goods (as per §2-704).

§2-711: Buyer's Remedies in General; Buyer's Security Interest in Rejected Goods:

Even though the Seller breached, the Buyer may be barred from using these remedies if:
a. The Seller properly tendered goods (as per §2-508)
and b. No delay was involved

(1) <u>Buyer's Remedies Permitting the Recovery of Money Damages</u>:
   a. The Buyer is entitled to §2-711 remedies when:
      1. The Seller fails to make delivery
      or 2. The Seller repudiates
      or 3. The Buyer rightfully rejects
      or 4. The Buyer justifiably revokes acceptance
   b. See §2-714 for remedies available to a Buyer if the goods were finally accepted.
   c. The §2-711 remedies apply with respect to:
      1. Any goods involved
      and 2. The whole contract (if the breach goes to the whole contract (see 2-612))
   d. **Buyer's Remedies** - The Buyer may:
      1. Cancel the contract
      and 2. Recover as much of the price as he has paid (whether or not he has canceled the contract)
      and 3. *Either:*
         (a) *"Cover"* and recover damages under §2-712 as to all the goods affected (whether or not they have been identified to the contract)
         or (b) Recover damages for non-delivery under §2-713.

(2) <u>Additional Remedies Which Permit Reaching the Goods Themselves</u>:
   a. Remedies - The Buyer may:
      (a) Recover the goods under §2-502 if the goods have been identified
      or (b) In a proper case obtain <u>specific performance</u> or <u>replevy</u> the goods as per §2-716
   b. These additional remedies apply when:
      1. The Seller fails to deliver
      or 2. The Seller repudiates

(3) <u>The Buyer's Security Interest In The Goods</u>:
    a. The Buyer has a Security Interest in goods which are *in his possession or control* in the amount of:
        1. That part of the price already paid by the Buyer
   or 2. Any expenses reasonably incurred in **inspection, receipt, transportation, care** and **custody** of the goods
    b. The Buyer may hold and resell (§2-706) such goods.
    c. This subsection applies if:
        1. The Buyer <u>rightfully rejected</u> the goods
   or 2. The Buyer <u>justifiably revoked</u> acceptance of the goods

§2-712: "Cover"; Buyer's Procurement of Substitute Goods:

(1) **"Covering"**:
    a. After a breach (within §2-711) the Buyer may "cover" by:
        1. Making any *reasonable purchase* of goods to substitute those due from the Seller
   or 2. Contracting to purchase such goods
    b. <u>Requirements</u> - "Covering" must be done:
        1. In good faith
   and 2. Without unreasonable delay
    c. <u>Note</u>: It is immaterial that hindsight may later prove that the method of cover used was not the cheapest or most effective.

(2) The Buyer may recover from the Seller the following as damages:

      The cost of cover
     - **The contract price**
     + **Any incidental or consequential damages** (as defined in §2-715)
     - **Expenses saved in consequence of the Seller's breach**

(3) Failure of the Buyer to cover within §2-712 does not bar the Buyer from any other remedy. (<u>Note</u>: Cover is not a mandatory remedy for the Buyer. The Buyer is always free to choose between cover and damages for non-delivery under **§2-713**.)

(Note: This subsection must be read in conjunction with §2-715. Moreover, the operation of §2-716 must be considered in this connection for availability of the goods to the particular Buyer for his particular needs is the test for that remedy and inability to cover is made an express condition to the right of the Buyer to replevy the goods.)

§2-713: Buyer's Damages for Non-Delivery or Repudiation:

This section applies only when and to the extent that the Buyer has not covered.

(1) <u>Calculation of Damages</u> (Subject to §2-723) - The measure of damages for non-delivery or repudiation by the Seller is:

> **The market price** (using the **market** in which the Buyer would have obtained cover and the **price** for goods of the same kind and in the same branch of trade) **at the time when the Buyer learned of the breach**
> - **The contract price**
> + **Any incidental or consequential damages** (as defined in §2-715)
> - **Any expenses saved in consequence of the Seller's breach**

(2) "<u>Market Price</u>" - The place where market price is to be determined is:
- a. The place for tender (if the goods never reached their destination)
- b. The place of arrival (if the goods are rejected or their acceptance is revoked after reaching their destination)

§2-714: Buyer's Damages for Breach in Regard to Accepted Goods:

(1) **Remedy:** The Buyer is permitted to recover his loss in *any reasonable manner* if:
- a. There is any non-conformity of tender (not only breaches of warranties but also any failure of the Seller to perform according to his obligations under the contract)
- and b. The loss resulted from the ordinary course of events from the Seller's breach
- and c. The goods have been accepted
- and d. The time for revocation of acceptance has gone by
- and e. The Buyer gave notification (as per §2-607(3))

(2) **Damages for Breach of Warranty:**
  a. <u>Measure</u>: Damages for breach of Warranty equal:

> **The value of the goods accepted at the time and place of acceptance**
>
> **– The value they would have had if they had been as warranted**

  b. <u>Exception</u>: When special circumstances show proximate damages of a different amount.

(3) **Incidental and Consequential Damages:** In a proper case any incidental and consequential damages under §2-715 may also be recovered.

§2-715: Buyer's Incidental and Consequential Damages:

(1) **Incidental Damages:** Reimbursement for the Buyer's incidental damages resulting from the Seller's breach include:
  a. <u>Expenses for Rejected Goods</u>: Expenses reasonably incurred in **inspection, receipt, transportation, care** and **custody** of goods rightfully rejected
  and b. <u>Expenses for Covering</u>: Any commercially reasonable **charges, expenses** or **commissions** in connection with covering
  and c. <u>Expenses for Delay or Breach</u>: Any other reasonable expense incident to the delay or other breach

(2) **Consequential Damages:** Consequential damages resulting from the Seller's breach include:
  (a) <u>Loss</u>: Any loss resulting from "general" or "particular" requirements:
    1. Conditions:
      a. The Seller had reason to know of the need for the requirement at the time of contracting
      and b. The Buyer could not reasonably have prevented such losses by covering or otherwise
    2. Note:
      a. "Particular" needs of the Buyer must generally be made known to the Seller.
      b. "General" needs must rarely be made known to charge the Seller with knowledge.
  and (b) <u>Injury</u>: Injury to person or property proximately resulting from any breach of warranty

105

§2-716: Buyer's Right to Specific Performance or Replevin:

(1) <u>Availability</u>: Specific performance may be decreed where:
    a. The goods are *unique* (The test is made in terms of the total situation which characterizes the contract, e.g., output and requirement contracts involving a particular or peculiarly available source or market)
  or b. *In other proper circumstances* (<u>Note</u>: Inability to cover is evidence of "other proper circumstances")

(2) <u>Terms of Specific Performance</u>: The decree for specific performance may specify terms and conditions relating to:
    a. Payment of the price
  or b. Payment of damages
  or c. Other relief as the court may deem just

(3) <u>Replevin</u>: The Buyer has a right of replevin in cases in which:
    a. Goods have been identified to the contract
  and b. *Either:*
        1. Cover is not reasonably available
    or 2. The circumstances reasonably indicate that an effort to cover will be unavailing
    or 3. The goods have been shipped under reservation (i.e. the Seller shipped the goods while retaining a Security Interest in them (as per §2-505)) and the Security Interest in the goods has been satisfied or tendered.

§2-717: Deduction of Damages from the Price:

a. The Buyer is permitted to deduct all or any part of the resulting damages from any part of the contract price still due if:
    1. The Seller breaches
  and 2. The Buyer gives notice of his intention to deduct all or part of the price

b. There is no formality of notice, and any language which reasonably indicates the Buyer's reason for holding up his payment is enough.

2) *Buyer's Remedies Upon Breach of Warranty:*

a) *Types of Warranties:*

OVERVIEW ─────────────────────────

Under Article 2 transactions, the Seller makes 2 types of
warranties to the Buyer:

- There are 2 types of warranties in the UCC:

  1. **Warranty of Title:** The Seller promises:
     a. Good Title: That he is transferring good title, and is
        doing so rightfully (§2-312(1)(a)).
     b. Free of Claims: The goods are free from any claims
        from the Seller's creditors (except for those that the Buyer
        knows about) (§2-312(1)(b)).
     c. No Infringements: Merchant sellers warrant that
        goods are delivered free from any rightful patent or
        trademark claims of a third person (unless Seller made the
        goods according to the Buyer's specifications) (§2-312(3)).

  2. **Warranty of Quality:** These are warranties regarding the
     goods themselves, and can either be expressed or
     implied:

     a) **Express Warranties:**
        - **"Express Warranties"** are statements relating to
          the goods which are part of the basis of the
          bargain (§2-313(1)(a)).
        - Form: The specific words *"warranty"* or
          "guarantee" need not be used. An Express
          Warranty may be created in the form of
          (§2-313(1),(2)):
          - An affirmation of fact
          - A promise
          - A description
          - A sample or model
        - The following do not create a warranty:
          - Statements of value or of the Seller's opinion
            or commendation of goods (ex: "Sales Puff")
            (§2-313(2)).
          - Modification: A statement made after the
            sale is closed that becomes part of the basis
            of the bargain may constitute a modification
            (§See 2-209).

b) Implied Warranties:
- **"Implied Warranties"** are warranties implied by law.
- Types of Implied Warranties:
  - *Warranty of Merchantability:*
    - The law imposes upon a Merchant Seller a warranty that the goods are of a *"merchantable" quality* (§2-314). (Note that this is in addition to the good faith requirement of §1-203 that even non-merchants are held to).
    - Goods are considered **"Merchantable"** when:
      - They are capable of passing without objection in the trade under the contract description (§2-314(2)(a)).
      - and For fungible goods, they must be of fair average quality (§2-314(2)(b).
      - and The goods must be *fit for the ordinary purposes* for which such goods are used (§2-314(2)(c)).
      - and The goods must be within the variations allowed by the agreement (§2-314(2)(d)).
      - and The goods have to be contained, packaged and labeled adequately (§2-314(2)(e)).
      - and The goods have to *conform* to the label (§2-314(2)(f)).

  - *Warranty of Fitness* (§2-315) - An implied warranty of fitness will be created if:
    - A Seller has reason to know of the particular use of the goods that the Buyer contemplates
    - and The Seller is aware that the Buyer is relying on the Seller's judgment.

§2-312: Warranty of Title:

(1) In a contract of sale, the Seller makes the following Warranties (subject to §2-312(2)):
    (a) **Good Title:**
        1. The title conveyed shall be good
      and 2. The transfer is rightful
    (b) **Goods Free of Liens:** The goods are delivered free from Security Interests or other liens (or encumbrances) which the Buyer had no knowledge of at the time the contract was created.

(2) **Modification or Exclusion:** A Warranty of Title may only be modified or excluded by:
    a) Specific language in the contract
    b) Circumstances which give the Buyer reason to know that
        1. The Seller does not claim title in himself
      or 2. The Seller is only purporting to sell the rights which he (or a third person) may have in the goods (ex: Seller sells goods "as is").

(3) **Goods Do Not Infringe Third Party Rights** - *Merchant Only*:
The Seller warrants that the goods do not infringe a third party's rights and will be delivered free from the rightful claim of any third person (ex: free from a patent or copyright infringement) if:
    a) The Seller is a *Merchant* regularly dealing in goods of the kind sold
    and b) The infringement does not arise out of the Seller's compliance with the Buyer's instructions (ex: Buyer tells Seller to apply a label which infringes an already existing copyrighted label to its goods).

§2-313 - Express Warranty by Affirmation:

(1) **Express Warranties** by the Seller are created as follows:

    (a) <u>Warranty That Goods Shall Conform to an Affirmation or Promise</u> - Created by *any affirmation of fact or promise:*
        1. Which is made by the Seller to the Buyer
      and 2. Relating to the goods
      and 3. Which becomes a significant part of the basis of the bargain

    (b) <u>Warranty That The Goods Shall Conform to their Description</u> - Created when any description of the goods becomes a significant factor in the basis of the bargain.

(c) <u>Warranty That Goods Shall Conform to Sample or Model</u> - Created when a sample or model becomes a significant factor in the basis of the bargain.

(2) **Substance Over Form**
    a. It is not necessary for Seller to use formal words such as *"warrant"* or *"guarantee"* to create an Express Warranty
    b. The following do not alone create express warranties:
        1. An Affirmation merely of the <u>value</u> of the goods
    or 2. A Statement purporting to be merely the Seller's <u>opinion</u>
    or 3. <u>Compliments or Commendations</u> of the goods (ex:"Sales Puff")

§2-314: Implied Warranty of Merchantability:

(1) **Implied Warranty:**
    a. A Warranty that the goods shall be merchantable is implied in a contract for their sale if:
        1. The Seller is a *Merchant*, selling goods of the kind sold
    and 2. There is no clause excluding or modifying such a warranty (as per §2-316)
    b. The serving of food or drink *for value* (regardless of where it is consumed) is considered a sale for purposes of this section.

(2) **Warranty of Merchantability:** Under the Warranty of Merchantability, the Seller warrants:
    (a) <u>Goods Fit Trade Description</u> - Goods must pass without objection in the trade under the contract description (ex: if in order to be considered Orange Juice, a drink must contain 75% juice from oranges, the contents of an "Orange Juice" container must be 75% juice from oranges).
    and (b) <u>Quality</u> - *Fungible Goods* must be of fair, average quality (within the description of such goods).
    and (c) <u>Fitness</u> - Must be fit for the *ordinary purposes* for which such goods are used (for particular purposes, see §2-315).
    and (d) <u>Uniformity</u> - They must have similar quality and characteristics (within variations permitted by the agreement) within each unit, and among all units involved in the contract.
    and (e) <u>Packaging</u> - The goods must be adequately contained, packaged, and labeled (as the agreement or nature of the product may require (ex: pills to be sold over the counter should be packaged in tamper-proof containers)).
    and (f) <u>Goods Fit Package Description</u> - Must conform to the Promise or Affirmations made on the container or label.

(3) Other implied warranties may arise from the Course of Dealing or Usage of Trade (unless excluded or modified as per §2-316)

§2-315: Implied Warranty of Fitness for a Particular Purpose:

The Seller impliedly promises the Buyer that the goods shall be fit for a particular purpose if:

    a) At the time the contract was created, the Seller had *reason to know* any particular purpose for which Buyer wanted to use the goods

and b) The Buyer relied on the Seller's skill or judgment to select or furnish suitable goods

and c) Such a warranty has not been excluded or modified (as per §2-316)

b) Disclaimers:

OVERVIEW ———————————————————

- Warranties can be disclaimed (§2-316).
- Requirements: *Specific, conspicuous* language in the contract mast be used to disclaim a warranty of title (§2-312(2)).

- **Disclaiming Express Warranties:**
  - Words or conduct creating the warranty and words or conduct negating or limiting the warranty shall be construed consistently (subject to §2-202; §2-316).
  - Unreasonable disclaimers will not be recognized as valid (§2-316(1)).

- **Disclaiming Implied Warranties:**
  Implied warranties can be disclaimed in one of 4 ways:
  - Specific Disclaimer Clauses:
    - For a Warranty of Merchantability, the word "merchantability" must be mentioned and the disclaimer, if written, must be conspicuous (See §1-201(10) (it can also be oral) (§2-316(2)).
    - For a Warranty of Fitness for a Particular Purpose the disclaimer must be in writing and conspicuous (§2-316(2)).
  - Goods "As-Is" - If goods are sold "as is" (or similar language), there are no implied warranties (§2-316(3)(a)).
  - **Limiting Implied Warranties**
    - Buyer's Inspection: Implied Warranties will be limited to defects which the Buyer should have reasonably discovered (under the circumstances) if:
      - The Buyer inspects (to his satisfaction) the goods or the sample model before entering into the contract
      - or ■ The Buyer refuses to examine the goods
    - Course of Dealing and Custom and Usage in the Trade can limit implied warranties (§2-316(3)).

§2-316: Exclusion or Modification of Warranties:

(1) Consistent Construction of Words and Conduct:
    a. The following shall be construed *consistently* whenever possible:
        1. Words or Conduct relating to the <u>creation</u> of an Express Warranty
        2. Words or Conduct tending to <u>negate</u> or <u>limit</u> such warranties
    b. Negation or Limitation of such warranties are invalid to the extent that a consistent construction is unreasonable (subject to §2-202 (Parole Evidence)).

(2) Requirements of Excluding or Modifying Implied Warranties (subject to §2-316(3))**:**
    a. <u>To Exclude or Modify an Implied Warranty of Merchantability</u>:
        1. The language must <u>mention merchantability</u>
        and 2. The language must be <u>conspicuous</u> if in writing
    b. <u>To Exclude or Modify an Implied Warranty of Fitness</u>:
        1. The exclusion must be <u>in writing</u>
        and 2. The language must be <u>conspicuous</u>
    c. <u>To Exclude ALL Implied Warranties of Fitness</u>: Language must be very clear (ex: "There are no warranties which extend beyond the description on the face hereof").

(3) Rules Regarding Excluding Implied Warranties:
<u>Notwithstanding §2-316(2)</u> (above):
    (a) All implied warranties may be excluded by the use of language which, in common understanding:
        1) Calls the Buyer's attention to the exclusion of warranties
        and 2) Makes it clear that there are no implied warranties (unless the circumstances indicate otherwise (ex: sold "as is" or "with all faults"))
    (b) **Buyer's Inspection:** Implied Warranties will be limited to defects which the Buyer should have reasonably discovered (under the circumstances) if:
        1. The Buyer inspects (to his satisfaction) the goods or a sample model before entering into the contract
        or 2. The Buyer refuses to examine the goods
    (c) An Implied Warranty can also be Excluded or Modified by:
        1) The Course of Dealing (as per §1-205)
        or 2) The Course of Performance (as per §2-208)
        or 3) The Usage of Trade (as per §1-205)

(4) **Limitations for Breach of Warranty:** Remedies for breach of warranty may be limited in accordance with the provisions dealing with:
  a) Liquidation or Limitation of Damages (§2-718)
  b) Contractual Modification of Remedy (§2-719)

§2-317: Cumulation and Conflict of Implied or Express Warranties:

1. Warranties (whether express or implied) shall be construed to be *cumulative* and *consistent with each other*, whenever reasonable.

2. If such a construction is unreasonable, the *intention of the parties* shall determine which warranty is dominant.

3. <u>Rules in Determining the Intention of the Parties</u> (with regard to conflicting warranties):
  (a) <u>Exact or Technical Specifications of the Goods</u> displace an inconsistent sample, model, or general language of the goods' description.
  (b) <u>A Sample From An Existing Bulk</u> displaces inconsistent general language or description of the goods.
  (c) <u>An Express Warranty</u> displaces inconsistent, implied warranties (other than the implied warranty of fitness for a particular purpose (§2-315)).

§2-318: Third Party Beneficiaries of Warranties:

This section shall be omitted if The United States Congress adopts it (as of 1995 it has not).

ALTERNATIVE A
1. A Seller's express or implied warranties extend to:
   a) Any natural person in the Buyer's family or household
   and b) Any guest in the Buyer's home
2. The Seller will be held responsible for breach of warranty to the third party if:
   a) It is reasonable to expect such a person to use, consume, or be affected by the goods (ex: A Seller should expect a third party to sit on a Buyer's dining room chair, but the Seller probably would not expect a third party to use the Buyer's dishwasher).
   and b) That person is injured by the breach of the warranty.
3. The Seller may not exclude or limit the warranties to third persons.

ALTERNATIVE B
1. A Seller's express and implied warranties extend to any natural person in the Buyer's family or household if:
   a) It is reasonable to expect such a person to use, consume, or be affected by the goods
   and b) That person is injured by the breach of the warranty.
2. The Seller may not exclude or limit its liability to third persons.

ALTERNATIVE C
1. A Seller's express and implied warranties extends to any person if:
   a) It is reasonable to expect such a person to use, consume, or be affected by the goods
   and b) That person is injured by the breach of the warranty.
2. The Seller may not exclude or limit its liability to third persons if the warranty is meant to extend to that person.

c) Breach of Warranty:

OVERVIEW ────────────────────────

- Requirements For Buyer to Recover for Breach of Warranty:
  - The Buyer must show that the breach was the *Proximate Cause* of the loss (§2-715(2)(a),(b)).
  - The Buyer must prove that he gave *Notice* of the breach of warranty within a reasonable time after the breach should have been discovered (§2-607(3)(a)).
  - If the Buyer is sued by a third party, he must give the Seller an opportunity to defend himself (§2-607(5)(a)).

- **Remedies for Breach of Warranty:**
  - Prior to Acceptance - breach is treated like a failure to perform the contract (See "Buyer's REMEDIES" and "Seller'S REMEDIES"):
  - After Acceptance - Buyer can:
    - **Recover:**
      - Loss in value because of the breach in warranty; the measure is (§2-714(2)):

      The value of the goods accepted at the time and place of acceptance
      - The value they would have had if they had been as warranted

      and ■ Consequential and Incidental Damages (§2-714(2)) (See "DAMAGES"):

      and ■ Costs and expenses reasonably incurred incidental to the Seller's breach (§2-715(1)).
    - or **Revoke Acceptance** (See "REVOCATION") in some cases (§2-714(2)).

V.LIMITATIONS WHEN BUYER OR SELLER IS ENTITLED TO DAMAGES AS A REMEDY:

OVERVIEW

When a Buyer or Seller chooses to sue for damages,the following limitations apply:

A. Available Damages:
  1. **Expectancy Damages** (§2-709; §2-715):
  - Expectancy damages attempt to put the non-breaching party in *as good of position as he would have been had there not been a breach.*
  - Common law has long held that the appropriate damages for breach of contract is Expectancy Damages. This has been adopted by the UCC (see §2-709 and §2-715).
  - The UCC will not punish a breaching party simply because it breached. It will only award damages for *Actual Losses* incurred by the non-breaching party as a result of the breach.
  - Thus, when a Buyer "covers," he may not sue the Seller for damages if he buys his substitute goods at a cheaper price that he would have under the contract; in such a case the Buyer did not incur a loss.
  - Since most sales transaction involve nothing more than profit seeking, expectancy damages are most appropriate as they can adequately compensate for losses
  - However, once a party suffers non-monetary losses (such as *goodwill*), expectancy damages do not adequately make the non-breaching party whole. In such situations other remedies (such as Specific Performance (§2-716)) may be made available.

- **Normal Measures for Expectancy Damages**:

  - **Seller's Expectancy Damages:**

        Contract Price
    - Resale/Market Price
    - Incidental Expenses
    + Expenses Avoided

  - **Buyer's Expectancy Damages**

        Price of Substitute goods
    - Contract Price
    - Incidental Expenses
    + Expenses Avoided

  - <u>Lost Sales</u>: Only Sellers are entitled to the profit they would have made on the goods if they can prove that they are *"lost volume sellers"* (i.e. that they can profitably sell as many goods as they buy or produce).

2. **Liquidated Damages** (§2-718(1)):
   - Parties often agree in their contract to set an appropriate amount of liability each party will incur if it breaches the contract. Such provisions are known as **"Liquidated Damages Provisions."**
   - Liquidated Damages Provisions will not always be enforced:
     - The Liquidated Damages must be *reasonable* in light of (§2-718):
       - The <u>Actual Loss</u> resulting from the breach
       and - The <u>Anticipated Loss</u>, as predicted when the contract was made
     - Liquidated Damages cannot be **"Penalties"** - Any award *unreasonably disproportionate* to the Actual <u>Damages</u> incurred will be considered a **"Penalty,"** and will NOT be enforced (§2-718(1)).

3. **Emotional Damages** - are prohibited unless the purpose of the contract was to protect a person from emotional distress

4. **Punitive Damages** - are rarely awarded. Some courts allow them when Fraud is involved or the Buyer is a Consumer.

5. **Reliance and Restitution:** Although the UCC does not explicitly provide for damages of Restitution or Reliance it represents the interests inherent in them.

   - <u>Restitution</u>: Restitution damages aim at putting the parties in status quo and pay them for services rendered ("quantum meruit"). Article 2 provides for specific types of restitution: <u>Replevin</u> (§2-716), <u>Restitution Rights</u> (§2-705), and the Buyer's obligation to pay Seller for the reasonable price of the goods when price is not determinable (§2-305).

   - <u>Reliance</u>: Reliance damages attempt to compensate a party for losses incurred in reliance of a certain expectation. Article 2 allows only certain types of Reliance damages: <u>Incidental Damages</u>, compensation for <u>Loss in Value</u> if a Seller must Resell or a Buyer must Cover, and, under certain circumstances, <u>Waiver</u>, if a party relies on an ineffective Modification.

6. **Specific Performance/Replevin:** Courts rarely award parties Replevin or Specific Performance; the UCC and common law only allow it if other remedies are *inadequate*. They strongly "urge" the parties to mitigate (i.e. reduce) damages (see "Mitigation" below).

B. <u>Other Limitations</u>:

1. <u>Foreseeability</u> - The breaching party will only be responsible for the *reasonably foreseeable* damages occurring in the *"ordinary course" of events* (<u>Hadley v. Baxendale</u>).

2. <u>Measurability</u> - Damages must be measurable.

3. <u>Mitigation</u>: Although a party is not required to mitigate (i.e. try to reduce the amount of damages), it cannot recover <u>Consequential Damages</u> if it does not make a *reasonable attempt* to mitigate.
   - A Buyer can mitigate by <u>Covering</u> (as per §2-712).
   - A Seller can mitigate damages by <u>Reselling</u> its goods (as per §2-706).

§2-716: Buyer's Right to Specific Performance or Replevin:

(1) <u>Availability</u>: Specific performance may be decreed where:
    a. The goods are *unique* (The test is made in terms of the total situation which characterizes the contract, e.g., output and requirement contracts involving a particular or peculiarly available source or market)
  or b. *In other proper circumstances* (<u>Note</u>: Inability to cover is evidence of "other proper circumstances")

(2) <u>Terms of Specific Performance</u>: The decree for specific performance may specify terms and conditions relating to:
    a. Payment of the price
  or b. Payment of damages
  or c. Other relief as the court may deem just

(3) <u>Replevin</u>: The Buyer has a right of replevin in cases in which:
    a. Goods have been identified to the contract
  and b. *Either:*
        1. Cover is not reasonably available
     or 2. The circumstances reasonably indicate that an effort to cover will be unavailing
     or 3. The goods have been shipped under reservation (i.e. the Seller shipped the goods while retaining a Security Interest in them (as per §2-505)) and the Security Interest in the goods has been satisfied or tendered.

§2-718: Liquidation or Limitation of Damages; Restitution:

(1) **Liquidated Damages Clauses:**
    a. In an agreement, liquidated damage clauses for breach by either party are allowed.
    b. <u>Requirement</u> - The amount involved has to be reasonable in the light of:
        1. The anticipated or actual harm caused by the breach
     and 2. The difficulties of proof of loss
     and 3. The inconvenience or non-feasibility of adequate compensation with another remedy
    c. A term fixing unreasonably large liquidated damages is considered a *"penalty"* and is void.

(2) **Restitution of Buyer's Payments:** Where the Seller justifiably withholds delivery of goods because of the Buyer's breach, the Buyer may recover restitution in an amount equal to:
    (a) <u>Liquidated Damages</u>:

       Buyer's Payments

       - What the Seller is entitled to (in accordance with subsection (1))

    or (b) If there are no liquidated damages clauses in the agreement for the Seller's damages, *the lower of*:
        1. $500
       or 2. **Buyer's Payments - 20% of the value of the total performance** (for which the Buyer is obligated under the contract)

(3) **Reduction of Buyer's Restitution:** The Buyer's right to recover under subsection (2) may be reduced by the amount the Seller establishes:
    (a) A right to recover damages under Article 2 other than §2-718(1)
    or (b) The amount or value of any benefits the Buyer received by reason of the contract (directly or indirectly)

(4) **"Buyer's Payments":** For purposes of subsection (2), the "Buyer's payments" includes:
    a. The reasonable value of goods received by the Seller as payment (in part performance)
    or b. The proceeds of their resale (provided the Seller does not have notice of the Buyer's breach before reselling the goods; if so, his resale is subject to the conditions in §2-706)

§2-709: Action for the Price:

(1) <u>Buyer Fails to Pay</u>: When the Buyer fails to pay the price as it becomes due, the Seller may recover the following (+ any incidental damages under §2-710):

    (a) **Accepted/Destroyed Goods:**

         1. <u>Accepted Goods</u> - The price of the goods

         2. <u>Destroyed Goods</u> - The price of the goods, if:

            a. The goods were conforming goods,

      and b. The goods were destroyed within a commercially reasonable time after risk of loss has passed to the Buyer

  and (b) **Identified Goods:** The price of goods identified to the contract if:

         1. The Seller is unable after *reasonable effort* to resell the goods at a reasonable price

      or 2. The circumstances reasonably indicate that such effort will be unavailing

(2) <u>Seller's Requirements With Respect to Identified Goods</u>:

    a. Seller must hold goods which have been identified to the contract for the Buyer if:

         1. The Seller is suing the Buyer for their price

      and 2. The goods are still in the Seller's control

    b. <u>Resale</u>: If resale becomes possible, the Seller may resell the goods at any time before the judgment (price) is collected.

    c. <u>Buyer's Rights</u>:

         1. The net proceeds of any such resale must be credited to the Buyer.

         2. Payment of the judgment entitles the Buyer to any goods not resold.

(3) Even if a Seller is not entitled to the price (under §2-709) he may be awarded <u>damages for non-acceptance</u> (under §2-708) if the Buyer:

    a. Wrongfully rejected the goods

    or b. Wrongfully revoked acceptance of the goods

    or c. Has failed to make a payment due

    or d. Has repudiated (as per §2-610)

§2-715: Buyer's Incidental and Consequential Damages:

(1) **Incidental Damages:** Reimbursement for the Buyer's incidental damages resulting from the Seller's breach include:

    a. <u>Expenses for Rejected Goods</u>: Expenses reasonably incurred in **inspection, receipt, transportation, care** and **custody** of goods rightfully rejected

and b. <u>Expenses for Covering</u>: Any commercially reasonable **charges, expenses** or **commissions** in connection with covering

and c. <u>Expenses for Delay or Breach</u>: Any other reasonable expense incident to the delay or other breach

(2) **Consequential Damages:** Consequential damages resulting from the Seller's breach include:

    (a) <u>Loss</u>: Any loss resulting from "general" or "particular" requirements:

        1. Conditions:

            a. The Seller had reason to know of the need for the requirement at the time of contracting

        and b. The Buyer could not reasonably have prevented such losses by covering or otherwise

        2. Note:

            a. "Particular" needs of the Buyer must generally be made known to the Seller.

            b. "General" needs must rarely be made known to charge the Seller with knowledge.

and (b) <u>Injury</u>: Injury to person or property proximately resulting from any breach of warranty

VI. CARRIER'S AND WAREHOUSEMAN'S OBLIGATIONS:

OVERVIEW

- A **"Carrier"** is a <u>third party</u> hired to ship goods (a "Carrier" cannot be an employee or entity of the Buyer or Seller).
    - The Carrier usually issues a **Bill of Lading** as a receipt that he has taken the goods for shipment.
    - The Carrier is obligated to "return" the goods (i.e. ship them) to the person holding the Bill of Lading (see "BILLS OF LADING" below).

- A **"Bailee"** is someone who holds and watches the goods. Usually the Bailee is a Warehouseman who is in the business of storing goods.
    - The Bailee usually issues a **Warehouse Receipt** or other **Document of Title** as a receipt that he is storing such goods in his warehouse.
    - The Bailee is obligated to return the goods to the person holding the Document of Title or Warehouse Receipt.

- The Carrier or the Bailee has an obligation to deliver the goods to the person "entitled" to them (§7-403; §7-404)
    - The Carrier will usually listen to changes of instructions from a Consignee (Buyer), although it is not obligated to (§7-303).
    - If the Consignor's (Seller's) instructions contradict the consignee (Buyer), the Carrier will usually listen to the Consignor (Seller) (§7-303).

- <u>Stopping Delivery</u>: The Carrier may stop delivery of goods In Transit if:
    - The Buyer is insolvent (§2-705)
    - Diversion occurs (as per §7-303)

- <u>Liability of Carrier/Bailee</u> - The Carrier will be liable for the goods if (§7-403; §7-404):
    - It Delivers them to the wrong person
    - It Delivers them without the appropriate documents (ex: Bill of Lading / Documents of Title).

124

- **Liability of the Warehouseman** -
    - Warehouseman is liable for Negotiable DOT's it writes (§7-203)
    - A Warehouseman is required to deliver the goods to:
        - **The Holder** - of a Negotiable DOT
        - or **The Consignee** - of a Non-Negotiable DOT
            (or others, upon notice by Consignor (see §7-303-diversion)).
    - The Warehouseman will be liable for the goods if (§7-403; §7-404):
        - It Delivers them to the wrong person
        - or It Delivers them without the appropriate documents

- **Canceling the Bill:** The Carrier must cancel the negotiable BOL upon delivery (or note cancellation on face) (§7-403).

---

§7-303: Diversion; Reconsignment; Change of Instruction:

(1) **Instructions Carrier May Obey:**
    i) The carrier may deliver the goods to a person or destination other than that stated in the Bill of Lading (**"BOL"**) (or may otherwise dispose of the goods) on instructions from *either*:
        (a) The holder of a Negotiable BOL
        or (b) The Consignor (on a Non-negotiable BOL) - regardless of what the Consignee says
        or (c) The Consignee (on a Non-negotiable BOL) *unless*:
            1. The consignor's instructions contradict instructions by the consignee
            or 2. The goods have already arrived at the billed destination
            or 3. The Consignee is in possession of the BOL
        or (d) The Consignee (on a Non-negotiable BOL) - if he is entitled to dispose of the goods against the consignor.
    ii) This section applies unless the BOL otherwise provides

(2) Negotiated Bill: A person to whom a BOL is *duly negotiated*, can hold the bailee according to the original terms of the BOL, unless such instructions are noted in the Negotiable Bill, itself.

§7-309: Carrier's Duty of Care; Contractual Limitation on Carrier's Liability:

(1) **Negligence Standard:**
   a) A Carrier issuing a Bill of Lading must exercise the degree of care that a *reasonably careful man would under like circumstances:*
   b) This subsection doesn't limit a common carrier's liability for damages not caused by negligence, which any other laws may provide for.

(2) **Contractual Limitations on Damages:**
   a) Damages may be limited by a provision indicating the <u>maximum value</u> which the carrier will be liable for, only IF:
      1. <u>There is No Set Limitation Filed</u>, but the consignor is advised of an opportunity to declare a higher value (or a value as lawfully provided in the tariff)
      2. <u>There is a Set Limitation Filed:</u>
        a) The Carrier's charge is dependent on the value (ie- the more "insurance" the carrier takes, the more he'll charge the consignor)
      and b) The Consignor is given an opportunity to declare a higher value (or a value as lawfully provided in the tariff)

   b) A contract may not limit a carrier's liability for <u>Conversion</u> of the goods (for its own use)

(3) **Other Provisions:** The BOL may also contain *Reasonable* provisions indicating the <u>Time</u> and <u>Manner</u> of:
   a) Presenting claims based on the shipment
   or b) Instituting actions based on the shipment

§7-403: Obligations of Warehouseman or Carrier to Deliver:

(1) **Bailee's Defenses:** The <u>Bailee</u> must deliver the goods to the person *entitled to* them under the Document of Title ("**DOT**") if:

    i) The person entitled to the documents complies with sections (2) and (3) (below)

and ii) <u>NO DEFENSES:</u> The Bailee Cannot establish the following defenses:

    (a) **Goods Already Delivered**: That the Bailee already delivered the goods to a person whose receipt was *Rightful* against the claimant

or (b) **Bailee Not Liable:** That the bailee is not liable for any

    a) Damage to the goods

    or b) Delay

    or c) Loss

    or d) Destruction

Note for Some States: <u>Burden of Proof</u>: the person entitled to the Document has the Burden to prove that the Bailee was <u>Negligent</u> in order to preclude the Bailee's liability defenses.

or (c) **Previous Sale or Disposition**: there was a previous sale or disposition of the goods, either

    1. In lawful enforcement of a lien

    or 2. On the Warehouseman's lawful termination of storage

or (d) **Seller's Right to Stop Delivery:** That the Seller exercised his right to stop delivery (as per §2-705)

or (e) **Disposition:** Pursuant to §7-303 (or a tariff relating to such right) there was *either:*

    1. A Diversion

    or 2. A Reconsignment

    or 3. Other Disposition

or (f) **Personal Defense**: The Bailee had a <u>personal defense</u> against the claimant resulting from *either:*

    1. A Release

    or 2. A Satisfaction

    or 3. Any other fact affording a personal defense

or (g) **Any Other Lawful Excuse**

(2) A person claiming goods covered by a DOT ("Claimant") must Satisfy the Bailee's lien if:
   a) The Bailee requests
   or b) The Bailee is prohibited by law from delivering the goods until the charges are paid.

(3) **Receipt of Delivery:**
   a) Upon receipt of the goods, the claimant must surrender the Documents of Title (or any other outstanding Negotiable Documents covering the goods) so that the Bailee can:
      1) *Cancel* the Document - if Complete Delivery is made
      or 2) *Conspicuously* note the quantity delivered, if Partial Delivery is made
   b) If the Bailee doesn't do this, he will be liable to whom the note is duly negotiated
   c) **Exception:** If the Claimant is a person against whom the DOT offers No Right (as per §7-503(1))

(4) **"Person Entitled Under the Document"** - means, *either*
   a) Negotiable Instrument - A HOLDER of a Negotiable Instrument
   or b) Non-Negotiable Instrument - A Person to whom delivery is to be made, pursuant to *Written* instructions with a Non-Negotiable instrument.

§7-404: Not Liable for Good Faith Delivery:

1) A Bailee is not liable for misdelivering or disposing of goods if he:
   a) Had Good Faith
   and b) Observed *Reasonable Commercial Standards*
   and c) Delivered (or otherwise disposed of) goods according to the terms of the Document of Title (or pursuant to Article 7)

2) **Scope:** This rule applies even though:
   a) The person who gave the Bailee the goods had no authority to *either:*
      1. Acquire the Document
      or 2. Dispose of the Goods
   or b) The Person to whom the Bailee delivers the goods had no authority to receive them.

VII. *Passage of Title and Risk of Loss:*

A. *PROPERTY RIGHTS OF GOODS*

OVERVIEW

- Under the UCC, <u>title</u> is not a relevant factor in determining who has property rights in goods (§2-509 comment 1).
- <u>When Property Rights Transfer</u>:
  - Property rights transfer upon *Acceptance*
  - No transfer occurs if goods are *Rejected*
  - Transfer will be deemed to have never taken place (retroactively) if Acceptance is *Revoked*.
- The main problem arises when goods are in transit, or in the "process" of switching title. At such points, it is important to determine who has what rights in the goods.

---

§2-401: Passing of Title; Reservation for Security; Limited Application of This Section:

Preamble to §2-401 - Title Not a Consideration:
The Provisions of Article 2 apply regardless of who has title to the goods (unless the provisions refer to such title) when they deal with the <u>Rights</u>, <u>Obligations</u>, and <u>Remedies</u> of:
  a) A Buyer
  or b) A Seller
  or c) A Purchaser
  or d) Other third parties

(1) **Passing of Title**
  a) The title to goods shall pass from the Seller to the Buyer according to the manner and conditions *explicitly* agreed upon (subject to Article 2 and Article 9 (Secured Transactions)).
  b) <u>Identification Required</u>: Title to goods cannot pass until the goods are identified to the contract for sale (as per §2-501) (note: Future Goods cannot be the subject of a present sale).

    c) <u>Buyer's Rights Upon Identification</u>: The Buyer will acquire a Special Property Right (as limited by this Act) in the goods once they are identified, unless the parties *explicitly* agree otherwise.

    d) <u>Shipment by Reservation</u>: If a Seller ships or delivers goods under "*Reservation*" (i.e. he retains or reserves title in the goods) the Seller will have the same rights as he would if he had a Reservation of a Security Interest.

(2) **Passing of Title When Goods Are Physically Delivered**

    i) Title passes to the Buyer at the time and place at which Seller physically delivers the goods (i.e. completes performance) to the Buyer (unless otherwise *explicitly* agreed upon), even if:

        1. The Seller has reserved a Security Interest in the goods

    or 2. A Document of Title is to be delivered at a different time and place (i.e. they will not be delivered with the goods)

    ii) **Passing of Title in Bill of Lading Transactions:**

      (a) <u>Shipment Contract</u>: Title passes at the time and place of *Shipment* if:

        1. The contract requires/authorizes the Seller to send the goods to the Buyer

      and 2. The contract does not require the Seller to deliver them at their destination (ex: "FOB" - Seller only has to deliver goods to the carrier)

      (b) <u>Destination Contract</u>: Title passes on *tender* of the goods at the specified destination if the contract requires the Seller to deliver the goods at a particular destination.

(3) **Passing of Title When Goods Are To Be Delivered Without Being Moved:** This section applies to transactions where delivery is to be made without moving the goods (unless otherwise agreed):

    (a) <u>Delivery of Documents</u>: Title passes upon *delivery of the documents of title* if the Seller is to deliver them.

    (b) <u>No Delivery of Documents</u>: Title passes at the *time and place of contracting* if:

        1. The goods are identified when the contract is made

    and 2. No documents are to be delivered

(4) **Passing of Title When Buyer Rejects:**

    a) Title to the goods "revests" in the Seller if:

        1. The Buyer rejects or refuses to receive or retain the goods (whether or not it is justified)

    or 2. The Buyer properly revokes his acceptance of the goods

    b) Such revesting occurs by operation of law, and is not considered a "Sale."

B. *IDENTIFYING GOODS* (§2-501):

OVERVIEW

- Before Property rights in goods can pass, the goods must be **Identified** (§2-401(1); §2-501).
- Upon identification, certain *"Special Property Rights"* will transfer to the Buyer.
- Goods must be <u>in existence</u> before they can be identified.
- Goods (non-crops) can be identified in two ways:
    1. *When Contract Made* - when a contract is made, certain goods (in existence at the time of the contract) may be specified or set aside for that particular contract (ex: goods with certain serial numbers will be sold under the contract).
    2. *After Contract Made* - when contract is made simply for a type of good (ex:Panasonic VCR's model 613), but the exact pieces to be sent to the Buyer (ex: the exact serial numbers of the VCR's to be shipped) are determined at a *later time*.
- **Substitution:** The Seller can substitute already identified goods, *unless* (§2-501;§2-502):
    - The Seller <u>Defaults</u>
    - or ▪ The Seller becomes <u>Insolvent</u>
    - or ▪ The Seller Notifies the Buyer that <u>Identification is Final</u>

---

§2-501: Insurable Interest in Goods; Manner of Identification of Goods:

(1) **Identification of Goods:**
   a) <u>Creation of Buyer's Interest</u> - Once <u>existing</u> goods are identified to a contract the Buyer obtains an *Insurable Interest* and a *Special Property Interest* in the goods.
   b) <u>Non-Conforming Goods</u> - The Buyer will maintain such interests in identified goods even if the goods are non-conforming; he then has the option of returning or rejecting them.
   c) <u>Manner of Identification</u>:
      1. <u>Agreed Mode of Identification</u>: Identification can be made at any time and in any manner *explicitly agreed to* by the parties.

2. <u>No Specified Mode of Identification</u>: If the parties did not explicitly agree how the goods are to be identified, identification shall occur as follows:
   (a) *Sale of Already Identified Existing Goods:* Identification shall occur *when the contract is made* if the contract is for the sale of goods which are already existing and identified.
   (b) *Sale of Future Goods:* Identification shall occur when the Seller designates specific goods as goods for the contract (ex: when they are shipped, marked or set aside for the Buyer) if the contract is for the sale of future goods (which are not crops or goods falling under (c)).
   (c) *Sale of Crops and Animals:*
      1. <u>Crops</u> - Identification shall occur when the crops are planted or become "growing crops" (if the contract is for the sale of crops to be harvested within the longer of <u>12 months</u> after or the next harvest season after the contract is made).
      2. <u>Unborn Animals</u> - Identification shall occur when the young are conceived (if the contract is for the sale of unborn young to be born within <u>12 months</u> after the contract is made).

(2) **Seller's Insurable Interest:**
   a) The Seller shall retain an <u>Insurable Interest</u> in the goods as long as the Seller has *either:*
      1. Title to the goods
      or 2. A Security Interest in the Goods
   b) <u>Substitute Goods</u>: The Seller may substitute other goods for those already identified if:
      1. Identification is by the Seller alone
      and 2. The Seller has not:
         a. Defaulted
         or b. Become insolvent
      and 3. The Seller has not yet notified the Buyer that the identification would be final.

(3) Nothing in this section impairs any insurable interest recognized under any other statute or rule of law.

C. *TERMS OF SHIPMENT:*

OVERVIEW ——————————————————————

- Once goods have been identified, title passes at the time agreed upon time (as intended in the contract) (§2-401(2)).
- If the parties' intent cannot be inferred from the contract, title passes when the <u>Seller has completed his obligations</u>.
- Terms of contract often determine when the Seller's obligations are completed.This, in turn, helps courts infer when the parties' *"intended"* title to pass.
- The contract terms listed below may be used as **"Price Terms"** (i.e. a term describing what is included in the price) and as **"Shipping Terms"** (i.e. a term describing when title and risk of loss pass, and what the Seller is obligated to do when shipping the goods). It is from these terms that courts often imply when title or risk of loss pass:

  - **FOB** - *Freight on Board* - Seller is obligated to send good to Carrier's rail (after which, he is no longer responsible for the goods) (§2-319(1))
  - **FAS** - *Freight Alongside* - Seller is obligated to make sure goods arrive alongside the ship (§2-319(2))
  - **C&F** - *Cost and Freight* - Seller pays for freight (§2-320)
  - **CIF** - *Cost, Insurance, Freight* - Seller pays for freight and insurance (§2-320)
  - **"Ex-Ship"** - Seller pays for freight to be delivered at a particular port of destination (§2-322)
  - **"No Arrival, No Sale"** - Seller pays for freight, and property rights only transfer if goods arrive (§2-324).
  - **Shipment by Reservation** - Seller retains a Security Interest in the goods and is issued a negotiable BOL, which is transferred to the Buyer through banking channels upon payment (usually with the use of a sight draft) (See "BILLS OF LADING" transactions below)

- Although the Seller may have completed his duties by the time the goods are delivered to the Carrier, he may still stop shipment of the goods under **§2-705** if:
  - Buyer is <u>Insolvent</u>
  - or Buyer's Check is <u>dishonored</u>

---

§2-319: F.O.B. and F.A.S.:

Preliminary Note: *The terms F.O.B. and F.A.S. will be construed as "Delivery Terms" even though they have been used as "Price Terms"* (unless the parties agree otherwise)

(1) **"F.O.B."** (Free on Board) - unless otherwise agreed, the term F.O.B. implies the following:
    (a) F.O.B.(Place of Shipment):
        The Seller has the following responsibilities:
           1. Deliver goods to their specified place of shipment (i.e. to the Carrier's possession) (as per §2-504)
      and 2. Pay for the shipment
      and 3. Bear the risk of putting the goods into the Carrier's possession
    (b) F.O.B.(Place of Destination):
        The Seller has the following responsibilities:
           1. Pay for the transport of the goods to the specified place of destination
      and 2. Bear the risk of transporting the goods to their specified destination
      and 3. Tender delivery of the goods to the Buyer (as per §2-503)
    (c) F.O.B.(Vessel, car, other vehicle) (either under (a) or (b)):
        1. Seller's Responsibility: The Seller has the following *additional* responsibilities:
           a. Pay for loading the goods on board
           b. Bear the risk of loading the goods on board
           c. Comply with §2-323 (regarding the form of the Bill of Lading)
        2. Buyer's Responsibility: The Buyer must name the particular vessel which the goods will be loaded upon.

(2) **"F.A.S. (vessel)"** (Free alongside) - unless otherwise agreed, the term F.A.S. implies that the Seller has the following responsibilities:
    (a) Pay for and bear the risk of *either:*
        1) Delivering the goods alongside the vessel (in the manner usual in that port)
      or 2) Delivering the goods on a dock designated and provided by Buyer
  and (b) Obtain and Tender a receipt for the goods, in which the Carrier promises to issue a BOL

(3) **Buyer's Obligation to Instruct Seller**

    a) The Buyer must seasonably give any needed instructions for delivery (unless otherwise agreed in an FAS, FOB(shipment), or FOB(vessel) contract), including:

        1. The loading berth of the vessel (if the terms are FOB or FAS)

        2. The name of the ship and its sailing date (in appropriate cases)

    b) <u>Buyer's Failure to Instruct</u> - If the Buyer fails to seasonably give the Seller the appropriate shipping instructions:

        1. The Seller may treat Buyer's failure to give instructions as a *Failure to Cooperate* (as per §2-311).

      and 2. The Seller may, at his option, move the goods in any reasonable manner in preparation for delivery or shipment.

(4) **Tender of Documents for FAS and FOB(vessel) Contracts:**

    a. The Buyer must make payment against tender of the required documents under an FOB(vessel) or FAS shipping contract (unless otherwise agreed).

    b. The Buyer may not demand delivery of the goods, nor may the Seller tender goods, in substitution of the documents.

<u>§2-320</u>: C.I.F. & C.& F.:

(1) **Definitions:**

    a) "<u>**C.I.F.**</u>" means that the Price includes:

        1. The cost of the Goods

      and 2. The Insurance

      and 3. The Freight (to the named destination)

    b) "<u>**C. & F.**</u>" means that the Price includes:

        1. The cost of the Goods

      and 2. The Freight (to the named destination)

(2) The Term "C.I.F. (destination)" (or its equivalent) implies that the Seller shall have the following responsibilities (unless otherwise agreed):

    (a) 1. Pay for putting the goods into possession of the Carrier (at the port for shipment)

    and 2. Bear the risk of putting the goods into possession of the Carrier (at the port for shipment)

    and 3. Obtain a Negotiable Bill of Lading covering the goods

and (b) 1. Load the goods

    and 2. Obtain a receipt from the Carrier (may be part of the BOL) showing that freight has been paid/provided for

and (c) Obtain a policy or certify insurance (including War Risk Insurance)

    1. The insurance must be of the type typical at the port of shipment

    2. The insurance contract must cover the goods in the BOL

    3. The beneficiary must be the Buyer or "whom it may concern"

    4. War risk premiums may be added to CIF price

and (d) Prepare an invoice of the goods and procure any other documents required to effect shipment (or to comply with the contract)

and (e) Forward and Tender all documents

    1. With *Commercial Promptness*

    2. In Due Form

    3. With any necessary indorsements to perfect the Buyer's rights

(3) Unless otherwise agreed, C&F has the same effect and obligations as a CIF contract, *except* for the insurance obligations.

(4) The Buyer must make payment against tender of the required Documents (unless otherwise agreed) under CIF and C&F contracts.

§2-321: C.I.F. or C&F: "Net Landed Weight"; "Payments on Arrival"; Warranty of Condition on Arrival:

This Section applies to contracts containing CIF or C&F terms.

(1) Price Based on Landed Weight
    a. The Seller must reasonably estimate the price if it is to be based on or adjusted according to its weight or quality (unless otherwise agreed).

    b. Sales based on quality or weight upon delivery are often denoted with such terms as:
        1. "Net Landed Weight"
        2. "Delivered Weights"
        3. "Out turn" quality or quantity of the goods

    c. <u>Payment Due</u>: The amount due on tender of the documents is the amount initially estimated by the Seller.

    d. After final price adjustments are made, a settlement for the balance must be made with *commercial promptness.*

(2) Risk of Deterioration
    a) The Seller shall have the <u>Risk of Ordinary Deterioration and Shrinkage</u> (and the like) while the goods are in transit if:
        1) An agreement (as described in (1) above) has been created
            (basing the price on the weight or quality of the goods upon delivery)
    or 2) A warranty of quality or condition of the goods on arrival has been created

    b) Such agreements have no effect on:
        1) The place or time of identification of goods to the contract (for sale or delivery)
    or 2) The passing of risk of loss

(3) Time For Payment
    a. <u>Inspection Before Payment</u>: The Seller must allow a preliminary inspection ("as feasible") of the goods *before* the Buyer makes payment if the contract allows payment to be made on or after the arrival of the goods (unless otherwise agreed).

    b. <u>Lost Goods</u>: Delivery of the documents and payment are due *when the goods would have arrived* if the goods are lost.

§2-322: Delivery "Ex-Ship":

(1) **"EX-SHIP"** (or equivalent language) means (unless otherwise agreed):
    a. That goods need not be delivered on a particular ship
  and b. Delivery will be made from a ship which has reached a place at the named port of destination (where goods of that kind are usually discharged).

(2) **Obligations under "Ex-Ship" Terms:**
    (a) <u>The Seller must</u>:
        1. Discharge all liens which arise out of carriage
     and 2. Furnish the Buyer with a direction that obligates the Carrier to deliver the goods
    (b) <u>Risk of Loss</u>: The Risk of Loss passes to the Buyer when:
        1. The goods leave the ship's tackle
      or 2. The goods are otherwise properly unloaded from the ship

§2-324: "No Arrival, No Sale" Term:

*The following sections govern the use of the term "**No Arrival, No Sale**" or terms of similar meaning (unless otherwise agreed):*

(a) **Obligations of the Seller**:
    1. The Seller must:
        a. Properly ship conforming goods
        b. Tender the goods on arrival (if they arrive by any means)
    2. <u>The Seller's Risk</u>: the Seller assumes no obligation that the goods will arrive, unless he has caused their non-arrival.

(b) **Buyer's Remedy:** The Buyer may proceed as if there had been *Casualty to Identified Goods* (as per §2-613) if:
    1. The Seller is not at fault
  and 2. *Either*:
        a. Some of the goods are lost
      or b. The goods have deteriorated (so as to no longer conform to the contract)
      or c. The goods arrive *after* the contract time

D. *RISK OF LOSS:*

OVERVIEW

- Risk of Loss also does not transfer immediately. Depending upon the agreement between the parties, the *Risk of Loss* will transfer between the Seller and the Buyer at a certain moment in time (§2-509; §2-510).
- It is important to determine when Risk of Loss passes, especially if goods get destroyed or damaged while in transit. The party with the Risk of Loss will be the one who must bear the responsibility for such damages incurred while in-transit.
- <u>Determining When Risk of Loss Passes</u>:
  - **Look to Intent of Parties** (often obtainable by looking at shipping terms).
  - **Shipping Terms:** If shipping terms are provided, we look to them as Risk of Loss rules (see §2-319 and §2-320) (see Transfer of Property above, and rules below).
  - If the parties don't specifically provide for Risk of Loss, one should look to **§2-509** and **§2-510** for guidance:
    - <u>Goods Shipped with a [3d party] Carrier</u>:
      - *Shipment Contract* - Risk of Loss passes to the Buyer when the goods arrive at the <u>*Carrier*</u> (§2-509(1)(a)).
      - *Destination Contract* - Risk of Loss passes to the Buyer only when the goods arrive at their <u>*Destination*</u> (as specified in the contract (usually Buyer's place)(§2-509(1)).
    - <u>Goods left with a [3d party] Bailee</u> (§2-509(2)):
      - *Negotiable Document Issued* - Risk of Loss passes to the Buyer when the Buyer <u>*receives*</u> the Document of Title
      - *Non-Negotiable Document Issued* - Risk of Loss passes to the Buyer when:
        1. The Buyer receives the Document of Title
        or 2. Seller sends Written directions to Carrier that Buyer is entitled to delivery of goods.
    - <u>All other Deliveries</u> (§2-509(3)): (ex: Buyer must pick up goods from Seller's place or Seller ships goods to Buyer with his own truck).
      - *Seller Merchant* - Risk of Loss passes to Buyer when he <u>*receives possession*</u> of the goods.
      - *Seller Non-Merchant* - Risk of Loss passes to Buyer upon <u>*Tender*</u> of Delivery.

- **Party in Breach** (§2-510)**:** If a party is in breach, the above Risk of Loss rules change:
  - ***Buyer Rightfully Rejects*** (i.e. Seller Breaches) - Risk of Loss remains on the Seller until the Seller Cures (as per §2-510) or the Buyer Accepts (In such case, Risk of Loss will be deemed to retroactively remained with the Seller (i.e. as if it had never passed Buyer)).

  - ***Buyer Rightfully Revokes*** - Risk of Loss will be deemed to have retroactively remained with the Seller (as if it had never passed to Buyer).
  - ***Buyer Breaches*** (wrongful repudiation) - Risk of Loss remains with the <u>Buyer</u> *"for a commercially reasonable time."*

- <u>Shipment by Reservation</u> - Shipment by Reservation has <u>no effect</u> on Risk of Loss (§2-509).

---

§2-509: Risk of Loss in the Absence of Breach:

(1) <u>Contracts Requiring or Authorizing Seller to Ship the Goods by the Carrier</u> (FOB Carrier):
  - (a) **Shipment Contract:** The Risk of Loss passes to the Buyer <u>when the goods are duly delivered to the Carrier</u> if the contract does not require the Seller to deliver the goods to a particular destination (even if the shipment is under "<u>Reservation</u>" (as per §2-505))
  - (b) **Destination Contract:** The Risk of Loss passes to the *Buyer* <u>when the goods are so tendered to *enable the Buyer to take delivery*</u> if:
    1. The contract does not require the Seller to deliver the goods to a particular destination.
    and 2. The goods are tendered while in the possession of a Carrier

140

(2) <u>When Goods are held by a Bailee to be Delivered without Being Moved</u> - Risk of Loss passes to the *Buyer* when:
    (a) He received a <u>Negotiable Document of Title</u> covering the goods
    or (b) The Bailee acknowledges the Buyer's right to possess the goods
    or (c) He received a <u>Non-Negotiable Document of Title</u> (or other written direction to deliver (as per §2-503(4)(b))

(3) <u>All other cases</u> - Risk passes to *Buyer*:
    a) *When he receives the goods* - if Seller is a Merchant
    b) *Upon Tender of Delivery* - if Seller is not a Merchant

(4) This section is subject to:
    a) Agreements of the parties
    b) §2-327 (Sale on Approval)
    c) §2-510 (Effect of Breach on Risk of Loss)

§2-510: Risk of Loss with Breach:

(1) **Seller's Breach:**
    Risk of loss remains on the <u>Seller</u> until *Cure* or *Acceptance* if:
    a) Tender or Delivery fails to conform to the contract
    and b) The non-conformity gives rise to a *Right of Rejection*

(2) **Buyer's Revocation of Acceptance**:
    The Buyer may treat the risk of loss as the Seller's *from the beginning of the contract* (as if risk of loss never passes to the Buyer)
    a) If the Buyer rightfully *revokes* acceptance
    and b) To the extent the Buyer's insurance is deficient

(3) **Buyer's Breach:**
    The Seller may treat the risk of loss as the <u>Buyer's</u> (To the extent the Seller's insurance was deficient) for a *commercially reasonable time* if:
    a. The goods were already identified to the contract
    and b. The goods conformed to the contract
    and c. The Buyer Repudiates/Breaches before risk of loss passes to him

VII. *ACCEPTANCE, REJECTION, & REVOCATION*

A. *ACCEPTANCE OF GOODS:*
OVERVIEW ———————————————————

- Once a Buyer Accepts the goods:
   1. Buyer may no longer reject them (he may only "Revoke" acceptance under certain circumstances (§2-607(2)) (see "REVOCATION" below).
   and 2. Seller is entitled to payment (§2-507 (upon tender); (§2-607 (upon acceptance); §2-709 (can sue if not paid)).

- Acceptance may be made in 3 ways (§2-606):
   1. *Expression* - The Buyer tells the Seller that he accepts the goods
   or 2. *Silence* - The Buyer doesn't reject the goods (look to industry for time period on non-rejection)
   or 3. *Action* - The Buyer does something to show he owns the goods (ex: he sells some of the goods)

- Acceptance does not bar the Buyer's claim for damages (for nonconforming goods, late delivery, etc.); Buyer need only give Seller <u>notice</u> of Seller's breach within a reasonable time after the Buyer discovered (or *should have* discovered) the non-conformity (§2-607(3)(a)).

---

§2-606: Acceptance Of Goods:

(1) Acceptance of Goods occurs when Buyer:
   (a) Signifies to Seller (after reasonable opportunity to inspect them) that *either*:
      1. The goods conform to the contract
      or 2. The Buyer will take or retain the goods even though there is a non-conformity
   or (b) Fails to make an effective rejection (as per §2-602(1)) after a reasonable opportunity to inspect
   or (c) Does any act inconsistent with Seller's ownership (i.e. if such an act is wrongful, acceptance is only at the Seller's option)
(2) Acceptance of part of a "commercial unit" is considered acceptance of the whole unit.

§2-607: Effect of Acceptance:

(1) **Price of Accepted Goods:** The Buyer must pay the *contract price* (i.e. the price of the goods as stated in the contract) for any goods accepted.

(2) **Rejection and Revocation:**
  a. Goods cannot be <u>rejected</u> after they have been accepted.
  b. Goods cannot be <u>revoked</u> due to a non-conformity if they were accepted with knowledge of the non-conformity *unless* the Buyer *reasonably assumed* that the Seller would fix the non-conformity.
  c. Acceptance itself does not impair other Article 2 remedies for non-conforming goods.

(3) **Acceptance of Tender:** If tender has been accepted:
  (a) <u>Breach</u>:
     1. The Buyer must notify the Seller of any breach within a reasonable time after discovering such a breach (or a reasonable time after he *should have* discovered it).
     2. If the Buyer does not notify the Seller of such breach within a reasonable time, the Buyer will be barred from any remedy.
  (b) <u>Infringement</u>:
     1. The Buyer must notify the Seller of any litigation against the Buyer if:
        a) The Buyer is sued as a result of the Seller's breach
        and b) The claim is for infringement (or the like (as per §2-312(3))
     2. If the Buyer does not send the Seller such notice within a reasonable time after the Buyer learns of the litigation, the Buyer will not be able to use any remedies against the Seller to recover the liability damages arising out of the litigation.

(4) **Burden of Proof:** The <u>Buyer</u> has the burden of proving a breach with respect to the accepted goods.

(5) **When Buyer is Sued for Seller's Wrong:** When the Buyer is sued for an obligation (ex: breach of warranty) which his Seller may be responsible for:

    (a) The facts determined in the suit against the Buyer will be binding in any similar suit which the Buyer may start against the Seller if:

        1) The Seller is *answerable* to the Buyer for the breach of obligation

        and 2) The Buyer sent the Seller a <u>written</u> notice of the litigation

        and 3) The notice gave the Seller an opportunity to defend himself in the case and described the consequences of not appearing

        and 4) The Seller neglected to defend himself within a reasonable time after he received the notice

    (b) <u>Infringement</u>:

        1) The original Seller may demand that his Buyer give him control of the litigation (including settlement).

        2) The Buyer will not be able to use any remedies against the Seller to recover the liability damages arising out of the litigation if:

            a. The claim was one of infringement (or the like (as per §2-312(3))

            and b. The original Seller demanded control of the litigation

            and c. The Seller's demand was in <u>writing</u>

            and d. The Seller agreed to pay for:

                1. All litigation expenses

                and 2. Any adverse judgment

            and e. The Buyer does not turn the case over to the Seller within a reasonable time after receiving the Seller's demand.

(6) **Applicability:** Subsections (3), (4) and (5) (above) apply to any obligation of a Buyer to hold the Seller harmless against infringement (or the like (as per §2-312(3))).

§2-608: Revocation of Acceptance:

(1) **When Buyer May Revoke:** The Buyer may revoke his acceptance if:
  - i) A non-conformity *substantially impairs* the value of the goods to the Buyer
  - and ii) *Either*:
    - (a) He has accepted the goods assuming that the Seller would cure the non-conformity, but the Seller neglected to do so *seasonably*
    - or (b) He accepted the goods without knowing of the non-conformity either because:
      - 1. It was difficult to discover the non-conformity before acceptance
      - or 2. The Seller's assurances induced him to accept

(2) **Time of Revocation:**
  - a) Revocation of acceptance must occur within a reasonable time:
    - 1. After the Buyer discovers *or should have discovered* the non-conformity
    - and 2. Before there is any *substantial change* in the condition of the goods (which is not caused by their own defects)
  - b) Revocation is not effective until the Buyer notifies the Seller of it.

(3) **Effect of Revocation:** A Buyer who properly revokes has the same rights and duties as if he had rejected them.

B. *REJECTION:*

OVERVIEW ─────────────────────────────

- The Buyer may reject goods if the Seller does not make *"Perfect Tender"* (§2-601).

- **Perfect Tender Rule** (§2-601):
    - Unlike the common law, which requires a party to tender only *Substantial Performance*, Article 2 requires the parties to make *"Perfect Tender*." Thus, the Buyer may reject goods if there is *any* deviation or defect in the goods (i.e. they are different from what Seller promised).
    - Courts are very strict with the Perfect Tender Rule (which is often unfair to Seller, because this rule makes its very easy for the Buyer to get out of the contract)
    - Seller has a <u>Right to Cure</u> (§2-508(1)) if non-conforming goods are delivered before the specified delivery date (Seller may fix and redeliver conforming goods by the specified delivery date, so long as it did not make the mistake intentionally).

- Buyer must state the reasons why he is rejecting the goods (§2-605(1)).

- After rejection, Buyer may not make an act of acceptance (§2-606) or else the Buyer will be considered to have Accepted the goods (as per §2-602) (i.e. If Buyer uses rejected goods in a manner inconsistent with rejection, he will be considered to have reaccepted them (and can only resort to revocation)).

- <u>Requirements for Rejection</u>:
    1) Buyer must expressly Reject the goods (§2-602) and cannot be passive (as it can with Acceptance (§2-606)).
    and 2) Buyer must notify Seller of rejection within a reasonable time after receiving the goods (§2-602).
    and 3) Buyer must specify a reason for rejecting the goods (§2-605(1)).

- **Buyer's Obligation upon Rejection** (§2-603):
  - Buyer must inform Seller why he is rejecting the goods (§2-605(1)).
  - Storage: The Buyer has a duty to hold the goods until the Seller can arrange for them to be removed (§2-602(2)(b)).
  - *Merchant Duties*: Upon rejection a Merchant Buyer must:
    1. Contact the Seller to:
       - Inform the Seller that he has Rejected the goods
       - and ▪ Get instructions on returning or disposing of the rejected goods
    2. If the Seller does not give the Buyer instructions regarding the rejected goods, the Buyer must:
       - Take a **§2-711** Security Interest in the goods
       - and ▪ Resell them (any profits above the Buyer's damages must go to Seller)

  - Buyer may *"Cover"* - Buyer may buy substitute goods elsewhere (§2-712; §2-713) and charge the Seller for the difference in price (Cover price - Contract price) (See "Buyer's REMEDIES" for more detail).
  - Lost Sales: The UCC does not compensate for *"lost sales"* of a Buyer (although it does for Sellers).

  - Remedies Upon Rejection: **§2-711(3)** discusses what remedies are available to a Buyer upon rejection (See "BUYERS REMEDIES").

---

§2-601: Buyer's Rights on Improper Delivery:

1. **Remedies For Imperfect Tender:** If the goods or the tender of delivery *in any way* fail to conform to the contract, then Buyer may:
   - (a) Reject the whole shipment
   - or (b) Accept the whole shipment
   - or (c) Accept any "commercial unit," and reject the rest
2. This rule is subject to
   - a) §2-612 (Breach of Installment Contracts)
   - b) Liquidated Remedy Agreements (under §2-718 and §2-719)

§2-606(1) Failure to Make An Effective Rejection:

(1) Acceptance of Goods occurs when Buyer:
- (a) Signifies to Seller (after reasonable opportunity to inspect them) **that** *either*:
  - 1. The goods conform to the contract
  - or 2. The Buyer will take or retain the goods even though there is a non-conformity
- or (b) Fails to make an effective rejection (as per §2-602(1)) after a reasonable opportunity to inspect
- or (c) Does any act inconsistent with Seller's ownership (i.e. if such an act is wrongful, acceptance is only at the Seller's option)

§2-602: **Manner and Effect of Rightful Rejection:**

(1) **When to Reject:**
- a) The Buyer must seasonably notify the Seller that it is rejecting the goods.
- b) Rejection will be ineffective if it is not made within a *reasonable time* after delivery or tender occurs.

(2) **Buyer's Rights and Obligations** (subject to §2-603 and §2-604):
- (a) After rejection, any "exercise of ownership" over the goods (by the Buyer) is considered *wrongful* against the Seller.
- and (b) The Buyer will have an obligation to hold the goods with *reasonable care* for a reasonable time *after* rejection (in order to allow the Seller to remove them) if:
  - 1. The Buyer has taken physical possession of the goods before he rejected them
  - and 2. The Buyer does not have a Security Interest in the goods (as per §2-711(3))
- and (c) The Buyer has no further obligations with regard to rightfully rejected goods (unless he is a Merchant, in which case §2-603 applies).

(3) **Seller's Rights:** The Seller's rights in *wrongfully* rejected goods are governed by §2-703 (Seller's Remedies).

§2-603: Merchant Buyer's Rightful Rejection:

(1) Buyer's Duties Upon Rejection:

  a) After rejection, any <u>Merchant</u> Buyer must follow any *reasonable instruction* received from the Seller, with respect to such goods if:

     1. If Seller has no agent or place of business where goods are rejected

    and 2. After rejection goods are still in the Buyer's possession or control

  b) Upon rejection, the Buyer must make reasonable efforts to sell the goods for the Seller if:

     1. The Seller has no agent or place of business where goods are rejected

    and 2. After rejection goods are still in the Buyer's possession or control

    and 3. The Seller left no other *reasonable instructions*

    and 4. The goods are perishable or threaten to speedily decline in value

  c) Instructions are not reasonable if, on the Buyer's demand, indemnity for expenses is not forthcoming.

  d) This subsection is subject to any S/I in the Buyer (as per §2-711(3)).

(2) Reimbursement to Buyer:

  When the Buyer sells goods under §2-603(1), he is entitled to <u>reimbursement</u> from the Seller (or out of the proceeds of the sale) for:

    a. Reasonable selling expenses

    b. Reasonable expenses incurred in caring for the goods

    c. Selling Commissions, if they are:

     1. Not included in expenses

    and 2. *Either:*

      a) Reasonable in the trade/industry

     or b) A Reasonable Sum (if no industry norm), *not to exceed 10% of gross proceeds.*

(3) Buyer's Standard of Good Faith:

  a) The Buyer is held to a standard of *Good Faith.*

  b) Good Faith conduct will not be considered Acceptance, Conversion, or a basis of an action for damages.

§2-605: Waiver of Buyer's Right to Reject:

(1) If Buyer does not give specific reasons for rejecting goods, he waives the right to reject them (based on that defect) if:

i) The defects are ascertainable by reasonable inspection

and ii) *Either*:

(a) The Seller could have fixed the problem seasonably (if the reason was stated)

or (b) <u>Between Merchants</u> - the *Merchant* Seller has requested a written statement of defects from the *Merchant* Buyer

(2) **Payment Against Documents:** Recovery of payments for defects apparent on the face of documents will be <u>precluded</u> if payment is made:

a) Against the documents

and b) *"Without reservation"*

C. *REVOCATION:*
OVERVIEW

- A Buyer may Revoke its acceptance of goods only under limited circumstances.
- The *Perfect Tender Rule* (§2-601) will not apply once goods are accepted since the Buyer had an obligation to inspect the goods before acceptance; it is for that reason that revocation cannot be made as easily as rejection.
- **Availability of Revocation:** The Buyer may only Revoke his acceptance of the goods if *either:*

  - *Seller Gave Assurance* - Buyer accepted the goods knowing of their defects, but Seller promised to fix them (§2-608((1)(a)).
  - or ■ *Defects Were Hidden* - Buyer did not know of the defects (nor should he have known) upon acceptance (§2-608(1)(b)).

- **Time of Revocation:** Revocation must be made within a *reasonable time* after discovering the non-conformity (§2-608(2)).

- **Substantial Changes:** If Buyer made a substantial change to the goods, he cannot revoke acceptance unless the impairment/defect caused the "change" (ex: A car crash would be considered a Substantial Change (car no longer in original condition); if the car crashed due to the Buyer's negligence the Buyer could not later revoke his acceptance of the car; if the car crashed because there was a defect in the braking system, the Buyer could revoke acceptance since it was the defect which caused the crash).

- Revocation is a form of rejection, and just as with rejection, the Buyer may not make an act of acceptance (as per §2-606) after revocation has occurred (or else Buyer will be considered to have accepted the goods again (as per §2-602)).

- Remedies Upon Revocation: **§2-711(3)** discusses what remedies are available to a Buyer upon revocation (See "BUYERS REMEDIES").

§2-608: Revocation of Acceptance:

(1) **When Buyer May Revoke:** The Buyer may revoke his acceptance if:
  i) A non-conformity *substantially impairs* the value of the
  goods to the Buyer
and ii) *Either*:
  (a) He has accepted the goods assuming that the Seller would
  cure the non-conformity, but the Seller neglected to
  do so *seasonably*
  or (b) He accepted the goods without knowing of the
  non-conformity either because:
  1. It was difficult to discover the non-conformity
  before acceptance
  or 2. The Seller's assurances induced him to accept

(2) **Time of Revocation:**
  a) Revocation of acceptance must occur within a reasonable time:
  1. After the Buyer discovers *or should have discovered* the
  non-conformity
  and 2. Before there is any *substantial change* in the condition of
  the goods (which is not caused by their own defects)
  b) Revocation is not effective until the Buyer notifies the Seller of it.

(3) **Effect of Revocation:** A Buyer who properly revokes has the same
  rights and duties as if he had rejected them.

IX. *GOOD FAITH PURCHASERS AND BUYERS IN THE ORDINARY COURSE:*

OVERVIEW ————————————————————

A. Special Property Rights

- A Recurring theme throughout the UCC is the concept of the "Innocent Owner." The term "Innocent Owner" is an E-Z Rules term created to encompass the many types of people who may take greater rights in property than the person selling the property had.

- The UCC affords special rights to "innocent owners":
  - Normally, a **Derivation Rule** applies to all transfers of property. According to this rule, a person may only acquire the property rights of the person it received the property from (i.e. the Seller cannot sell more than he owns!) (ex: If Seller only owns 50% of his car, he cannot sell the *entire* car to Buyer; Seller may only sell his 50% interest in the car. Thus, under normal conditions, even if Buyer thought he was buying the entire car he will only have rights in 50% of the car.)
  - Under certain circumstances the UCC allows certain parties to take *more* rights than what the Seller had. They can usually take their property *free from all other interests* in it.

  - The following are the 5 types of **Innocent Owners** afforded such special property rights under the UCC:

    - ***Good Faith Purchaser*** - referred to in Articles 2 and 6 (Regarding Sale of Goods and Bulk Sales).

    - ***Buyer in The Ordinary Course of Business*** - referred to in Articles 2 and 9 (Regarding the Sale of Goods and Security Interests).

    - ***Holder by Due Negotiation*** - referred to in Article 7 (Regarding Warehouse Receipts and other Documents of Title) (see "HOLDER BY DUE NEGOTIATION" below).

    - ***Holder in Due Course*** - referred to in Articles 3 and 4 (Regarding Checks and other Negotiable Instruments).

    - ***Bona Fide Purchaser*** - referred to in Article 8 (Regarding Securities).

■ For purposes of Contracts for the Sale of Goods the relevant types of innocent owners which must be considered are the <u>Good Faith Purchaser</u> and <u>The Buyer in the Ordinary Course</u> when dealing with goods; however, the <u>Holder by Due Negotiation</u> is also a relevant party to the Sales transaction since he can take the goods away from the actual Buyer or Seller of the goods if a Bill of Lading, Warehouse Receipt, or other Document of Title has been issued for the goods.

B. <u>The Good Faith Purchaser</u> (§2-403)

■ <u>Requirements to be Classified as a GFP</u>: The Seller of the goods must have:
    1) Paid **value** for the goods
  and 2) Bought the goods in **Good Faith** (i.e. the Buyer must deal with *honesty in fact* in the transaction (§1-201(19))).
  and 3) Bought from a Seller who received goods under a ***Transaction of Purchase*** (as per §1-201(32)).

  ■ *Seller's* <u>Transaction of Purchase</u>:
    In order for this "innocent owner" rule to apply, the person selling the goods to the GFP had to have obtained the goods under a *"Transaction of Purchase."*

      ■ Therefore, if a Seller has obtained its goods by fraud, yet still under a purchasing arrangement, the Seller has met the good faith requirement.
      ■ If the Seller actually stole the goods (no transaction took place) then the goods can never be resold to a Good Faith Purchaser (even if the GFP purchased it from an innocent party who purchased it from the thief).

    ■ <u>Merchant v. Non-Merchant</u>: A Merchant has a higher degree of good faith. He must (§1-203(1)(b)):
        1. Deal with Honesty in Fact
      and 2. Observe Reasonable Commercial Standards of Fair Dealing in the trade.

C. The Buyer in The Ordinary Course
(§1-201(9)):

- Requirements to be Classified as a BIOC:
    - Ordinary Purchase - Buyer must have bought goods from *inventory*
    - From a Merchant - Buyer must have purchased the goods from a Seller *typically engaged in selling goods of that kind*
    - Sale - The Buyer must have bought the goods under a *Sales transaction*
    - New Value - New Value (as per §1-201(44)) must be exchanged for the goods
    - Good Faith
    - No knowledge that the purchase in violation of any security Interests in the goods

D. Rights of the GFP and BIOC:

- A BIOC will always be a GFP, by definition; yet to qualify as a BIOC, he must also:
    - A Buyer - the BIOC must take the goods by Sale (while a GFP can take by any means of Purchase (ex: Although a Secured Party can qualify as a GFP, it cannot qualify as a BIOC, since a Secured Party is not a Buyer) (§2-403(1); §1-201(9)).
    - Buy the goods from the inventory of a Merchant
    - Buy the goods without knowledge of an existing security interest in the goods (although a GFP will probably have to live up to this standard as well to qualify under the Good Faith requirement).

- **Rights of the GFP**: A GFP will acquire all title to goods it purchases to the extent paid for.

- **Rights of a BIOC**: The BIOC has greater rights than a GFP:
    - A BIOC will acquire all title to goods it purchases (to the extent paid for).
    - A BIOC can defeat a Security Interest in goods (while a GFP cannot).
    - A BIOC can take goods free from an Entruster (while a GFP cannot (see "Entrustment" below)).

157

E. Entrustment (§2-403(2),(3)):

- If a person stores ("entrusts") his goods with a *Merchant*, that Merchant has a right to *transfer all rights* in those goods to a **Buyer in the Ordinary Course of Business** (not a GFP) (§2-403(2)).
- The *Entrustment rule* only applies if the goods are sold to a **BIOC** (not a GFP):
  - Secured Parties are not buyers (although they are purchasers).
  - If Non-BIOC's resell the goods which they bought from the Entruster to a BIOC, the BIOC Buyer will NOT take free (since the person taking the goods from the entruster wasn't a BIOC).

- Entrustment can occur in various situations:
  1) When a Seller allows the Buyer to keep the goods in his warehouse until the Buyer can pay for them (so that the Seller would not have to take a Security Interest in the goods).
  2) When a Buyer buys the goods, yet allows the Seller to keep them until the Buyer is ready to pick them up (if a BIOC comes in the next day and buys the same goods, the BIOC has rights to the goods).
  3) When a Buyer or Seller stores their goods with a third party who also sells the same kind of goods (ex: Celia asks Isaac to store her mink coat; Isaac has a mink coat vault in the back of his fur coat store; If Isaac sells the mink coat to Susan, a BIOC, Susan will have the right to keep Celia's mink coat).

§2-403: Good Faith Purchaser of Goods:

(1) **Derivation Rule:**
   a) <u>A Full Purchaser</u> - A purchaser of goods acquires all title which his transferor had or had the power to transfer.
   b) <u>The Purchaser of Limited Interest</u> - acquires only the rights of the interest he actually purchases.
   c) <u>Exception - THE GOOD FAITH PURCHASER</u>:
      1) A person with a Voidable Title has the power to transfer a good title if:
         a. The transferee Purchased it in <u>Good Faith</u>
         b. The Purchaser has paid <u>Value</u> (as per §1-204(44))(therefore, gifts and judicial liens are no good)
      2) This exception will apply when goods have been delivered under a <u>Transaction of Purchase</u> (i.e. not theft), even if:
         (a) The transferor was deceived as to the purchaser's identity
         or (b) The delivery was in exchange for a check which is later dishonored
         or (c) It was agreed that the transaction was to be a *"cash sale"*
         or (d) The delivery was obtained through <u>Fraud</u> (which would be punishable as larceny under the criminal law)

(2) **Merchant as Bailee** - A person automatically obtains the right to <u>Transfer all Rights</u> in goods (even if he doesn't own all the rights in those goods), if:
      a. Someone *"entrusts"* the person with possession of the goods
   and b. The person is a <u>Merchant</u>, dealing with goods of the kind entrusted
   and c. The Merchant sells the goods to a Buyer In the Ordinary Course ("BIOC") (as per §1-201(9))

(3) **"Entrusting"**
   a) "Entrusting" includes:
      1) Any delivery
      and 2) Any acquiescence in retention of possession

   b) These are considered "entrusting" *regardless of*:
      1) Any agreement between the parties (for the Merchant not to sell the goods)
      or 2) Whether or not the "entrusting" or disposition was motivated by Fraud

(4) **Rights of Other Purchasers:**
   a. Rights of other purchasers are governed by Articles 9 and 7.
   b. Article 6 also governs the rights of other purchasers.

§1-201(9): **Buyer in the Ordinary Course of Business:**

1. A "Buyer In The Ordinary Course" ("BIOC") is a
   Person/Organization (not a Pawnbroker) who buys goods:
   a) In Good-Faith (see §1-201(19))
   and b) Without knowledge that purchase is in violation of
   someone else's other ownership rights or S/I
   and c) From a 'Merchant' - someone in the business of selling
   those goods (except a pawnbroker)
   and d) In the *Ordinary Course*- passing of title *for value* (ie- a
   SALE) in a typical transaction (ex: inventory, not equipment)
   and e) For **Value**

2. Anyone selling minerals, oil, or gas (at wellhead or minehead) is
   considered to be in the business of selling goods of that kind.

3. How goods may be Bought
   a) For Cash
   or b) By Exchange of property
   or c) On Credit - secured or unsecured
   or d) Receiving goods/title under a pre-existing contract for sale

4. Goods are NOT considered Bought if
   a) They are given as a security for a debt
   b) They are given as partial or total satisfaction of a debt
   c) They are Bulk Transfers

§1-201(19): **Good Faith:**

"Good Faith" means Honesty in Fact in the Conduct or
Transaction Concerned. (see also §2-103(b) for Merchants)

§1-201(32): **Purchase:**

A **"Purchase"** is any _Voluntary Transaction_ creating an interest in property, <u>including a:</u>

     1. Sale (ie- involving a Buyer and Seller)
or 2. Discount
or 3. Negotiation
or 4. Mortgage
or 5. Pledge (ex: a Secured party)
or 6. Lien (ex: a Secured party)
or 7. Issue or Re-issue
or 8. Gift (donee)

§1-201(33): **Purchaser:**

A **"Purchaser"** is a Person" who takes by _purchase"_
(ex: a buyer, a Security Interest holder,etc... (as per §1-201(32))

§2-103(1)(a) **"Buyer"**

A **"Buyer"** is a person who buys or contracts to buy goods.

§2-104(1): **"Merchant"**

A person is considered a "Merchant" if he is _either:_
    a) <u>Dealer</u>: A person who _deals_ with goods of the kind
or b) <u>Expert</u>: A person who _either:_
      1) Holds himself out as having _knowledge or skill_
        peculiar to the type of goods involved in the
        transaction
    or 2) Employs an Agent, Broker, or other Intermediary who
        holds himself out as having such _knowledge_ or _skill_

§1-201(44): Value:

1) A Person is deemed to give **"Value"** if he acquires his rights *either*:
    (a) In return for either:
           1. A Binding Commitment to **Extend Credit** (ex: L/C)
        or 2. An Extension of **Immediately Available Credit**
    or (b) A Security for total or partial **Satisfaction** of a
           pre-existing claim
    or (c) By accepting delivery pursuant to a pre-existing
           contract for purchase
    or (d) In return for any "sufficient" consideration

2) This section is subject to:
    a) §3-303 (Negotiable Instruments)
    b) §4-208; §4-209 (Bank Collections)

X. *DOCUMENTS OF TITLE AND LETTERS OF CREDIT:*

A. *DOCUMENTS OF TITLE:*

OVERVIEW

- <u>Documents of Title</u> are used to "transform" property rights in goods to "paper," so people can transfer title of goods easier (without having to transfer possession every time people want to transfer interests).
- Since documents of title are such a common occurrence in the sales transaction, they are imperative to the study of any sale. Article 7 governs the law of documents of title and must be integrated with the rules of Article 2.

- <u>Bills of Lading</u> and <u>Warehouse Receipts</u> are the most common Documents of Title.
    - <u>Bill of Lading</u> ("BOL") - A BOL is a document issued by a *Carrier* when it takes the goods for shipment. The BOL is issued so that the Seller does not lose title to goods while they are in transit (in the Carrier's possession).
    - <u>Warehouse Receipt</u> ("W/R") - A W/R is issued by a *Bailee* (usually a Warehouseman) when it takes the goods for storage. The W/R is issued so that the Seller does not lose title to goods while stored in the Bailee's warehouse (and in the Bailor's possession).

- <u>Payment and Acceptance</u> (§2-310):
    - In a document transaction, the Buyer pays for the goods when the *Documents* arrive (not when the goods arrive) (§2-512).
    - **Payment is Not Acceptance** (§2-512(2)): If goods are non-conforming, Buyer may reject them under §2-601 and then sue for his money back (§2-711).
    - The Buyer, thus, loses his right to inspect the goods before payment (§2-512) (he may protect himself by requiring a professional inspector's document).

§2-310(c): Delivering Documents of Title:

Unless otherwise agreed, if delivery is authorized and made by delivering Documents of Title, then payment is due at the time and place where the Buyer is to receive the Documents (regardless of where the goods are to be received).

§2-512: Payment by Buyer Before Inspection:

(1) **Payment Required Before Inspection:** If a contract requires goods to be paid for before inspection (ex: Seller will tender documents), a non-conformity of the goods will not be an excuse for non-payment, *unless*:

> (a) The non-conformity appears without inspection (i.e. when the goods are delivered, the non-conformities are very obvious)
>
> or (b) The circumstances would justify an injunction against honoring the Seller's tender of the required documents (as per §5-114)

(2) **Effects of Payment Before Inspection:**

> a. PAYMENT (as per §2-512(1)) DOES NOT CONSTITUTE ACCEPTANCE.
> b. Payment does not impair the Buyer's right to inspect the goods (before accepting them).
> c. Payment does not impair any of the Buyer's remedies.

§2-513: Buyer's Right to Inspect Goods:

(1) **Buyer's Right to Inspection of Goods:**

> a) The Buyer has a right to inspect the goods before payment or acceptance if the goods are:
>> 1. Tendered
>> or 2. Delivered
>> or 3. Identified to the contract for sale
> b) The Buyer has a right to inspect the goods:
>> 1. At any reasonable place and time
>> and 2. In any reasonable manner
> c) When the Seller is required or authorized to send the goods to the Buyer, the inspection may be after their arrival.
> d) This subsection may be changed by agreement of the parties, and is subject to §2-513(3).

(2) <u>Expense of Inspection</u>:
    a) Expenses must be borne by the Buyer.
    b) If the goods do not conform and are rejected, the Buyer may recover inspection expenses from Seller.

(3) **No Right to Inspect:**
    i) The Buyer is not entitled to inspect the goods before payment if the contract provides:
        (a) For delivery *"C.O.D."* (or on other similar terms)
    or (b) For payment against DOT's (except where such payment is due only after the goods are to become available for inspection)
    ii) This subsection may be changed by agreement of parties, and is subject to §2-321(3) (dealing with C.I.F. contracts).

(4) **Fixed Place/Method of Inspection:**
    a) A place or method of inspection fixed by the parties is presumed to be *exclusive*.
    b) Unless otherwise agreed, such an agreement does not:
        1. Postpone identification
    or 2. Change the place for delivery
    or 3. Shift the passing of risk of loss
    c) <u>If compliance with fixed terms becomes impossible</u> -
        Buyer shall have a right to inspect (as per §2-513), unless the fixed place/method was clearly intended as an *indispensable condition,* failure of which avoids the contract.

§2-514: When Documents Deliverable on Acceptance; When on Payment:

1) <u>Documents Delivered Upon Acceptance</u> - Documents (against which a draft is drawn) are to be delivered to the <u>Drawee</u> upon *Acceptance* of the draft if:
    a) The Draft is payable more than <u>3 Days</u> after presentment
    and b) The Parties do not otherwise agree

2) <u>Documents Delivered Upon Payment</u> - Documents (against which a draft is drawn) are to be delivered to the <u>Drawee</u> upon *Payment* of the draft if:
    a) The Draft is not payable more than <u>3 Days</u> after presentment
    and b) The Parties agree

B. *HOLDER BY DUE NEGOTIATION* ("HDN")

OVERVIEW ─────────────────────────────

A Holder by Due Negotiation is similar to a Holder in Due Course (the "innocent owner" of a Negotiable Instrument (see "INNOCENT OWNER").

- Requirements to be Classified as an HDN (§7-501):
    1. **Holder:** The HDN must be a Holder (as per §1-201(20))
  and 2. **Due Negotiation:** The DOT must be *"Duly Negotiated"* to the holder:
    - a) Negotiation: The Holder must take the Document of Title by *Negotiation* (as per §7-501(1))
    - and b) Purchase - The Holder must take by *Purchase* (as per §1-201(32))
    - and c) New Value - the Holder must have taken the DOT for *New Value* (as per §1-201(44)) - it cannot involve receiving the DOT in settlement or payment for a previous monetary obligation (i.e. "antecedent debt").
    - and d) *Regular Course of Business Financing* - both parties must be Merchants (§7-501 official comment 1)
    - and e) Good Faith - The Holder must have demonstrated *Honesty in Fact* and *Reasonable Commercial Standards* (as per §2-103 (stricter standard of good faith required since both parties must be merchants)).

- **Rights of the HDN** (§7-502; §7-503):
  - The Holder by Due Negotiation (as per §7-501) will usually take priority in the goods, even against someone in possession of the goods.
  - An HDN will get title to goods subject to (§7-502 ("HDN Rule")).
  - Possession of Goods v. Possession of DOT (§7-503):
    - Situations occasionally arise when an unscrupulous Warehouseman will issue a DOT to someone and then sell the goods to another person (ex: Owner sends goods to Warehouseman for storage. In return, Warehouseman gives Owner a Warehouse Receipt. Nevertheless, the next week, Warehouseman sells the goods to Buyer, who immediately takes the goods home with him. Soon after, Owner returns to the Warehouse to redeem his Warehouse receipt for the goods, but learns that they had been sold to someone).

    - **DOT Superior:** In such a situation, the person holding the Document of Title will take priority over a Person in Possession of the goods *unless* the person possessing the DOT:
      1. Was issued the DOT after the goods had been sold
      or 2. Put the Goods into the Stream of Commerce: Entrusted goods to a Merchant (Note: a personal shipper (i.e. one directly employed by the Merchant) would not qualify under this exception, since "*To Ship*" or "*To Store*" refers only to someone who is a professional shipper/Warehouseman who issues a BOL/DOT (see §2-403(3)).
      or 3. Acquiesced the Goods in Procurement: (ex: Buyer leaves the goods in Seller's warehouse after he bought them)

- Forgery: If signatures on a DOT are not legitimate, the DOT will not be valid, even to an HDN ((§7-504 (no forgery); §7-501(1)(indorsement to negotiate); see §1-201(39) for definition of "signed")).

- **Regular Course of Business:**
  - DOT's Require negotiation to be in the *"Regular Course of Business"* (i.e. between merchants) (§7-501; §7-504 official comment).
  - Regular Course of Business v. Ordinary Course of Business
    - *Ordinary Course* - Sold by a Merchant (someone in the business of selling such goods).
    - *Regular Course* - Both sides are Merchants/ professionals (as most Negotiations are).

- **Warranties upon Negotiation of Document of Title** (§7-507):
  The transferor of a DOT makes the following Warranties:
    1) The Transferor has a legal right to transfer the goods which the DOT represents.
    2) The Documents are genuine.
    3) The Transferor has no knowledge of any act that would impair the validity or worth of the document.

---

§7-501: Due Negotiation:

(1) **Manner of Negotiation:**

    a) <u>Named Person:</u> A *Negotiable* Document of Title "running" to the order of a named person, can be negotiated *only* if:

        a) <u>Indorsement</u> - The identified person in the document Indoreses it

     and b) <u>Delivery</u> - The document is delivered into the possession of the holder

    b) <u>Bearer:</u> If the instrument is indorsed in blank (ie "to Bearer" or has a "blank indorsement"), it can be negotiated by *delivery* alone.

(2) <u>Delivery as Negotiation:</u>

    (a) A Negotiable Document of Title may also negotiated by <u>Delivery alone</u> if it "runs" to bearer (by its original terms).

    (b) A Document of Title will be considered as if it had been negotiated if it is delivered to the *identified person*.

(3) <u>Special Indorsement:</u> If a negotiable DOT has been indorsed to an identified person, the special indorsee must <u>Indorse</u> and <u>Deliver</u> it to negotiate it.

(4) **"Due Negotiation"**: Requirements for a Negotiable Document
    of Title to be *"duly negotiated"* :
      a) It is Negotiated (in the manner stated above in this section) to a
        Holder (as per §1-201(20))
   and b) The Holder takes by ***Purchase*** (as per §1-201(32))
   and c) It is Purchased:
        1. In **Good Faith** (as per §1-201(19))
     and 2. **Without any Notice** of another person's claims or
         defenses against the document
     and 3. For **Value** (as per §1-201(44))
     and 4. In the *Regular Course of Business or financing* (ie-
         from a merchant)
   and d) It does NOT involve receiving the document in
      settlement or payment of a money obligation.

(5) **Non-Negotiable Documents:** Indorsement of a Non-Negotiable
    Document neither makes it negotiable nor adds to the
    transferee's rights

(6) **Naming Person to Notify upon Arrival:** The naming of a
    person (in a negotiable DOT) to be notified when goods
    (represented by the DOT) arrive does not:
      a) Limit the negotiability of the bill
   nor b) Constitute notice to a purchaser of the bill the named
      person has any interest in the goods.

§7-502: Rights Acquired by Due Negotiation:

(1) **Rights by Due negotiation:** A person acquires the following rights if a Negotiable Document has been *Duly Negotiated* to him (subject to §7-205 and §2-703):

    (a) Title to the Documents

and (b) Title to the Goods

and (c) All rights accruing under the law of agency and estoppel (including rights to goods delivered to the bailee after the document was issued)

and (d) 1. The Direct Obligation of the *Issuer* to <u>Hold</u> or <u>Deliver</u> the Goods according to the terms of the Document <u>FREE of any defense or claim by the issuer</u> (except those arising under the terms of the Document or Under Article 7)

    2. <u>Delivery Order Cases:</u> The Bailee's Obligation accrues only when

        a) The Bailee accepts its obligation

    and b) The obligation acquired by the holder is that the <u>Issuer</u> (and any indorser) will procure the acceptance of the Bailee

(2) **Title and Rights** (subject to §7-503)

    a) Title and rights acquired by negotiation will not be defeated by

        1) Any stoppage (of the goods represented by the document)

    or 2) By surrender of the goods by the Bailee

    b) Title and rights acquired by negotiation will not be impaired, even if

        1) Negotiation (or any prior negotiation) constituted a breach of duty

        2) Any person has been deprived of possession of the document by:

            a) Misrepresentation

         or b) Fraud

         or c) Accident

         or d) Mistake

         or e) Duress

         or f) Loss

         or g) Theft

         or h) Conversion

        3) A Previous sale (or other transfer of the goods or document) has made a third person.

§7-503: Defeated Documents of Title:

(1) <u>Interests before Issuance:</u>   A DOT confers no right in goods against a person who:
      (a) Didn't delivered or entrust such goods (or DOT covering them) to a merchant (as per §2-403)
  and (b) Didn't acquiesce title in the procurement by the Bailor (or his nominee) of any DOT
  and (c) Had a legal or perfected S/I in the goods *before* the Document was issued

(2) <u>Unaccepted Delivery Orders:</u>
      a) Title to goods based upon an *unaccepted delivery order* is subject to the rights of anyone to whom a Negotiable warehouse receipt or BOL (covering such goods) has been *Duly Negotiated.*
      b) Such a title may be defeated under §7-504 to the same extent as the rights of the Issuer or a Transferee from the Issuer.

(3) <u>BOL issued to a Freight Forwarder</u>
      a) Title to goods based on a BOL issued to a Freight Forwarder is subject to the rights of anyone to whom a bill issued to the Freight Forwarder is *Duly Negotiated*
      b) Delivery by the carrier (in accordance with Part 4 of Article 7) pursuant to its own BOL, discharges the carrier's obligation to deliver.

C. *BILLS OF LADING:*

OVERVIEW

- **"Bill of Lading"** ("BOL") - A BOL is a document issued by a *Carrier* who it takes the goods for shipment. The BOL is issued so that the Seller does not lose title to the goods while they are in transit (i.e. in the Carrier's possession).
- **The BOL Transaction:**
  - If the BOL is <u>*Negotiable*</u>:
    - The Carrier will issue the Seller a Bill of Lading, to *"Seller's Order."*
    - Subsequently, the Seller will indorse the BOL and *negotiate* it to the Buyer.
    - In order to get the goods, the Buyer must present the BOL upon delivery.
    - <u>Problems</u>:
      - Seller is not assured payment.
      - Seller often cannot send the BOL to Buyer before the goods arrive.
      - The Buyer can't inspect goods before accepting them from the Carrier (§2-323).

- **The Sight Draft Transaction:**
    - The Sight Draft Transaction tries to alleviate the above mentioned problems.
    - Procedure:
        - The Seller will *draw* a "draft" (ex: a check) **against the Buyer** (this way, Seller writes a "check" out to himself, ordering the Buyer (instead of Seller's bank) to pay Seller):
            - Parties on the Draft:
                - Drawer = Seller
                - Payee = Seller
                - Drawee/Payor = Buyer

            - Since the Seller is the Drawer, the Buyer (as payor) is only liable to pay the Seller by the terms of the contract (and until the Buyer signs the draft he is not liable by the terms of the draft, as specified in Articles 3 and 4).
        - The Seller indorses the *Negotiable BOL* and the Draft (making it a "<u>Sight Draft</u>").

        - <u>The Seller Sends the Documents to the Buyer through the Banking Channels</u>:
            - The Seller gives his Bank the Sight Draft and the Negotiable BOL.
            - The Seller's Bank gives the Sight Draft and BOL to Buyer's Bank.
            - Buyer's Bank tenders the BOL to the Buyer upon Acceptance of the Draft (i.e. Buyer indorses the draft, binding himself to pay it under Article 3 and 4).
        - Once the Carrier arrives with the goods the Buyer exchanges the BOL with the Carrier for the goods.
        - The Seller enforces the accepted Draft against the Buyer.

- Payment and Acceptance (§2-310):
    - In a document transaction the Buyer pays for the goods when the *Documents* arrive (not when the goods arrive) (§2-512; §2-507).
    - The Buyer, thus, loses his right to inspect the goods before payment (he may protect himself by requiring a professional inspector's document) (§2-512;§2-513(3)).
    - **Payment is Not Acceptance:** Buyer may reject goods under §2-601 and then sue for his money back after (even after it has paid for the goods) (§2-512(2)).

- **Dishonor**:
  - A Sight Draft is considered *dishonored* if it is not paid within <u>3 days</u> after <u>Due Presentment</u> (as per §3-502(c) and §3-502(b)(2)).
  - <u>Due Presentment</u>:
    - Due Presentment may be made orally, electronically, in writing or in any other *commercially reasonable manner* (§3-501(a)(1)).
    - Presentment is effective when demand for payment is *Received* by the Drawer (i.e. the Buyer).
  - Presentment - A <u>Collecting Bank</u> (a bank which takes the Seller's draft for collection purposes) presents the draft by sending the Drawee (the Buyer) a notice that the bank is holding the draft for payment (§4-212(a)).
  - <u>Presenting Bank</u> - A Presenting Bank (the Bank enforcing the check directly against the Buyer or Buyer's Bank) has added duties to inform Seller of dishonor (§4-503); if the Presenting Bank accepts Personal Checks as payment for the draft, it will be liable if the check is dishonored (pre-1993 §4-211(1)(d); although new §4-213 doesn't say this, it would probably violate §4-202's Duty of Care for Banks).

- <u>Problem with the Sight Draft Transaction</u>:
  Under a Sight Draft transaction, the Buyer only has to *Accept* the draft (by signing it) before the bank releases the Bill Of Lading to the Buyer; however, the Buyer doesn't have to actually pay the Draft until Seller enforces it; thus, there is still a risk that the Buyer can "skip town" or go bankrupt and never pay it. The Letter of Credit transaction (detailed below) tries to eliminate this risk by holding a bank responsible for payment (since banks are presumed to be more reliable than others (see "LETTERS OF CREDIT" below)).

---

§2-323: Bill of Lading:

(1) **Requirements of the Bill of Lading**

    a. The Seller must obtain a <u>Negotiable Bill of Lading</u> (unless otherwise agreed) if:

        1. The contract involves an *overseas* shipment

    and 2. The terms are FOB(vessel), CIF or C&F

    b. <u>Contents of the Negotiable Bill of Lading</u>:

        1. FOB - must state that goods have been loaded on board.

        2. CIF or C&F - must state that the goods have been received for shipment.

(2) **Multi-Part Documents**

    i) When a Bill of Lading has been issued in a <u>set of parts</u>, only one part need be tendered *unless:*

        a) The agreement expressly requires a full set to be tendered

    or b) *Both*

        1. The Buyer demands a full set to be tendered

        and 2. The documents are <u>not</u> to be sent from abroad

    ii) <u>The following rules apply even if the contract expressly requires a full set of documents to be tendered</u>:

        (a) Due tender of a single part of the BOL is acceptable to cure improper delivery (as per §2-508(1))

    and (b) <u>Documents sent from abroad</u>: If the documents are sent from abroad, the person tendering an incomplete set of documents may require payment upon furnishing an <u>indemnity</u> (which the Buyer deems to have been made in good faith), even if the full set is demanded.

(3) **"Overseas"** - an "overseas" contract or shipment is one:

    a) Involving shipment by <u>water</u> or <u>air</u>

  and b) That is subject to commercial, financial, or shipping practices characteristic of *international deep water commerce,* either by Usage of Trade or Agreement.

). *LETTERS OF CREDIT:*

)VERVIEW———————————————

The Letter of Credit Transaction:

- The Letter of Credit ("L/C") Transaction has become very popular in recent years, especially between geographically distant parties.
- The L/C transaction helps ensure that the Seller will get paid upon delivery of the goods.
- The Letter of Credit is a document which requires the Buyer's Bank to pay the Seller (or Seller's Bank) upon the occurrence of certain conditions. These conditions are usually nothing more than a *checklist* of documents which must be received in order for the Buyer's Bank to release the funds to the Seller.

Applicable Law: Letter of Credit transactions are usually governed by international treaties, banking laws, and the <u>Uniform Customs and Practices for Documentary Credits and Demand Guarantees</u> ("UCP"). Article 5 of the UCC briefly summarizes the rights and liabilities of the parties involved, yet subjects itself to any accepted statute or treaty governing Letters of Credit (§5-102(3)).

Article 5 has recently been amended (in 1995); the rules discussed below reflect Article 5 in its amended form.

Procedure:

- The Buyer's Bank makes a loan to the Buyer before opening (i.e. creating) the L/C.
- The Buyer's Bank opens an L/C with the Seller's Bank (or Seller), promising to pay the Seller upon tender of the documents specified in the L/C.
- The Seller's Bank usually "writes" the L/C and specifies the list of documents required by the Buyer in order for it to *"release"* (i.e. pay) the L/C. (These documents usually include a Bill of Lading, an invoice, applicable visas required for the goods to enter the country, and certificates of approval from an outside source.)
- Once the Buyer's Bank receives the appropriate documents it "releases" the Letter of Credit, and pays the Seller.

Liabilities of the Parties:

The Issuing Bank (Buyer's Bank):

- The Issuing Bank must pay the Seller's Bank upon fulfillment of the L/C's conditions (§5-108(a)).
- The Issuing Bank has no obligation to interpret the Merchant's customary practices when determining whether the conditions of the L/C have been fulfilled (in order to make the Buyer pay) (§5-108(f)(3)).
- According to the UCP, the Issuing Bank may pay the Seller's Bank as long as all documents are *not inconsistent* with the L/C (though there is no need for them to be identical).

The Seller's Bank - A Seller's Bank can have 2 levels of responsibility, depending on the L/C's terms:

- A *Confirming Bank* is liable to pay the Seller for a L/C once it approves the L/C, even if the Issuing Bank fails to pay. (The L/C must specify that Seller's Bank is a Confirming Bank, otherwise it will be presumed an Advising Bank (§2-325).)
- An *Advising Bank* is not liable to the Seller; it just advises that the L/C's conditions are fulfilled and pays the Seller once the Issuing Bank pays it.

The Buyer:

- Liable to the Seller under its contract with the *Seller* for the price of the goods.
- Liable to reimburse the *Issuing Bank* for any loan made to pay the L/C to the Seller's Bank (§5-108(i)(1)), once the Issuing Bank has actually paid the Seller.

The Independence Doctrine:
- Although the terms of the L/C usually reflect the underlying contract between the Buyer and Seller, payment of the L/C is a totally *separate* obligation.
- ***The Letter of Credit is enforceable even if the contract between the Buyer and Seller is invalid or breached.***
- A Bank may not look at the validity of the documents or the underlying contract used to fulfill the L/C's conditions.

Fraud Exception (§5-109(a)):
- When *Material* Fraud is involved a party may obtain a court injunction to stop its Bank from paying the L/C.
  - Fraud includes:
    - Forgery
  - and • Fraud in the Transaction
  - Fraud in Transaction: Even if Fraud exists in the transaction, the Bank may still be obligated to pay the Letter of Credit (§5-114(2)):
    - **Bank Must Pay** - if the Person to whom the Bank owes the Money to is a beneficiary specified in §5-108(a)(1).
    - **Bank May Pay** - if, in acting in good faith, it decides to honor or dishonor the L/C based upon the condition of the documents.
    - **Bank May Not Pay** - if the court issues an injunction (or similar relief) enjoining the Issuer from honoring the L/C. The use of such relief is strictly limited by §5-109(b) in order to preserve the independent nature and reliability of payment from the L/C.
- If there is an underlying Draft, the Bank can attempt to stop Payment according to the "Stop Payment Order" rules (§4-303), but cannot stop payment once the Issuing Bank has accepted the Draft.

Other Rules:
- L/C's are presumed *irrevocable* (§2-325(3)).
- L/C's must be *seasonably provided*, or the Buyer will be deemed to have repudiated his obligation to pay (§2-325(1)).
Payment by L/C *"suspends"* the obligation to pay (under the contract) (§2-325(2)). Only upon Dishonor of the L/C may the Seller demand Payment directly from the Buyer (§2-325(2)).

2-325: Letter of Credit:

) Failure of a Buyer to seasonably provide an agreed Letter of Credit is a breach of the contract for sale.

) **L/C as Payment:**

    a) The delivery of a proper L/C to the Seller *suspends* the Buyer's obligation to pay.

    b) If the L/C is dishonored, the Seller may require Payment directly from Buyer upon *seasonable notification*.

) Definitions:

    a) **"Letter of Credit"** (or "banker's credit") - means (unless otherwise agreed) an irrevocable credit issued by a financing agency of good repute.

    b) **"Confirmed Credit"** - means that the credit carries the direct obligation of a financing agency which does business in the Seller's financial market.

5-108: Issuer's Rights and Obligations:

) **Issuing Bank's Obligations:**[1]

    1) **When Issuer Must Honor**: An Issuer Bank[2] shall honor a Presentation only if it appears to comply with the terms of the Letter of Credit (as determined by the "Standard Practice" referred to in §5-108(e)).

    2) **When Issuer Does Not Have to Honor**:

        i) Fraud Exception The Bank does not have to comply if there is evidence of Fraud (as per §5-109).

    3) Non-Compliance: An Issuer shall Dishonor a Presentation that does not comply with the Letter of Credit, *unless*:

        a) The Applicant otherwise directs the Issuer

        b) Otherwise provided where there is a Transfer by Operation of Law (as per §5-113).

---

ormer §5-114(2) did not requires "strict compliance" as Amended §5-108(a) does. Strict Compliance is to be determined by the court (and not a jury) pursuant to the "Standards of Practice" required under §5-108(e hese rules also apply to Confirming Banks (see Off. Comment 1).

b) Time Limits:
    1) <u>Time Limit</u>: An Issuer must honor, accept, or notify, by the earlier of
        i) A *Reasonable Time*
        ii) <u>7 Business Days</u> after receiving documents (upon Presentation)
    2) <u>Application of Time Limit</u>: The above time limit applies to the following:
        i) *Honoring an L/C*
        ii) *Accepting a Draft*, (or incurring a "deferred obligation") - if the L/C provides
           for the L/C to be completed more than 7 Business Days after
           Presentation.
        iii) *Give Notice* to the Presenter - of any discrepancies in the Presentation

c) Failure to Give Notice of Discrepancies - If the Issuer fails to timely notify the
    Presenter of a discrepancy, the Issuer may not use such discrepancy as a basis for
    Dishonoring the L/C (except as provided in §5-108(d)). [3]

d) Failure to Give Notice of Fraud - Even if the Issuer fails to timely notify the
    Presenter of a discrepancy (as per §5-108(b)) or that there may be <u>Fraud</u>, <u>Forgery</u>, or
    that the L/C has <u>expired</u>, the Issuer may still assert Expiration or Fraud and
    Forgery (as per §5-109(a)) as a basis for dishonor.

e) Issuer's Standard of Practice -
    1. <u>Standard of Care</u> - An Issuer shall observe *Standard Practice of Financial
       Institutions* that regularly issue Letters of Credit.
    2. Whether an Issuer has met this standard is an issued to be determined by the
       court (and not a jury).
    3. The court shall allow the parties a reasonable opportunity to present evidence
       of the "standard practice".

Former Article 5 did not have such notice requirements.

Independent Significance: An Issuer is not responsible for:
- (1) <u>The Underlying Contract</u> - the performance or nonperformance of the underlying contract
- (2) An act or omission of others[4]
- (3) <u>Trade Terms</u> - Observance or knowledge of usage of a particular trade (unless should know under "Standard Practice" as determined in §5-108(e) above)

Nondocumentary Conditions - The Issuer shall <u>ignore</u> any conditions in an Undertaking (constituting an L/C under §5-102(a)(10)) which are <u>Nondocumentary conditions</u> (ex: conditions to payment which are not evidenced by documents to be presented to Issuer)

Dishonor - If an Issuer has Dishonored an L/C, it shall do the following:
- 1) Return the documents
- or 2) *Both*;
     - a) Hold the documents (at the disposal of the Presenter)
     - and b) Send the Presenter notice that such documents are being held by the Issuer

Issuer's Rights - After appropriately honoring an L/C, the Issuer will have the following rights:
- (1) <u>Reimbursement</u> - the Issuer is entitled to Reimbursement by the Applicant no later than the <u>date of Issuer's Payment</u> of the L/C.[5]
- (2) <u>Free & Clear Documents</u> - the Issuer takes the documents free any claims from the:
     - i) Beneficiary
     - ii) Presenter
- (3) <u>Limited Right of Recourse</u> - the Issuer may not assert a right of recourse against the Drawer or Indorser of a Draft (under §3-414 or §3-415)

Former §5-109 limited this to Drafts, Demands, Documents in Possession of Others and Documents in Transit
Former §5-114(3) entitled reimbursement at least 1 day *Before* any Acceptance under the L/C matured.

(4) <u>No Restitution for Mistake</u> - the Issuer will be precluded from obtaining restitution for money paid (or value given) by Mistake:
    a) *To the Extent* the Mistake concerns
        i) Discrepancies in the documents (which the Issuer should have spotted)
        ii) Discrepancies in Tender (which was apparent on the face of the documents presented)
    b) Unless otherwise provided for in Warranties (§5-110) or with Subrogation Rights (arising under §5-177).

(5) <u>Discharge</u> - The Issuer will be discharged of its obligations to the Applicant, *to the extent* of its performance under the L/C *unless* the Issuer honored a presentation with a forged signature of a Beneficiary required to sign a presented document.

5-109: Fraud or Forgery:

) **Fraudulent Presentation -**
    i) <u>Scope:</u> The following rules apply if
      a) a document that is presented appears to comply, on its face, to the L/C
  and b) *Either*:
        1) A required document is <u>Forged</u> or <u>Materially Fraudulent</u>[6]
        2) Honor of the Presentation would facilitate a Material Fraud by the Beneficiary (hurting the Issuer or Applicant)**:**

    ii) <u>Rules of Honoring with Forged/Fraudulent Documents:</u>
        (1) **Protected Beneficiaries:** The Issuer shall <u>Honor</u> the presentation if Honor is demanded by:
          or (i) A <u>Nominated Person</u> if:
              a. It was given <u>Value</u>
            and b. In <u>Good Faith</u>
            and c. <u>Without Notice </u>of Forgery
          or (ii) A <u>Confirmer </u>- who has honored its confirmation in Good Faith

---

Former Article 5 did not specify that the fraud had to be a "Material Fraud"

or (iii) A <u>Holder in Due Course</u> if:

    1. It is the Holder of a Draft drawn under the L/C

    and 2. The draft was taken *After* Acceptance by the Issuer (or Nominated Party)

or (iv) An <u>Assignee</u> of the Issuer's or Nominated Person's <u>Deferred Obligation</u> (as per §5-108(b)(2)) if:

    1. It was taken for <u>Value</u>

    and 2. <u>Without Notice</u> of Forgery

    and 3. *After* the Obligation was incurred by the Issuer (or Nominated Person)

and (2) **Issuer's Discretion**- the Issuer may honor or dishonor the presentation while acting in <u>Good Faith</u>.

) Injunctions:

The court may <u>not</u> temporarily or permanently enjoin the Issuer from Honoring Presentation (or it may grant similar relief against the Issuer or other persons)[7] <u>unless</u> the court finds that:

(1) <u>Applicable Law Allows Relief</u>: The relief is <u>not prohibited</u> under the law applicable to the Accepted Draft or Deferred Obligation.

and (2) <u>Adequate Protection</u>: The Beneficiary, Issuer, or Nominated Person (who may be adversely affected by the injunction) is *adequately protected* against any loss it may incur as a result of the relief.

and (3) <u>State Law Satisfied</u>: All the requirements for the particular relief under state law have been met.

and (4) <u>Applicant Likely to Succeed</u>:

    1. The Applicant is *more likely than not* to succeed under its claim of forgery or material Fraud

    and 2. The person demanding honor doesn't qualify for protection under §5-109(a)(1).

and 5) An Applicant claims that a Required Document:

    a. Is Forged

    or b. Is Materially Forged

    or c. Would facilitate a Material Fraud by the Beneficiary (hurting the Issuer or Applicant).

Former §5-114 only restrained a court's power to grant an injunction. Amended Article 5 also restricts the courts from granting "similar relief," which includes attachment, declaratory judgment, and interpleaders

THE
E-Z RULES
FOR
ARTICLE 2

E-Z RULES TABLE OF CONTENTS

ARTICLE 2 SALES

PART 1   SHORT TITLE, GENERAL CONSTRUCTION AND SUBJECT MATTER

PART 2   FORM, FORMATION AND READJUSTMENT OF CONTRACT

PART 3   GENERAL OBLIGATION AND CONSTRUCTION OF CONTRACT

PART 4   TITLE, CREDITORS AND GOOD FAITH PURCHASERS

SECTION   **DESCRIPTION**   **PAGE**

PART 6   BREACH, REPUDIATION AND EXCUSE

SECTION	DESCRIPTION	PAGE

PART 7   <u>**REMEDIES**</u>

DEFINTIONS

§1-201(9): Buyer in the Ordinary Course of Business:

1. A "Buyer In The Ordinary Course" ("BIOC") is a
   Person/Organization (not a Pawnbroker) who buys goods:
   a) In Good-Faith (see §1-201(19))
   and b) Without knowledge that purchase is in violation of
   someone else's other ownership rights or S/I
   and c) From a 'Merchant' - someone in the business of selling
   those goods (except a pawnbroker)
   and d) In the *Ordinary Course*- passing of title *for value* (ie- a
   SALE) in a typical transaction (ex: inventory, not equipment)
   and e) For **Value**

2. Anyone selling minerals, oil, or gas (at wellhead or minehead) is
   considered to be in the business of selling goods of that kind.

3. How goods may be Bought
   a) For Cash
   or b) By Exchange of property
   or c) On Credit - secured or unsecured
   or d) Receiving goods/title under a pre-existing contract for sale

4. Goods are NOT considered Bought if
   a) They are given as a security for a debt
   b) They are given as partial or total satisfaction of a debt
   c) They are Bulk Transfers

§1-201(19): Good Faith:

"Good Faith" means <u>Honesty in Fact</u> in the Conduct or
Transaction Concerned. (see also §2-103(b) for Merchants)

§1-203: Good Faith:

"Every contract or duty within this Act imposes an obligation of
Good Faith in its performance or enforcement"   (see §1-201(19))

§1-201(20): Holder:

1. <u>With Respect to a **Negotiable Instrument:**</u>
    a) *Instruments Payable to "Bearer"* - The person in
       Posession of the instrument is the Holder
    b) *Instruments Payable to an Identified person* - the idetified
       person is the Holder (ie- has possession)

2. <u>With Respect to a **A Document of Title:**</u>
    The Holder is the person in <u>Posession</u> of the Document if the
    goods are deliverable to:
       a) The "Bearer"
    or b) The order or the person in posession of the Document

§1-201(24) Money:

"**Money**" is a medium of exchange authorized or adopted by a
domestic or foreign government, and includes a Monetary
Unit of Account established by either:
       a) An intergovernmental organization
    or b) By agreement between one or more nations

§1-201(32): Purchase:

A **"Purchase"** is any _Voluntary Transaction_ creating an interest in property, <u>including a:</u>
  1. Sale (ie- involving a Buyer and Seller)
  or 2. Discount
  or 3. Negotiation
  or 4. Mortgage
  or 5. Pledge (ex: a Secured party)
  or 6. Lien (ex: a Secured party)
  or 7. Issue or Re-issue
  or 8. Gift (donee)

§1-201(33): Purchaser:

A **"Purchaser"** is a Person" who takes by _purchase"_
  (ex: a buyer, a Security Interest holder,etc... (as per §1-201(32))

§1-201(39): Signed:

Includes any Symbol executed or adopted by someone **intending** to _authenticate_ a writing.

§1-201(43): Unauthorized:

1. An unauthorized signature is made without <u>Actual</u>, <u>Implied</u>, or <u>Apparent</u> authority.
2. A Forgery is a type of unauthorized signature

§1-201(44): Value:

1) A Person is deemed to give **"Value"** if he acquires his rights *either*:
    (a) In return for either:
        1. A Binding Commitment to **Extend Credit** (ex: L/C)
      or 2. An Extension of **Immediately Available Credit**
    or (b) A Security for total or partial **Satisfaction** of a pre-existing claim
    or (c) By accepting delivery pursuant to a pre-existing contract for purchase
    or (d) In return for any "sufficient" consideration

2) This section is subject to:
    a) §3-303 (Negotiable Instruments)
    b) §4-208; §4-209 (Bank Collections)

ARTICLE 2

PART 1:
SHORT TITLE, GENERAL CONSTRUCTION AND SUBJECT MATTER

§2-101: Short Title:

"This Article shall be known and may be cited as **Uniform Commercial Code** - Sales."

§2-102: Scope:

1. This Article applies to transactions in goods unless the context provides otherwise.
2. This Article does not apply to any transaction which is intended to act only as a <u>security transaction</u> (even though it is in the form of an unconditional contract to sell).
3. This Article does not impair or repeal any statute regarding sales to special classes of buyers (ex: consumers, farmers, etc.).

§2-103: Definitions:

(1) <u>Definitions Applicable to Article 2</u> (unless the context requires otherwise):
   (a) **"Buyer"** - a person who buys or contracts to buy goods.
   (b) **"Good Faith"** - *For a Merchant* - requires both:
     1. Honesty in fact
   and 2. The observance of *reasonable commercial standards* of fair dealing in the trade
   (c) **"Receipt"** [of goods] - means taking *Physical Possession.*
   (d) **"Seller"** - a person who sells or contracts to sell goods.

(2) <u>Index to Other Definitions Applying to Article 2</u>:
   a. "Acceptance" - §2-606
   b. "Banker's Credit" - §2-325
   c. "Between Merchants" - §2-104
   d. "Cancellation" - §1-106(4)
   e. "Commercial Unit" - §2-105
   f. "Confirmed Credit" - §2-325
   g. "Conforming to Contract" - §2-106
   h. "Contract for Sale" - §2-106
   i. "Cover" - §2-712
   j. "Entrusting" - §2-403
   k. "Financing Agency" - §2-104
   l. "Future Goods" - §2-105
   m. "Goods" - §2-105
   n. "Identification" - §2-501
   o. "Installment Contract" - §2-612
   p. "Letter of Credit" - §2-325
   q. "Lot" - §2-105
   r. "Merchant" - §2-104
   s. "Overseas" - §2-323
   t. "Person in Position of Seller" - §2-707
   u. "Present Sale" - §2-106
   v. "Sale" - §2-106
   w. "Sale on approval" §2-326
   x. "Sale or Return" §2-326
   y. "Termination" - §2-106

(3) <u>Index to Applicable Definitions From Other Articles</u>
   a. "Check" - §3-104
   b. "Consignee" - §7-102
   c. "Consignor" - §7-102
   d. "Consumer Goods" - §9-109
   e. "Dishonor" - §3-507
   f. "Draft" - §3-104

(4) Article 1 contains general definitions and principles of construction and interpretation that apply throughout this Article.

§2-104: "Merchants"; Other Definitions:

(1) **"Merchant"** - A person is considered a "Merchant" if he is *either:*
    a) <u>Dealer</u>: A person who *deals* with goods of the kind
  or b) <u>Expert</u>: A person who *either:*
        1) Holds himself out as having <u>*knowledge or skill*</u>
          peculiar to the type of goods involved in the
          transaction
      or 2) Employs an Agent, Broker, or other Intermediary who
          holds himself out as having such *knowledge* or *skill*

(2) **"Financing Agency"** - A Bank, Finance Company or other
    person who *either*:
      a. Makes advances against goods or documents of title,
        in the *Ordinary Course of Business*
  or b. Intervenes in the Ordinary Course (by arrangement with either the
      Seller or Buyer) to make or collect payment due or claimed
      under a contract for sale as by:
        1) Purchasing or paying the Seller's draft
      or 2) Making advances against the Seller's draft
      or 3) Taking the Seller's draft for collection (whether or not
        documents of title accompany the draft)
  or c. Similarly intervenes between Sellers and Buyers with respect
      to the goods (as per §2-707)

(3) **"Between Merchants"** - This term refers to any transaction
    where both parties are deemed to have the *knowledge* and
    skill of merchants.

§2-105: Definitions:

(1) **"Goods"** - all things which are *movable at the time they are
identified to a contract.*

    a) <u>The Following are "Goods"</u>:
        1. Unborn young animals
        2. Growing crops
        3. Other identified things attached to realty (as described in
         §2-107: "Goods to be Severed From Realty")

    b) <u>The Following are NOT "Goods"</u>:
        1. Money in which the price of the contract is to be
         paid
        2. Investment Securities (see Article 8)
        3. Things in Action

(2) **"Future Goods"** - goods which are NOT *both* Existing and Identified
    a) Goods must be *both* **Existing** and **Identified** before any interest in them can pass.
    b) An alleged *"present sale"* of Future Goods (or any interest in them) is considered a contract To Sell.

(3) **Sale of Partial Interest:** One may sell (or contract to sell) a *partial interest* in goods if they are existing, identified goods (one may not sell a partial interest in Future Goods).

(4) **Bulk Fungible Goods:**
    a) An undivided share in an Identifiable Bulk of Fungible Goods is considered *sufficiently identified* in order to be sold (although the exact quantity in the Bulk is not determined).
    b) A Seller may sell the interest he has in such bulk goods in any agreed upon proportion or quantity (measured by number, weight or other measure). The Buyer will become an Owner in Common.

(5) **"Lot"** - A parcel or single article which is the subject matter of a separate sale or delivery (*whether or not it is sufficient to perform the contract*).

(6) **"Commercial Unit"** -
    a. Some thing is considered a "Commercial Unit" if:
      1. It is a unit of goods which, by commercial usage, is a single whole (for purposes of sale)
    and 2. Division of such a unit would *materially impair* the character or value on the market or in use

    b. A Commercial Unit May Include:
      1) A single article (ex: machine)
      2) A set (ex: assortment of sizes, a suite of furniture)
      3) A quantity of articles (ex: a bale, gross, or carload)
      4) Any other unit treated in use (or in the relevant market) as a single whole

§2-106: Definitions:

(1) **General Definitions:**
   a. Limitation to Present and Future Sales of Goods: In this Article (unless the context otherwise requires) the terms *"contract"* and *"agreement"* are limited to those relating to the present or future sale of goods.
   b. **"Contract for Sale"** - includes both:
      1. A Present Sale of goods
    and 2. A contract to sell goods at a Future Time.
   c. **"Sale"** - a sale consists of the passing of title from the Seller to the Buyer for a price (as per §2-401).
   d. **"Present Sale"** - a sale which is accomplished by the making of the contact.

(2) **"Conforming to Contract":** Goods or conduct (including any part of performance) will be deemed to *"conform to the contract"* when they are in accordance with the obligations under the contract.

(3) **"Termination"**
   a. "Termination" occurs when either party puts an end to the contract - pursuant to a power created by the terms of the contract or an applicable law (ie - not because of a party's breach).
   b. Obligations upon Termination
      1. *Bilateral Executory Obligations* - all obligations which are still executory on both sides are *discharged*.
      2. *Rights based on Performance or Breach* - any right based on prior breach or prior performance will survive after termination.

(4) **"Cancellation"**
   a. "Cancellation" occurs when a party puts an end to the contract because of the other party's breach.
   b. Effect of Cancellation: Cancellation has the same effect as *termination*, except that the canceling party retains the right to any remedy for:
      1. Breach of the *whole* contract
    or 2. Any unperformed balance

§2-107: Goods to Be Severed From Realty; Recording:

(1) Goods Severed by Seller:

a. The following is considered a Contract for the Sale of Goods (and therefore governed by Article 2) so long as the material being sold is to be *severed* (i.e. removed) from the Realty (on which they are sold) by the <u>Seller</u>:

    1. A contract for the sale of Natural Resources (including minerals, oil and gas) to be removed from the realty

    or 2. A contract for the sale of a Structure (or its materials) to be removed from the realty

b. Until such "goods" are severed from the Realty a puported sale of such material is:

    1. Effective as a *Contract to Sell*

    2. Not effective as a *Transfer of Interest*

(2) Goods Severed by Buyer or Seller:

a. The following will be considered a Contract for the Sale of Goods if the material is to be severed by the <u>Buyer</u> or the <u>Seller</u>:

    1. A contract to sell <u>Growing Crops</u> (apart from the land)

    2. A contract to sell <u>Timber</u> to be cut

    3. Other things attached to realty and capable of severance without material harm to the property (but not described in 2-107(1))

b. Such contracts are deemed Contracts for the Sale of Goods even though the "goods" form part of the Realty at the time the contract was made (therefore, the parties can effect a present sale *before* severance (by identifying the actual goods sold under the contract)).

(3) Rights of Third Parties:

a. The provisions of this section are subject to any Third Party Rights (provided by the laws relating to Realty Records).

b. If a contract for sale is executed and <u>recorded</u> as a *Document Transferring an Interest in Land*, it shall constitute notice to Third Parties of the Buyer's rights under the contract for sale.

PART 2:

FORM, FORMATION AND READJUSTMENT OF CONTRACT

§2-201: Formal Requirements of a Contract:

(1) **Statute of Frauds**:
   a. A Contract for the Sale of Goods for ≥ **$500** must be in **writing** to be enforceable by way of action or defense (except as otherwise provided in this section).
   b. The Writing Requirement:
       1. The writing need only indicate that a contract for sale has been made between the parties.
       2. The writing must be <u>signed</u> by the party against whom enforcement is sought (or his authorized agent or broker (ex: if Seller is suing Buyer, Buyer's signature must be on the writing)).
       3. A writing is not insufficient if it omits or incorrectly states an agreed upon term.
   c. The Contract will not be enforceable under §2-201(1) beyond the quantity of goods shown in such writing.

(2) **Contract Between Merchants:**
   a. Merchant's Confirmation: A Merchant may satisfy the requirements of writing (§2-201(1)) by sending the other Merchant party a confirmation of the contract.
   b. Notice of Objection: The confirmation will be an effective writing unless the party receiving the confirmation gives the sender a *written notice of objection* within <u>10 Days</u> after it received the confirmation.
   c. If the party receiving the confirmation does not properly object to it, it will be effective if:
       1. The writing is in confirmation of the contract
   and 2. It is also sufficient to hold the sender responsible
   and 3. It is sent within a *reasonable time* after the contract was created
   and 4. The party receiving the confirmation has reason to know its contents

(3) A contract which does not satisfy the writing requirements in
   §2-201(1) (but is valid in all other respects), will still be enforceable if:

    (a) <u>The Goods Are To Be Specially Manufactured</u>:
        1. The goods are to be specially manufactured for the
           Buyer
   and 2. The goods are not suitable for sale to others in
           the *Ordinary Course of the <u>Seller's</u> Business*
   and 3. The Seller has either substantially begun their
           manufacture or made commitments to obtain
           them:
              a. *Before* any notice of repudiation was received
          and b. Under circumstances which reasonably indicate
              that the goods are for the Buyer

  or (b) <u>An Admission Is Made</u>
        1. If the party against whom enforcement is sought
           admits (in his pleadings, testimony, or otherwise in court) that
           a contract for sale was made, the writing requirement
           will be satisfied.
        2. The contract is only enforceable (under this provision) up to
           the quantity of goods admitted.

  or (c) <u>The Goods Under The Contract Have Been Accepted</u>
        1. Payment has been made and accepted
     or 2. Goods have been received and accepted (as per §2-606)

§2-202: Final Written Expressionl; Parol or Extrinsic Evidence:

1. <u>Final Written Expression</u>: The following are considered Final
   Written Expressions of the parties:
    a. Agreed upon terms reflected in a <u>Confirmatory Memorandum</u>
  or b. Terms set forth in a <u>Writing</u> which were intended to be a
    Final Expression of their agreement (on those terms)

2. **Writing Cannot Be Contradicted:** The terms of a Final Written
   Expression CANNOT be contradicted by evidence of any:
    a. Prior Agreement
  or b. Contemporaneous Oral Agreement

3. **Writing May Be Explained:** A Final Written Expression may,
   however, be *explained* or *supplemented* by:
    (a) The Course of Dealing or Usage of Trade (§1-205) or by the
        Course of Performance (§2-208)
  and (b) Evidence of consistent additional terms, *unless* the court finds
        the writing was intended by both parties as a <u>complete</u> and
        <u>exclusive</u> statement of all the terms of the agreement

§2-203: Seals Inoperative:

The common law rules relating to <u>Sealed Instruments</u> do not apply to:
   1. A writing evidencing a contract for sale
or 2. An offer to buy or sell goods

§2-204: Formation of a Contract:

(1) **Creation of Contract:** A Contract for the Sale of Goods may be created by:
   a. The conduct of *both* parties (which recognizes the existence of such a contract)
or b. Any other manner sufficient to show agreement (written, oral or otherwise (subject to Statute of Frauds (§2-201))).

(2) **Time of Creation Not Certain:** An agreement sufficient to constitute a contract for sale may be found even though the exact moment the contract was created is undetermined.

(3) **Open Terms:**
   A contract will not fail for *indefiniteness* if one or more terms are left open, if:
   a. The parties have intended to make a contract
and b. There is a reasonably certain basis for giving an appropriate remedy

§2-205: Firm Offers:

1. **"Firm Offer"** - an offer which:
   a. Is made by a <u>Merchant</u>
and b. Is evidenced by a <u>Signed</u> Writing
and c. By its terms, gives assurance that the offer will be held open

2. A Firm Offer is <u>not revocable</u> for lack of consideration.

3. **Effectiveness of Firm Offer:**
   a. The period of time in which a Firm Offer is irrevocable is either:
      1. For the time stated in the Firm Offer
      2. For a *reasonable time*, if no time is stated
   b. The period of irrevocability may not exceed <u>3 Months</u>

4. <u>Firm Offer on Offeree's Form</u>: Any terms of assurance in a Firm Offer which is made on a form supplied by the <u>offeree</u> must be separately signed by the offeror.

§2-206: Offer and Acceptance in Formation of Contract:

(1) Unless otherwise <u>unambiguously</u> indicated by the language or circumstances:

- (a) **An Offer to Make a Contract:**
    1. An offer to make a contract is considered to be *inviting* acceptance.
    2. <u>Mode of Acceptance</u>: Acceptance to such an offer may be made *in any manner and by any medium* reasonable under the circumstances.

- (b) **An Order or Other Offer to Buy Goods for Prompt Shipment:**
    1. An order or offer to buy goods for prompt or current shipment is considered to be *inviting* acceptance.
    2. <u>Mode of Acceptance</u>: Acceptance to such an offer may be made either by:
        - a. A prompt promise to ship
        - or b. Prompt or Current Shipment (of conforming or non-conforming goods)
    3. <u>Shipment of Non-Conforming Goods</u>: The shipment of non-conforming goods does not constitute acceptance of the Buyer's offer if the Seller *seasonably* notifies the Buyer that the shipment was offered only as an "accommodation" to the Buyer.

(2) <u>Reasonable Time of Acceptance</u>: An offeror who is not notified of acceptance within a *reasonable time* may treat the offer as having lapsed before acceptance even if the beginning of the offeree's performance was a reasonable mode of acceptance.

§2-207: Additional Terms in Acceptance or Confirmation (Counteroffer):

(1) Acceptance With Different Terms:
   a) The following operates as an acceptance even if it states <u>additional</u> or <u>different</u> terms from the offer if it is made as a:
      1. Definite and seasonable expression of acceptance which is sent within a reasonable time
   or 2. Written Confirmation which is sent within a reasonable time
   b) If Acceptance is expressly made conditional to the offeror's acceptance of the offeree's additional or different terms, then it is considered a counteroffer (and not an acceptance).

(2) Additional Terms:
   i) <u>Between Non-Merchants</u>: Additional terms shall be construed as *proposed additions* to the contract.
   ii) <u>Between Merchants</u>: Additional terms shall become part of the contract *unless:*
      (a) The Offer expressly limits acceptance to the terms of the offer
   or (b) The additional terms materially alter the offer
   or (c) Notification of objection to the additional terms has already been given (or is given within a reasonable time after notice of the additional terms is received)

(3) Contracts Implied By Conduct:
   a. <u>Conduct</u> by both parties which recognizes the existence of a contract is sufficient to establish a contract for sale (even though the writings of the parties do not otherwise establish one).
   b. <u>Terms of Contracts Implied from Conduct</u>: The terms of such a contract (implied by the parties' conduct) shall be:
      1. Those terms on which the writings of the parties agree
   and 2. Any supplementary terms incorporated under any other provision of this Act

§2-208: **Construction of Contract:**

(1) **When Course of Performance Relevant:** The Course of Performance (accepted or acquiesced in without objection) will be relevant in determining the meaning of the agreement between the parties when:
    a. The contract for sale involves repeated occasions for performance by either party
    and b. The non-performing party knows the nature of the other party's performance
    and c. The non-performing party had an opportunity to object to the nature of that performance

(2) **Interpretation of Contract:**
    a) When interpreting the terms of a contract, the following factors shall be construed to be consistent with each other *whenever reasonable:*
        1. The Express Terms of the agreement
        and 2. Any Course of Performance
        and 3. Any Course of Dealing
        and 4. Any Usage of Trade

    b) When it is unreasonable to read the above factors consistently, then:
        1. The Express Terms - shall be used to construe the "Course of Performance"
        and 2. The Course of Performance - shall be used to construe both
            a) The "Course of Dealing"
            and b) The "Usage of Trade" (as per §1-205)

(3) The Course of Performance shall be relevant to show the existence of a waiver or modification of any term inconsistent with such Course of Performance (subject to §2-209).

§2-209: Modification, Rescission and Waiver:

(1) **No Consideration Required for Modification**: A modification of a sales contract does not require consideration to be binding.

(2) **Writing Requirement:**
    a. An agreement cannot be rescinded or modified without a signed writing if the original agreement:
        1) Is in <u>writing</u>
      and 2) Is <u>signed</u>
      and 3) Requires that modifications or rescissions be made with a signed writing
    b. Such a term (requiring a modification or rescission to be in writing) must be <u>separately signed</u> if:
        1) One party is not a Merchant
      and 2) The term is on a form supplied by the party who is a Merchant

(3) **Statute of Frauds Requirement:**
    The requirements of the Statute of Frauds (§2-201) must be satisfied if the modified contract falls under §2-201(1) (i.e. it is or is modified to be a Contract for the Sale of Goods for ≥ $500).

(4) **Creation of Waiver**: Although an attempt to modify or rescind a contract fails (because it is not a signed writing (§2-209(2) or (3) above)), it can operate as a <u>Waiver.</u>

(5) **Retraction of Waiver:**
    a. A party who has made a waiver affecting an *executory portion* of a contract may retract the waiver by giving reasonable notice to the other party that <u>Strict Performance will be required</u> of any term waived.
    b. In order for the retraction of the waiver to be effective, the other party <u>must receive the notification</u> requiring strict performance.
    c. A party will not be able to retract such a waiver if it would be unjust in view of a <u>*material change of position*</u> in reliance on the waiver.

§2-210: Delegation of Performance; Assignment of Rights:

(1) Delegation:
    a. A party may perform his duty through a <u>delegate</u> unless:
        1. The other party has a substantial interest in having
           his original promisor perform or control the acts
           required by the contract
      or 2. The parties otherwise agree
    b. Delegation of performance <u>does not</u> relieve the delegating party
       of any <u>duty to perform</u> or <u>liability for breach.</u>

(2) Assignment:
    a. All the rights of a Seller or Buyer may be assigned *unless*:
        1. The parties otherwise agree
      or 2. The assignment would *either*:
           a) *Materially Change the Duty* of the other party
              (ex: Seller, is a N.Y. company. It promises to ship goods to
              Buyer in NJ; Buyer cannot assign his rights to Assignee
              without Seller's consent if Assignee is a Hong Kong company,
              since it would cost Seller substantially more to ship its goods
              to Hong Kong and to set up and enforce a payment system)
          or b) *Materially Increase the Burden or Risk* imposed
             on the other party
          or c) *Materially Impair the Chance of Return Performance*
             to the other party (ex: Buyer assigns his obligation to
             Assignee, who has a poor credit history)
    b. <u>Assignment Despite Agreement</u>: The following rights can be
       assigned even if the parties agreed otherwise:
        1. A right to damages for breach of the *whole contract*
        2. A right arising out of the Assignor's due performance of
           his *entire* obligation

(3) Prohibiting Assignment: A clause prohibiting the assignment of
    "the contract" is to be construed as barring *only* the delegation to
    the consignee of the assignor's <u>performance</u> (unless the circumstances
indicate otherwise).

(4) Effect of Assignment:
    a. The following terms denote an "Assignment of Rights" (unless the language or circumstances indicate otherwise):
        1. An assignment of "the contract"
        2. An assignment of "all my rights under the contract"
        3. An assignment in similar general terms
    b. Terms of Assignment:
        1. Such an assignment is a delegation of performance of the assignor's duties to the assignee.
        2. Acceptance by the assignee constitutes a promise by the assignee to perform those duties.
        3. This promise is enforceable by either the assignor or the other party (to the original contract).

(5) Demand for Assurance:
    Upon delegation to the assignee, the non-assigning original party may, without prejudice:
        a. Treat any assignment which delegates performance as creating a reasonable grounds for insecurity (as per §2-609)
    and b. Demand assurances from the assignee (as per §2-609) that any delegated duties will be performed

213

PART 3

General Obligation and Construction of Contract

§2-301: General Obligations of Parties:

1. <u>Obligation of the Seller</u>: **Transfer** and **Deliver** the goods in accordance with the contract.

2. <u>Obligation of the Buyer</u>: **Accept** and **Pay** for the goods in accordance with the contract.

§2-302: Unconscionable Contract or Clause:

(1) **Treatment of Unconscionable Contracts or Clauses**: If the court finds (as a matter of law) a contract or any clause of the contract to have been *unconscionable* <u>at the time it was made</u>, the court may:
   a. Refuse to enforce the entire contract
   or b. Refuse to enforce only the unconscionable portions of the contract
   or c. Limit the application of any unconscionable clause to avoid any unconscionable result

(2) **Proving Unconscionability**:
   a. When a contract clause appears unconscionable, or when a party claims it is unconscionable, the parties shall have a reasonable opportunity to present evidence (to aid the court in making its determination).
   b. Evidence presented to the court may include evidence as to:
      1. The <u>commercial setting</u> of the contract
      and 2. The <u>purpose</u> of the contract
      and 3. The <u>intended effect</u> of the contract

§2-303: Allocation or Division of Risk:
Where this Article allocates a risk or burden between the parties and uses the term "unless otherwise agreed", an agreement between the parties may:
   1. Shift the allocation of risk and burden
   or 2. Divide the risk or burden among themselves

§2-304: Price Payable:

(1) **Payment with Money or Goods**:
    a. The price of a contract may be payable in Money or otherwise.
    b. If the contract is payable in goods (in whole or in part), each party is considered a Seller of the goods which he is to transfer.

(2) **Payment with Realty**:
    a. All contracts may be paid with interests in realty.

    b. <u>Applicable Laws Governing Contracts for the Sale of Goods Which Are Paid with Realty</u>:
        1. Article 2 governs:
            a) The Seller's obligations with reference to the goods
        and b) Laws relating to the Transfer of the goods
        2. Article 2 will not govern:
            a) Laws relating to the Transfer of Interest in the Realty
        and b) The transferor's obligations in connection with the Transfer of the Realty

§2-305: Open Price Term

(1) **Price Unsettled:**
    i) If the parties intend, they can conclude a contract for sale even if they have not yet settled on a price (subject to §2-305(4) below).
    ii) The price of the contract shall be a *reasonable price* <u>at the time for delivery</u> if:
        (a) Nothing is said about the price
    or (b) The price is left to be agreed upon by the parties, and they fail to agree
    or (c) The price is to be fixed in terms of some agreed market which has not been set or recorded (or other standard as set or recorded by a third person or agency (ex: setting the price of cotton at $5.00 over the COMEX price on the date of delivery)) (see §2-305(3) below for the effects of not fixing price).

(2) A **"price to be fixed by the Seller/Buyer"** - means a price fixed by him in <u>Good Faith.</u>

(3) Fault of a Party:

If the price of a contract is left to be fixed (other than by agreement of the parties), and that price fails to be fixed due to the fault of one party, the other party may:

    1. Treat the contract as canceled

or 2. Fix a reasonable price on his own

(4) Failure of Contract:

a) There will be <u>no contract</u> if the parties intend not to be bound unless the price is fixed or agreed upon, and it is not.

b) <u>Consequences If Contract Fails Due to Absence of Price</u>:

    1. <u>Buyer's Obligations</u> - the Buyer must:

        a. Return any goods already received

    or b. If the Buyer is unable to return the goods she must Pay the Seller the *reasonable value* of the goods <u>at the time of delivery</u>

    2. <u>Seller's Obligations</u> - The Seller must return any portion of the price paid on account.

§2-306: Output, Requirements, and Exclusive Dealings Contracts

(1) Output & Requirement Contracts:

a. <u>Terms Measuring Quantity</u>:

    1. **"Output Term"** - a term which measures the qua~~ contract by the Seller's output (ie "Total Produc~

    2. **"Requirement Term"** - a term which me~ of the contract by the requirements ~ Needs" contrcat).

b. <u>Good Faith Requirement</u>:

    1. "Output" and "Require~ and requirements ~

    2. <u>Estimates</u> - if~ include~ *dispropc*

        a) Ten~

    or b) Dem~

    3. In absence of~ more than an~ or requirement

        a) Tendered b~

    or b) Demanded b~

(2) **Exclusive Dealings** - *"Best Efforts Test"*:
   A lawful agreement by either a Seller or Buyer for Exclusive
   Dealing (in the kind of goods concerned) creates the following
   obligations (unless otherwise agreed):
   - a) Exclusive Right to Sell: Obligation by the Seller to use its *Best Efforts* to supply the goods
   - b) Exclusive Right to Buy: Obligation by Buyer to use its *Best Efforts* to promote the sale of such goods

§2-307: Delivery in Single Lot or Several Lots:

1) Single Delivery: Unless otherwise agreed:
   - a. All goods called for by a contract for sale must be Tendered in a single delivery.
   - and b. Payment is due only upon such tender.

2) If the circumstances allow either party to make or demand delivery in separate lots, then the price can be *apportioned* and *demanded* for each delivery.

§2-308: Absence of Specified Place for Delivery:

When Seller is not required or authorized to deliver goods through a Carrier (as in §2-504), the place for delivery shall be (unless otherwise agreed):
   - (a) The Seller's place of business (or if he has none, his residence)
   - (b) Contracts for Identified Goods: at the place where the identified goods were located at the time of the contract if:
      - 1. The contract is for the sale of identified goods
      - and 2. At the time the contract was created, the parties knew that the identified goods were in some place other than Seller's place

   Contracts Calling for Delivery of Documents:
   Documents of title may be delivered through customary banking channels.

§2-309: Absence of Specified Time Provisions:

(1) **Implied Reasonable Time:** The time for <u>shipment</u> or <u>delivery</u> (or any other action under a contract) shall be a *"reasonable time"* (unless otherwise agreed upon or provided for in this Article).

(2) **Termination of Contracts With Indefinite Duration:**
    a. A contract will be valid for a *reasonable time* if:
        1. It provides for successive performances
    and 2. It is indefinite in duration
    b. Such a contract, however, may be terminated *at any time* by either party (unless otherwise agreed).

(3) **Termination of a Contract by One Party:**
    a. A party terminating the contract must offer the other party a reasonable notification of termination (which must actually be *received* by the other party to be effective) if:
        1. Only one party terminates the contract
    and 2. The termination is not the result of the occurrence of an agreed upon event.
    b. An agreement waiving such notification of termination is invalid if its use would be unconscionable.

§2-310: Open Time for Payment or Running of Credit; Authority to Ship Under Reservation:

(a) **When Payment is Due**: Unless otherwise agreed, payment is due at the <u>time and place at which the Buyer is to receive the goods</u> (not at the point of delivery, except as in §2-310(c))

(b) **Shipment by Reservation:**
    1. If the Seller is authorized to send the goods, he may ship them under *Reservation* (unless otherwise agreed)
    2. <u>If the Goods are Shipped under Reservation:</u>
        a. The Seller may tender the Documents of title
        b. The Buyer may inspect the goods after their arrival and before payment is due (unless such inspection is inconsistent with the terms of the contract (see §2-513))

(c) **Delivering Documents of Title:**
Unless otherwise agreed, if delivery is authorized and made by delivering Documents of Title, then payment is due at the <u>time and place where the Buyer is to receive the Documents</u> (regardless of where the goods are to be received).

(d) **Shipment on Credit:**
1) If the Seller is authorized or required to ship the goods on credit, the credit-period *normally* begins from the <u>time of shipment</u> (unless otherwise agreed).
2) <u>Extended Credit Period</u>: The starting date of the credit period may be delayed by:
a) Post-dating the invoice
or b) Delaying the dispatch of the invoice

§2-311: Options and Cooperation Respecting Performance:

(1) **Details of Performance Absent:**
a) An agreement for Sale (which is otherwise sufficiently definite to be considered a contract under §2-204(3)) will not be invalidated if it leaves particular details of performance to be specified by one of the parties.
b) Any such details must be made in *Good Faith,* and within the limits set by *"commercial reasonableness".*

(2) **Parties Specifying Details**:
Unless otherwise agreed, the following details may be decided by certain parties:
a. <u>The Buyer</u> may decide how to assort the goods (ex: Buyer may request that each 1 dozen package of colored ice cream cones contain 4 red cones, 2 blue cones, 3 green cones and 3 yellow cones).
b. <u>The Seller</u> may decide the details and arrangements of shipping (except as provided for in §2-319(1)(c) and §2-319(3)).

(3) **Remedies for Neglect:**
   i) A party may be eligible for §2-311 Remedies if:
      a) <u>The Other Party Fails To Make Specifications</u> (as per
        §2-311(2)) - Remedies will be available if:
          1. The other party's specifications would *materially
            affect* performance
      and 2. The other party neglects to seasonably make such
          specifications (ex: The Buyer was to tell the Seller   whether to
          ship goods by UPS or Federal Express by July 1st,   but neglected
          to do so).

     or b) <u>The Other Party Fails to Cooperate</u> - Remedies will be
        available if:
          1. The other party's cooperation is necessary to the
            agreed performance
      and 2. The other party does not seasonably cooperate

  ii) <u>Available Remedies</u>: In such situations, the non-neglectful party:
      (a) Is excused for any resulting default in his own
         performance (in addition to all other remedies)
    and (b) May also *either:*
          1. Proceed to perform in any reasonable manner
       or 2. Treat the failure to cooperate or specify as a breach
          (by failure to deliver or accept goods upon his
          performance) <u>after</u> the time for a material part of his
          own performance

WARRANTIES:
(§2-312-§2-318)

§2-312: Warranty of Title:

(1) In a contract of sale, the Seller makes the following Warranties (subject to §2-312(2)):

    (a) **Good Title:**
        1. The title conveyed shall be good
     and 2. The transfer is rightful

    (b) **Goods Free of Liens:** The goods are delivered free from Security Interests or other liens (or encumbrances) which the Buyer had no knowledge of at the time the contract was created.

(2) **Modificaton or Exclusion:** A Warranty of Title may only be modified or excluded by:
    a) Specific language in the contract
    b) Circumstances which give the Buyer reason to know that
        1. The Seller does not claim title in himself
    or 2. The Seller is only purporting to sell the rights which he (or a third person) may have in the goods (ex: Seller sells goods "as is").

(3) **Goods Do Not Infringe Third Party Rights** - *Merchant Only*: The Seller warrants that the goods do not infringe a third party's rights and will be delivered free from the rightful claim of any third person (ex: free from a patent or copyright infringement) if:
    a) The Seller is a *Merchant* regularly dealing in goods of the kind sold
    and b) The infringement does not arise out of the Seller's compliance with the Buyer's instructions (ex: Buyer tells Seller to apply a label which infringes an already existing copyrighted label to its goods).

§2-313 - Express Warranty by Affirmation:

(1) **Express Warranties** by the Seller are created as follows:

    (a) Warranty That Goods Shall Conform to an Affirmation or Promise - Created by *any affirmation of fact or promise:*
        1. Which is made by the Seller to the Buyer
    and 2. Relating to the goods
    and 3. Which becomes a significant part of the basis of the bargain

    (b) Warranty That The Goods Shall Conform to their Description - Created when any description of the goods becomes a significant factor in the basis of the bargain.

(c) <u>Warranty That Goods Shall Conform to Sample or Model</u> - Created when a sample or model becomes a significant factor in the basis of the bargain.

(2) **Substance Over Form**
    a. It is not necessary for Seller to use formal words such as *"warrant"* or *"guarantee"* to create an Express Warranty
    b. The following do not alone create express warranties:
        1. An Affirmation merely of the <u>value</u> of the goods
    or 2. A Statement purporting to be merely the Seller's <u>opinion</u>
    or 3. <u>Compliments or Commendations</u> of the goods (ex:"Sales Puff")

§2-314: Implied Warranty of Merchantability:

(1) **Implied Warranty:**
    a. A Warranty that the goods shall be merchantable is implied in a contract for their sale if:
        1. The Seller is a *Merchant*, selling goods of the kind sold
    and 2. There is no clause excluding or modifying such a warranty (as per §2-316)
    b. The serving of food or drink *for value* (regardless of where it is consumed) is considered a sale for purposes of this section.

(2) **Warranty of Merchantability:** Under the Warranty of Merchantability, the Seller warrants:
    (a) <u>Goods Fit Trade Description</u> - Goods must pass without objection in the trade under the contract description (ex: if in order to be considered Orange Juice, a drink must contain 75% juice from oranges, the contents of an "Orange Juice" container must be 75% juice from oranges).
    and (b) <u>Quality</u> - *Fungible Goods* must be of fair, average quality (within the description of such goods).
    and (c) <u>Fitness</u> - Must be fit for the *ordinary purposes* for which such goods are used (for particular purposes, see §2-315).
    and (d) <u>Uniformity</u> - They must have similar quality and characteristics (within variations permitted by the agreement) within each unit, and among all units involved in the contract.
    and (e) <u>Packaging</u> - The goods must be adequately contained, packaged, and labeled (as the agreement or nature of the product may require (ex: pills to be sold over the counter should be packaged in tamper-proof containers)).
    and (f) <u>Goods Fit Package Description</u> - Must conform to the Promise or Affirmations made on the container or label.

(3) Other implied warranties may arise from the Course of Dealing or Usage of Trade (unless excluded or modified as per §2-316)

§2-315: Implied Warranty of Fitness for a Particular Purpose:

The Seller impliedly promises the Buyer that the goods shall be fit for a particular purpose if:

    a) At the time the contract was created, the Seller had *reason to know* any particular purpose for which Buyer wanted to use the goods

and b) The Buyer relied on the Seller's skill or judgment to select or furnish suitable goods

and c) Such a warranty has not been excluded or modified (as per §2-316)

§2-316: Exclusion or Modification of Warranties:

(1) **Consistent Construction of Words and Conduct:**
    a. The following shall be construed *consistently* whenever possible:
        1. Words or Conduct relating to the <u>creation</u> of an Express Warranty
        2. Words or Conduct tending to <u>negate</u> or <u>limit</u> such warranties
    b. Negation or Limitation of such warranties are invalid to the extent that a consistent construction is unreasonable (subject to §2-202 (Parole Evidence)).

(2) **Requirements of Excluding or Modifying Implied Warranties** (subject to §2-316(3))**:**
    a. <u>To Exclude or Modify an Implied Warranty of Merchantability</u>:
        1. The language must <u>mention merchantability</u>
     and 2. The language must be <u>conspicuous</u> if in writing
    b. <u>To Exclude or Modify an Implied Warranty of Fitness</u>:
        1. The exclusion must be <u>in writing</u>
     and 2. The language must be <u>conspicuous</u>
    c. <u>To Exclude ALL Implied Warranties of Fitness</u>: Language must be very clear (ex: "There are no warranties which extend beyond the description on the face hereof").

(3) **Rules Regarding Excluding Implied Warranties:**
Notwithstanding §2-316(2) (above):
(a) All implied warranties may be excluded by the use of language which, in common understanding:
1) Calls the Buyer's attention to the exclusion of warranties
and 2) Makes it clear that there are no implied warranties
(unless the circumstances indicate otherwise (ex: sold "as is" or "with all faults"))
(b) **Buyer's Inspection:** Implied Warranties will be limited to defects which the Buyer should have reasonably discovered (under the circumstances) if:
1. The Buyer inspects (to his satisfaction) the goods or a sample model before entering into the contract
or 2. The Buyer refuses to examine the goods
(c) An Implied Warranty can also be Excluded or Modified by:
1) The Course of Dealing (as per §1-205)
or 2) The Course of Performance (as per §2-208)
or 3) The Usage of Trade (as per §1-205)

(4) **Limitations for Breach of Warranty:** Remedies for breach of warranty may be limited in accordance with the provisions dealing with:
a) Liquidation or Limitation of Damages (§2-718)
b) Contractual Modification of Remedy (§2-719)

§2-317: Cumulation and Conflict of Implied or Express Warranties:

1. Warranties (whether express or implied) shall be construed to be *cumulative* and *consistent with each other*, whenever reasonable.

2. If such a construction is unreasonable, the *intention of the parties* shall determine which warranty is dominant.

3. Rules in Determining the Intention of the Parties (with regard to conflicting warranties):
(a) Exact or Technical Specifications of the Goods displace an inconsistent sample, model, or general language of the goods' description.
(b) A Sample From An Existing Bulk displaces inconsistent general language or description of the goods.
(c) An Express Warranty displaces inconsistent, implied warranties (other than the implied warranty of fitness for a particular purpose (§2-315)).

§2-318: Third Party Beneficiaries of Warranties:

This section shall be omitted if The United States Congress adopts it (as of 1995 it has not).

ALTERNATIVE A
1. A Seller's express or implied warranties extend to:
   a) Any natural person in the Buyer's family or household
   and b) Any guest in the Buyer's home
2. The Seller will be held responsible for breach of warranty to the third party if:
   a) It is reasonable to expect such a person to use, consume, or be affected by the goods (ex: A Seller should expect a third party to sit on a Buyer's dining room chair, but the Seller probably would not expect a third party to use the Buyer's dishwasher).
   and b) That person is injured by the breach of the warranty.
3. The Seller may not exclude or limit the warranties to third persons.

ALTERNATIVE B
1. A Seller's express and implied warranties extend to any natural person in the Buyer's family or household if:
   a) It is reasonable to expect such a person to use, consume, or be affected by the goods
   and b) That person is injured by the breach of the warranty.
2. The Seller may not exclude or limit its liability to third persons.

ALTERNATIVE C
1. A Seller's express and implied warranties extends to any person if:
   a) It is reasonable to expect such a person to use, consume, or be affected by the goods
   and b) That person is injured by the breach of the warranty.
2. The Seller may not exclude or limit its liability to third persons if the warranty is meant to extend to that person.

DELIVERY TERMS:
§2-319: F.O.B. and F.A.S.:

Preliminary Note: *The terms F.O.B. and F.A.S. will be construed as "Delivery Terms" even though they have been used as "Price Terms"* (unless the parties agree otherwise)

(1) **"F.O.B."** (Free on Board) - unless otherwise agreed, the term F.O.B. implies the following:
    (a) F.O.B.(Place of Shipment):
        The Seller has the following responsibilities:
            1. Deliver goods to their specified place of shipment
                (i.e. to the Carrier's possession) (as per §2-504)
        and 2. Pay for the shipment
        and 3. Bear the risk of putting the goods into the Carrier's possession
    (b) F.O.B.(Place of Destination):
        The Seller has the following responsibilities:
            1. Pay for the transport of the goods to the specified place of destination
        and 2. Bear the risk of transporting the goods to their specified destination
        and 3. Tender delivery of the goods to the Buyer (as per §2-503)
    (c) F.O.B.(Vessel, car, other vehicle) (either under (a) or (b)):
            1. Seller's Responsibility: The Seller has the following *additional* responsibilities:
                a. Pay for loading the goods on board
                b. Bear the risk of loading the goods on board
                c. Comply with §2-323 (regarding the form of the Bill of Lading)
            2. Buyer's Responsibility: The Buyer must name the particular vessel which the goods will be loaded upon.

(2) **"F.A.S. (vessel)"** (Free alongside) - unless otherwise agreed, the term F.A.S. implies that the Seller has the following responsibilities:
    (a) Pay for and bear the risk of *either:*
        1) Delivering the goods alongside the vessel (in the manner usual in that port)
      or 2) Delivering the goods on a dock designated and provided by Buyer
  and (b) Obtain and Tender a receipt for the goods, in which the Carrier promises to issue a BOL

(3) Buyer's Obligation to Instruct Seller

a) The Buyer must seasonably give any needed instructions for delivery (unless otherwise agreed in an FAS, FOB(shipment), or FOB(vessel) contract), including:

1. The loading berth of the vessel (if the terms are FOB or FAS)
2. The name of the ship and its sailing date (in appropriate cases)

b) <u>Buyer's Failure to Instruct</u> - If the Buyer fails to seasonably give the Seller the appropriate shipping instructions:

1. The Seller may treat Buyer's failure to give instructions as a *Failure to Cooperate* (as per §2-311).

and 2. The Seller may, at his option, move the goods in any reasonable manner in preparation for delivery or shipment.

(4) Tender of Documents for FAS and FOB(vessel) Contracts:

a. The Buyer must make payment against tender of the required documents under an FOB(vessel) or FAS shipping contract (unless otherwise agreed).

b. The Buyer may not demand delivery of the goods, nor may the Seller tender goods, in substitution of the documents.

---

§2-320: C.I.F. & C.& F.:

(1) Definitions:
  a) "**C.I.F.**" means that the Price includes:
    1. The cost of the Goods
  and 2. The Insurance
  and 3. The Freight (to the named destination)
  b) "**C. & F.**" means that the Price includes:
    1. The cost of the Goods
  and 2. The Freight (to the named destination)

(2) The Term "C.I.F. (destination)" (or its equivalent) implies that the Seller shall have the following responsibilities (unless otherwise agreed):
  (a) 1. Pay for putting the goods into possession of the Carrier (at the port for shipment)
  and 2. Bear the risk of putting the goods into possession of the Carrier (at the port for shipment)
  and 3. Obtain a Negotiable Bill of Lading covering the goods
  and (b) 1. Load the goods
  and 2. Obtain a receipt from the Carrier (may be part of the BOL) showing that freight has been paid/provided for
  and (c) Obtain a policy or certify insurance (including War Risk Insurance)
      1. The insurance must be of the type typical at the port of shipment
      2. The insurance contract must cover the goods in the BOL
      3. The beneficiary must be the Buyer or "whom it may concern"
      4. War risk premiums may be added to CIF price
  and (d) Prepare an invoice of the goods and procure any other documents required to effect shipment (or to comply with the contract)
  and (e) Forward and Tender all documents
      1. With *Commercial Promptness*
      2. In Due Form
      3. With any necessary indorsements to perfect the Buyer's rights

(3) Unless otherwise agreed, C&F has the same effect and obligations as a CIF contract, *except* for the insurance obligations.

(4) The Buyer must make payment against tender of the required Documents (unless otherwise agreed) under CIF and C&F contracts.

§2-321: C.I.F. or C&F: "Net Landed Weight"; "Payments on Arrival"; Warranty of Condition on Arrival:

This Section applies to contracts containing CIF or C&F terms.

(1) Price Based on Landed Weight

    a. The Seller must reasonably estimate the price if it is to be based on or adjusted according to its weight or quality (unless otherwise agreed).

    b. Sales based on quality or weight upon delivery are often denoted with such terms as:

        1. "Net Landed Weight"

        2. "Delivered Weights"

        3. "Out turn" quality or quantity of the goods

    c. <u>Payment Due</u>: The amount due on tender of the documents is the amount initially estimated by the Seller.

    d. After final price adjustments are made, a settlement for the balance must be made with *commercial promptness*.

(2) Risk of Deterioration

    a) The Seller shall have the <u>Risk of Ordinary Deterioration and Shrinkage</u> (and the like) while the goods are in transit if:

        1) An agreement (as described in (1) above) has been created (basing the price on the weight or quality of the goods upon delivery)

    or 2) A warranty of quality or condition of the goods on arrival has been created

    b) Such agreements have no effect on:

        1) The place or time of identification of goods to the contract (for sale or delivery)

    or 2) The passing of risk of loss

(3) Time For Payment

    a. <u>Inspection Before Payment</u>: The Seller must allow a preliminary inspection ("as feasible") of the goods *before* the Buyer makes payment if the contract allows payment to be made on or after the arrival of the goods (unless otherwise agreed).

    b. <u>Lost Goods</u>: Delivery of the documents and payment are due *when the goods would have arrived* if the goods are lost.

§2-322: Delivery "Ex-Ship":

(1) **"EX-SHIP"** (or equivalent language) means (unless otherwise agreed):
    a. That goods need not be delivered on a particular ship
 and b. Delivery will be made from a ship which has reached a place at the named port of destination (where goods of that kind are usually discharged).

(2) **Obligations under "Ex-Ship" Terms:**
    (a) <u>The Seller must</u>:
        1. Discharge all liens which arise out of carriage
     and 2. Furnish the Buyer with a direction that obligates the Carrier to deliver the goods
    (b) <u>Risk of Loss</u>: The Risk of Loss passes to the Buyer when:
        1. The goods leave the ship's tackle
      or 2. The goods are otherwise properly unloaded from the ship

§2-323: Bill of Lading:

(1) **Requirements of the Bill of Lading**
    a. The Seller must obtain a <u>Negotiable Bill of Lading</u> (unless otherwise agreed) if:
        1. The contract involves an *overseas* shipment
    and 2. The terms are FOB(vessel), CIF or C&F
    b. <u>Contents of the Negotiable Bill of Lading</u>:
        1. FOB - must state that goods have been loaded on board.
        2. CIF or C&F - must state that the goods have been received for shipment.

(2) **Multi-Part Documents**
    i) When a Bill of Lading has been issued in a <u>set of parts</u>, only one part need be tendered *unless:*
        a) The agreement expressly requires a full set to be tendered
    or b) *Both*
        1. The Buyer demands a full set to be tendered
    and 2. The documents are <u>not</u> to be sent from abroad

    ii) <u>The following rules apply even if the contract expressly requires a full set of documents to be tendered</u>:
        (a) Due tender of a single part of the BOL is acceptable to cure improper delivery (as per §2-508(1))
    and (b) <u>Documents sent from abroad</u>: If the documents are sent from abroad, the person tendering an incomplete set of documents may require payment upon furnishing an <u>indemnity</u> (which the Buyer deems to have been made in good faith), even if the full set is demanded.

(3) **"Overseas"** - an "overseas" contract or shipment is one:
    a) Involving shipment by <u>water</u> or <u>air</u>
  and b) That is subject to commercial, financial, or shipping practices characteristic of *international deep water commerce,* either by Usage of Trade or Agreement.

§2-324: "No Arrival, No Sale" Term:

The following sections govern the use of the term "No Arrival, No Sale" or terms of similar meaning (unless otherwise agreed):

(a) **Obligations of the Seller**:
    1. The Seller must:
        a. Properly ship conforming goods
        b. Tender the goods on arrival (if they arrive by any means)
    2. The Seller's Risk: the Seller assumes no obligation that the goods will arrive, unless he has caused their non-arrival.

(b) **Buyer's Remedy:** The Buyer may proceed as if there had been *Casualty to Identified Goods* (as per §2-613) if:
    1. The Seller is not at fault
and 2. *Either*:
        a. Some of the goods are lost
    or b. The goods have deteriorated (so as to no longer conform to the contract)
    or c. The goods arrive *after* the contract time

§2-325: Letter of Credit:

(1) Failure of a Buyer to seasonably provide an agreed Letter of Credit is a breach of the contract for sale.

(2) **L/C as Payment:**
    a) The delivery of a proper L/C to the Seller *suspends* the Buyer's obligation to pay.
    b) If the L/C is dishonored, the Seller may require payment directly from Buyer upon *seasonable notification*.

(3) Definitions:
    a) **"Letter of Credit"** (or "banker's credit") - means (unless otherwise agreed) an irrevocable credit issued by a financing agency of good repute.
    b) **"Confirmed Credit"** - means that the credit carries the direct obligation of a financing agency which does business in the Seller's financial market.

§2-326: Consignment:

(1) If delivered goods may be *returned* by the Buyer (even though they conform), the transaction is considered *either*:

    (a) A **"Sale on Approval"** - if the goods are delivered primarily for use (ex: trial period)

    or (b) A **"Sale or Return"** - if the goods are delivered primarily for resale

(2) Effect of Classification (subject to (3) below):

    a) "Sale on Approval" goods are not subject to claims of the Buyer's creditors until goods are *accepted*

    b) "Sale or Return" goods are subject to claims of the Buyer' creditors while in the "Buyer's" *possession*

(3) "**Sale or Return**"

    i) Goods are deemed to be "Sale or Return" if:

        a) Goods are delivered to a person for the purpose of resale

      and b) The person (Consignee) maintains a place of business (where he deals in goods of the kind involved)

      and c) The Consignee sells the goods under a name other than the name of the person making the delivery (i.e. the Consignor).

    ii) Form over Substance: These provisions apply even if:

        a) Title is agreed not to pass until payment or resale

      or b) The contract uses words such as "on consignment" or "on memorandum"

    iii) EXCEPTIONS to "Sale or Return" Classification:

        (a) The person making the delivery complies with an applicable law providing for Consignor's interests to be *evidenced by a sign*.

      or (b) The person making delivery establishes that the person conducting business is known by creditors to be *"substantially engaged in selling the goods of others"* (ex: a known auction house).

      or (c) The person making delivery complies with filing provisions of Article 9.

(4) Any "or return" term of a contract for sale is considered:

    a) A separate contract for sale within the Statute of Frauds (§2-204)

    and b) To be contradicting the sale aspect of the contract (within the provisions for Parol or Extrinsic Evidence (as per §2-202))

§2-327: Special Incidents of Sale on Approval and Sale or Return:

(1) <u>Rules Governing Sales Made On *"Sale or Approval"*</u> (unless otherwise agreed):

    (a) **Risk of Loss and Title**: The Risk of Loss and Title pass to the Buyer upon acceptance (even if the goods are identified to the contract)

    (b) **Acceptance of Goods Sold on "Sale or Return"**

        1. Use of the goods consistent with the purpose of the trial offer is not considered acceptance

        2. Failure to seasonably notify the Seller of an intention to return the goods is considered acceptance.

        3. The Buyer will be deemed to have accepted *all* the goods under the contract if:

            a) The Buyer accepts *any* part of the goods under the contract

        and b) The goods conform to the contract

    (c) **Returning Goods:**

        1. After due notification to the Seller, the return of the goods shall be at the <u>Seller's</u> risk and expense.

        2. A *merchant* Buyer must follow any reasonable instructions of the Seller.

(2) <u>Rules Governing Sales Made on *"Sale or Return"*</u> (unless otherwise agreed):

    (a) **Apportionable:** The Buyer may return all or some of the goods if:

        1. They are returned seasonably

        and 2. They are in *substantially* their original condition

        and 3. They are returned in commercial units

    (b) **Return:** The <u>Buyer</u> shall bear the expense and risk of loss when returning the goods.

§2-328: Sale by Auction:

(1) In a Sale by Auction where goods are put up in lots, each lot is subject to a separate sale.

(2) <u>The Auction</u>:
    a. A Sale by Auction is complete when the auctioneer so announces (by fall of the hammer or other customary manner).
    b. <u>Auctioneer's Discretion</u>: If someone places a bid while the auctioneer's hammer is "falling", the auctioneer may:
        1. Reopen the bidding process
      or 2. Close the bidding process (and declare the goods sold to the person who bid <u>before</u> the hammer fell).

(3) **Reserve:**
    a. <u>Auction With Reserve</u> - In an auction with reserve, the auctioneer may withdraw the goods at any time before he announces the completion of the sale.
    b. <u>Auction Without Reserve</u> - Once the auctioneer takes bids, the article or lot may not be withdrawn - unless there are no bids within a *reasonable amount of time*.
    c. Goods sold by Auction are deemed to be put up for auction *"with reserve"*, unless it is explicitly stated that they are to be sold without reserve.
    d. <u>Retracting Bids</u>:
        1. A bidder may retract his bid at any time before the auctioneer announces the completion of the sale.
        2. Retraction of a bid <u>does not</u> automatically revive any previous bid.

(4) <u>Buyer's Option to Avoid Sale</u>:
    a. The Buyer, at his option, may avoid the sale or take the goods at the price of the last good faith bid before completion if:
        1) *Either:*
            i. The auctioneer knowingly receives a bid on the Seller's behalf
          or ii. The Seller makes or procures a bid himself
      and 2) There has not been notice that the Seller may bid on the goods.
    b. This section does not apply to any bid at a forced sale.

PART 4
TITLE, CREDITORS AND GOOD FAITH PURCHASERS

§2-401: Passing of Title; Reservation for Security; Limited Application of This Section:

Preamble to §2-401 - Title Not a Consideration:
The Provisions of Article 2 apply regardless of who has title to the goods (unless the provisions refer to such title) when they deal with the Rights, Obligations, and Remedies of:
- a) A Buyer
- or b) A Seller
- or c) A Purchaser
- or d) Other third parties

(1) **Passing of Title**
- a) The title to goods shall pass from the Seller to the Buyer according to the manner and conditions *explicitly* agreed upon (subject to Article 2 and Article 9 (Secured Transactions)).
- b) Identification Required: Title to goods cannot pass until the goods are identified to the contract for sale (as per §2-501) (note: Future Goods cannot be the subject of a present sale).
- c) Buyer's Rights Upon Identification: The Buyer will acquire a Special Property Right (as limited by this Act) in the goods once they are identified, unless the parties *explicitly* agree otherwise.
- d) Shipment by Reservation: If a Seller ships or delivers goods under "*Reservation*" (i.e. he retains or reserves title in the goods) the Seller will have the same rights as he would if he had a Reservation of a Security Interest.

(2) Passing of Title When Goods Are Physically Delivered
  i) Title passes to the Buyer at the time and place at which Seller physically delivers the goods (i.e. completes performance) to the Buyer (unless otherwise *explicitly* agreed upon), even if:
      1. The Seller has reserved a Security Interest in the goods
  or 2. A Document of Title is to be delivered at a different time and place (i.e. they will not be delivered with the goods)

  ii) **Passing of Title in Bill of Lading Transactions:**
      (a) <u>Shipment Contract</u>: Title passes at the time and place of *Shipment* if:
          1. The contract requires/authorizes the Seller to send the goods to the Buyer
      and 2. The contract does not require the Seller to deliver them at their destination (ex: "FOB" - Seller only has to deliver goods to the carrier)
      (b) <u>Destination Contract</u>: Title passes on *tender* of the goods at the specified destination if the contract requires the Seller to deliver the goods at a particular destination.

(3) Passing of Title When Goods Are To Be Delivered Without Being Moved: This section applies to transactions where delivery is to be made without moving the goods (unless otherwise agreed):
      (a) <u>Delivery of Documents</u>: Title passes upon *delivery of the documents of title* if the Seller is to deliver them.
      (b) <u>No Delivery of Documents</u>: Title passes at the *time and place of contracting* if:
          1. The goods are identified when the contract is made
      and 2. No documents are to be delivered

(4) Passing of Title When Buyer Rejects:
      a) Title to the goods "revests" in the Seller if:
          1. The Buyer rejects or refuses to receive or retain the goods (whether or not it is justified)
      or 2. The Buyer properly revokes his acceptance of the goods
      b) Such revesting occurs by operation of law, and is not considered a "Sale."

§2-402: Rights of Seller's Creditors Against Sold Goods:

(1) Buyer's Priority Over Seller's Creditors:
   a. Rights of the Seller's Unsecured Creditors are subject to the Buyer's rights to recover goods which have already been identified to the contract (as per §2-502 and §2-716).
   b. This subsection is subject to (2) and (3) below.

(2) Seller's Fraudulent Retention of Goods:
   a) The Seller's creditors may treat a sale or identification of goods as VOID if the Seller *fraudulently* retains possession of the goods (according to any rule of law in the state where the goods are located).
   b) A Seller is not considered to be fraudulently retaining possession of goods if:
      1. It is done in <u>Good Faith</u>
   and 2. It is done in the <u>*current course of trade*</u>
   and 3. The Seller is a <u>Merchant</u>
   and 4. The goods are held for no more than a *commercially reasonable time* after the sale or identification of the goods.

(3) Creditor's Rights Outside Article 2 Shall Govern:
   (a) Article 2 cannot reduce the rights of the Seller's creditors granted in Article 9 (Secured Transactions).
   (b) Article 2 cannot reduce the Seller's creditor's rights when:
      1. Goods are delivered or identified to the contract but not in the *current course of trade*.
   and 2. The Delivery or Identification is considered (according to the law of the state where the goods are located) either a:
         a) Fraudulent Transfer
      or b) Voidable Preference
   and 3. The goods are used either:
         a) As security for a pre-existing claim for money, security, or the like.
      or b) To satisfy (i.e. pay off) a pre-existing claim for money, security, or the like.

§2-403: Good Faith Purchaser of Goods:

(1) Derivation Rule:
- a) <u>A Full Purchaser</u> - A purchaser of goods acquires all title which his transferor had or had the power to transfer.
- b) <u>The Purchaser of Limited Interest</u> - acquires only the rights of the interest he actually purchases.
- c) <u>Exception - THE GOOD FAITH PURCHASER</u>:
  - 1) A person with a Voidable Title has the power to transfer a good title if:
    - a. The transferee Purchased it in <u>Good Faith</u>
    - b. The Purchaser has paid <u>Value</u> (as per §1-204(44))(therefore, gifts and judicial liens are no good)
  - 2) This exception will apply when goods have been delivered under a <u>Transaction of Purchase</u> (i.e. not theft), even if:
    - (a) The transferor was deceived as to the purchaser's identity
    - or (b) The delivery was in exchange for a check which is later dishonored
    - or (c) It was agreed that the transaction was to be a *"cash sale"*
    - or (d) The delivery was obtained through <u>Fraud</u> (which would be punishable as larceny under the criminal law)

(2) Merchant as Bailee - A person automatically obtains the right to <u>Transfer all Rights</u> in goods (even if he doesn't own all the rights in those goods), if:
- a. Someone *"<u>entrusts</u>"* the person with possession of the goods
- and b. The person is a <u>Merchant</u>, dealing with goods of the kind entrusted
- and c. The Merchant sells the goods to a Buyer In the Ordinary Course ("BIOC") (as per §1-201(9))

(3) "Entrusting"
- a) "Entrusting" includes:
  - 1) Any delivery
  - and 2) Any acquiescence in retention of possession

- b) These are considered "entrusting" *regardless of*:
  - 1) Any agreement between the parties (for the Merchant not to sell the goods)
  - or 2) Whether or not the "entrusting" or disposition was motivated by Fraud

(4) Rights of Other Purchasers:
- a. Rights of other purchasers are governed by Articles 9 and 7.
- b. Article 6 also governs the rights of other purchasers.

PART 5
PERFORMANCE

§2-501: Insurable Interest in Goods; Manner of Identification of Goods:

(1) **Identification of Goods:**
    a) <u>Creation of Buyer's Interest</u> - Once <u>existing</u> goods are identified to a contract the Buyer obtains an *Insurable Interest* and a *Special Property Interest* in the goods.
    b) <u>Non-Conforming Goods</u> - The Buyer will maintain such interests in identified goods even if the goods are non-conforming; he then has the option of returning or rejecting them.
    c) <u>Manner of Identification</u>:
        1. <u>Agreed Mode of Identification</u>: Identification can be made at any time and in any manner *explicitly agreed to* by the parties.
        2. <u>No Specified Mode of Identification</u>: If the parties did not explicitly agree how the goods are to be identified, identification shall occur as follows:
            (a) *Sale of Already Identified Existing Goods:* Identification shall occur *when the contract is made* if the contract is for the sale of goods which are already existing and identified.
            (b) *Sale of Future Goods:* Identification shall occur when the Seller designates specific goods as goods for the contract (ex: when they are shipped, marked or set aside for the Buyer) if the contract is for the sale of future goods (which are not crops or goods falling under (c)).
            (c) *Sale of Crops and Animals:*
                1. <u>Crops</u> - Identification shall occur when the crops are planted or become "growing crops" (if the contract is for the sale of crops to be harvested within the longer of <u>12 months</u> after or the next harvest season after the contract is made).
                2. <u>Unborn Animals</u> - Identification shall occur when the young are conceived (if the contract is for the sale of unborn young to be born within <u>12 months</u> after the contract is made).

(2) **Seller's Insurable Interest:**
    a) The Seller shall retain an <u>Insurable Interest</u> in the goods
        as long as the Seller has *either:*
           1. Title to the goods
      or 2. A Security Interest in the Goods
    b) <u>Substitute Goods</u>: The Seller may substitute other goods
        for those already identified if:
           1. Identification is by the Seller alone
      and 2. The Seller has not:
              a. Defaulted
          or b. Become insolvent
      and 3. The Seller has not yet notified the Buyer that the
            identification would be final.

(3) Nothing in this section impairs any insurable interest
    recognized under any other statute or rule of law.

§2-502: Buyer's Right to Goods on Seller's Insolvency:

(1) **Seller's Insolvency:**
    a. The Buyer may recover identified goods from the Seller
        if:
           1. The Seller becomes insolvent within <u>10 Days</u> after
              the Seller received the first installment on the price of
              the goods
      and 2. The Buyer:
              a. Has made (and kept) good a tender of any unpaid
                  portion of the price of the goods
          and b. Has paid part or all of the price of the goods
          and c. Has a Special Property Interest (as per §2-501)
    b. This section shall apply even though the goods have not been
        shipped.
    c. This section is subject to §2-502(2).

(2) **Buyer Identifies Goods:** If the Buyer has made the identification
    which creates the special property Interest he acquires the right to
    recover the goods <u>only if</u> the goods conform to the contract.

§2-503: Manner of Seller's Tender of Delivery:

(1) Tender of Delivery:
   i) <u>Requirements for Tender</u>:
      a) The Seller must <u>Put and Hold</u> conforming goods at the Buyer's disposition.
  and b) The Seller must give the Buyer any type of <u>notification</u> *reasonably necessary* to enable the Buyer to take delivery.
 and ii) <u>Manner, Place & Time of Tender</u>:
      Manner, time and place are determined by the agreement and Article 2, and specifically the following:
        (a) Time for Tender of Delivery:
          1. Tender must be at a *reasonable hour.*
          2. <u>If Goods</u> - they must be kept available for a sufficient period *reasonably necessary* for Buyer to take possession.
        (b) Place to Deliver: The Buyer must furnish a facility *reasonably suited* to receive the goods (unless otherwise agreed).

(2) Shipment by Seller: Where shipment is by Seller (as per §2-504), the Seller must tender according to the provisions of §2-504.

(3) Delivery at a Particular Destination: If Seller is required to deliver goods to a particular destination, the Seller must:
     a) Comply with §2-503(1)
  and b) Tender documents as per §2-503(4) and (5) (where appropriate)

(4) **Goods In A Bailee's Possession To Be Delivered Without Being Moved:**
  (a) <u>Tendering a Negotiable Document of Title</u> - Seller must *either:*
    1) Tender a Negotiable Document of Title (covering the goods)
    or 2) Have the Bailee acknowledge the Buyer's right to possession of the goods
  (b) <u>Tendering a Non-Negotiable Document of Title</u> (or written direction to the Bailee to deliver):
    1) A **Non-Negotiable DOT** or a **Written Direction to the Bailee** is sufficient to tender delivery unless the Buyer *seasonably objects*.
    2) Once the Bailee is notified of the Buyer's rights, the Buyer's rights will be fixed against the Bailee <u>and</u> all third persons.
    3) The <u>Seller</u> bears the risk of:
      a) Loss
      and b) Failure of Bailee to honor the non-negotiable document of title
      and c) Failure of Bailee to obey a written direction
    4) The Seller's risk remains until the Buyer has had a reasonable time to present the document or written direction.
    5) Tender is defeated by the Bailee's refusal to honor the instrument/written direction.

(5) **Contracts Requiring Seller to Deliver Documents:**
  (a) <u>Requirements of Documents</u>:
    1. The Seller must tender each required document.
    2. The documents must be:
      a) The actual documents required by the contract
      and b) In their correct form
    3. <u>Exception</u>: This section shall not apply to Bills of Lading in a set (see §2-323).
  (b) <u>Tendering with Banks</u>:
    1. Tender through customary banking channels is sufficient.
    2. If an accompanying draft is dishonored, the goods are deemed to be either:
      a. Rejected
      or b. Not accepted

§2-504: Shipment by Seller:

1. This Section applies only if:
   - a. The Seller is *required* or *authorized* to send the goods to the Buyer
   - and b. The contract doesn't require the Seller to deliver the goods to a particular destination
   - and c. The parties have not otherwise agreed

2. The Seller must (unless otherwise agreed):
   - (a) <u>Arrange for Goods to be Shipped</u>:
     - 1. Put the goods in the Carrier's possession
     - and 2. Make a contract for the transportation of the goods in a manner reasonable under the circumstances (considering the type of goods to be shipped (ex: frozen food, fragile glass)).
   - and (b) <u>Send Documents</u>: Obtain and *promptly deliver* or *tender* any documents (in due form) which:
     - i) Buyer may need to obtain possession of the goods (ex: BOL)
     - or ii) Are otherwise required by the agreement
     - or iii) Are otherwise required by Usage of Trade
   - and (c) <u>Promptly notify the Buyer of shipment</u>

3. The following are grounds for Rejection only if *material delay* or *loss* results:
   - a) Failure to make a proper shipping contract (as per §2-504(a))
   - or b) Failure to promptly notify Buyer of the shipment (as per §2-504(c))

§2-505: Seller's Shipment Under Reservation:

(1) **Goods Identified By Seller By or Before Shipment:**
  (a) <u>Negotiable BOL</u>: If the Seller has identified goods to a contract by or before shipment, then:
   1. The Seller may reserve a Security Interest in the goods by preparing a *Negotiable Bill of Lading* to his order (or otherwise).
   and 2. Making the Negotiable BOL to the order of the <u>Buyer</u> or a <u>Financing Agency</u> will not impair the reservation of the security interest (it only indicates the Seller's expectations of transferability of interest).
  (b) <u>Non-Negotiable BOL</u>: If the Seller has identified goods to a contract by or before delivery, then:
   1. *Unconditional Delivery*: A non-negotiable BOL naming the Seller or his nominee reserves possession of the goods as a security.
   2. *Conditional Delivery* (as per §2-507(2)): The Seller will not reserve himself a Security Interest if he uses a non-negotiable BOL which names the Buyer as the Consignee (even if the Seller retains possession of the BOL).

(2) **Seller's Reservation In Violation of Contract:**
  If the Seller's reservation of a Security Interest violates the contract of sale:
   a) The contract is considered an improper contract for transportation (as per §2-504).
   but b) The effectiveness of the contract is not impaired regarding:
    1. The rights given to the Buyer by the shipment and identification of the goods to the contract
    and 2. The Seller's powers as a Holder of a Negotiable Document

§2-506: Rights of Financing Agency:

(1) **Financing Agency's Rights From Purchase of Documentary Draft:**

    a. A Financing Agency may obtain a shipper's rights in the goods by paying or purchasing (for value) a Draft relating to the shipment of the goods (ex: a draft made against an invoice, a draft made against a delivery order).

    b. The rights the Financing Agency will obtain from the shipper include:

        1) The right to stop delivery

        2) The Shipper's right to have the draft honored by the Buyer

    c. The Financing Agency must pay <u>value</u> (as per §1-201(44)) for the draft.

    d. The Financing Agency may only acquire the shipper's right to the extent of the payment or purchase of the draft.

    e. These rights are in addition to the Financing Agency's own rights under the draft and any documents of title securing them.

(2) **Rights of Reimbursement**: A Financing Agency's rights in a draft will not be impaired by any defects in relevant documents if:

    a. The documents looked regular on their face

  and b. The defects were not discovered until after the Financing Agency purchased or honored the draft

  and c. The Financing Agency either:

        1) <u>Honored</u> the Draft in Good Faith

      or 2) <u>Purchased</u> the Draft under a commitment to the Buyer

      or 3) <u>Purchased</u> the Draft under the authority of the Buyer

§2-507: Effect of Seller's Tender; Delivery on Condition:

(1) **Effect of Tender:**
    a. <u>Buyer's Obligation</u>: Tender of delivery is a condition to the Buyer's obligation to:
        1. *Accept* the goods
      and 2. *Pay* for the goods (unless otherwise agreed)
    b. <u>Seller's Entitlement</u>: Tender entitles the Seller to:
        1. The Buyer's acceptance of the goods
      and 2. Payment (according to the contract)

(2) **Conditional Delivery:**
    The Buyer's rights to *retain* or *dispose of* the goods is conditional upon making payment due to the Seller, if:
        a. <u>Payment is due</u> upon delivery (of goods or documents of title) to the Buyer
      and b. <u>Seller demanded payment</u> upon delivery (of goods or documents of title) to the Buyer

§2-508: Cure By Seller for Improper Tender or Delivery; Replacement:

(1) **Non-Conforming Goods:** The Seller may seasonably notify the Buyer of his intention to cure, and may then ship conforming goods if:
    a) Goods are rejected because they are non-conforming
    b) The time for performance has not expired
    c) The Seller re-ships conforming goods before the expiration of performance (i.e. before the delivery date)

(2) **Goods Seller Deemed Conforming:** Seller may extend time of delivery and ship conforming goods if:
    a) The goods are rejected because they are non-conforming
    and b) The Seller had *reasonable grounds* to believe they would be acceptable (with or without a money allowance)
    and c) Seller seasonably notifies the Buyer
    and b) The extension is reasonable

§2-509: Risk of Loss in the Absence of Breach:

(1) <u>Contracts Requiring or Authorizing Seller to Ship the Goods by the Carrier</u> (FOB Carrier):

    (a) **Shipment Contract:** The Risk of Loss passes to the Buyer <u>when the goods are duly delivered to the Carrier</u> if the contract does not require the Seller to deliver the goods to a particular destination (even if the shipment is under "<u>Reservation</u>" (as per §2-505))

    (b) **Destination Contract:** The Risk of Loss passes to the *Buyer* <u>when the goods are so tendered to *enable the Buyer to take delivery*</u> if:

        1. The contract does not require the Seller to deliver the goods to a particular destination.

    and 2. The goods are tendered while in the possession of a Carrier

(2) <u>When Goods are held by a Bailee to be Delivered without Being Moved</u> - Risk of Loss passes to the *Buyer* when:

    (a) He received a <u>Negotiable Document of Title</u> covering the goods

    or (b) The Bailee acknowledges the Buyer's right to possess the goods

    or (c) He received a <u>Non-Negotiable Document of Title</u> (or other written direction to deliver (as per §2-503(4)(b))

(3) <u>All other cases</u> - Risk passes to *Buyer*:

    a) *When he receives the goods* - if Seller is a Merchant

    b) *Upon Tender of Delivery* - if Seller is not a Merchant

(4) This section is subject to:

    a) Agreements of the parties

    b) §2-327 (Sale on Approval)

    c) §2-510 (Effect of Breach on Risk of Loss)

§2-510: Risk of Loss with Breach:

(1) Seller's Breach:

Risk of loss remains on the <u>Seller</u> until *Cure* or *Acceptance* if:
   a) Tender or Delivery fails to conform to the contract
and b) The non-conformity gives rise to a *Right of Rejection*

(2) Buyer's Revocation of Acceptance:

The Buyer may treat the risk of loss as the Seller's *from the
beginning of the contract* (as if risk of loss never passes to the Buyer)
   a) If the Buyer rightfully *revokes* acceptance
and b) To the extent the Buyer's insurance is deficient

(3) Buyer's Breach:

The Seller may treat the risk of loss as the <u>Buyer's</u> (To the extent the
Seller's insurance was deficient) for a *commercially reasonable time* if:
   a. The goods were already identified to the contract
and b. The goods conformed to the contract
and c. The Buyer Repudiates/Breaches before risk of loss
     passes to him

§2-511: Tender of Payment:

(1) Tender of Payment is a condition to the Seller's duty to tender and complete any delivery (unless otherwise agreed).

(2) Tender of Payment is sufficient if it is made by any manner in the ordinary course of business, *unless:*
    a) Seller demands money (legal tender)
  and b) Seller gives an extension of time *reasonably necessary* for Buyer to comply

(3) Payment by check is *conditional* and is defeated if it is dishonored on due presentment (Subject to §3-802 (Effect of an Instrument on an Obligation)).

§2-512: Payment by Buyer Before Inspection:

(1) **Payment Required Before Inspection:** If a contract requires goods to be paid for before inspection (ex: Seller will tender documents), a non-conformity of the goods will not be an excuse for non-payment, *unless*:
    (a) The non-conformity appears without inspection (i.e. when the goods are delivered, the non-conformities are very obvious)
  or (b) The circumstances would justify an <u>injunction</u> against honoring the Seller's tender of the required documents (as per §5-114)

(2) **Effects of Payment Before Inspection:**
    a. PAYMENT (as per §2-512(1)) DOES NOT CONSTITUTE ACCEPTANCE.
    b. Payment does not impair the Buyer's right to inspect the goods (before accepting them).
    c. Payment does not impair any of the Buyer's remedies.

§2-513: Buyer's Right to Inspect Goods:

(1) **Buyer's Right to Inspection of Goods:**
  a) The Buyer has a right to inspect the goods before payment or
    acceptance if the goods are:
      1. Tendered
    or 2. Delivered
    or 3. Identified to the contract for sale
  b) The Buyer has a right to inspect the goods:
      1. At any reasonable place and time
    and 2. In any reasonable manner
  c) When the Seller is required or authorized to send the goods to
    the Buyer, the inspection may be after their arrival.
  d) This subsection may be changed by agreement of the parties,
    and is subject to §2-513(3).

(2) <u>Expense of Inspection</u>:
  a) Expenses must be borne by the Buyer.
  b) If the goods do not conform and are rejected, the Buyer may
    recover inspection expenses from Seller.

(3) **No Right to Inspect:**
  i) The Buyer is not entitled to inspect the goods before payment if
    the contract provides:
      (a) For delivery *"C.O.D."* (or on other similar terms)
    or (b) For payment against DOT's (except where such payment
        is due only after the goods are to become available for inspection)
  ii) This subsection may be changed by agreement of parties,
    and is subject to §2-321(3) (dealing with C.I.F. contracts).

(4) **Fixed Place/Method of Inspection:**
  a) A place or method of inspection fixed by the parties is presumed
    to be *exclusive*.
  b) Unless otherwise agreed, such an agreement does not:
      1. Postpone identification
    or 2. Change the place for delivery
    or 3. Shift the passing of risk of loss
  c) <u>If compliance with fixed terms becomes impossible</u> -
    Buyer shall have a right to inspect (as per §2-513), unless the
    fixed place/method was clearly intended as an *indispensable
    condition*, failure of which avoids the contract.

§2-514: When Documents Deliverable on Acceptance; When on Payment:

1) <u>Documents Delivered Upon Acceptance</u> - Documents (against which a draft is drawn) are to be delivered to the <u>Drawee</u> upon *Acceptance* of the draft if:

    a) The Draft is payable more than <u>3 Days</u> after presentment
and b) The Parties do not otherwise agree

2) <u>Documents Delivered Upon Payment</u> - Documents (against which a draft is drawn) are to be delivered to the <u>Drawee</u> upon *Payment* of the draft if:

    a) The Draft is not payable more than <u>3 Days</u> after presentment
and b) The Parties agree

§2-515: Preserving Evidence of Goods in Dispute:

(a) **Right To Inspect, Test or Sample:**
    Either party has the right to <u>Inspect</u>, <u>Test</u> and <u>Sample</u> the goods (including those that are in possession or control of the other party), if:
      1. <u>Notice</u>: The party reasonably notifies the other party that it intends to inspect, test or sample the goods.
    and 2. <u>Purpose of Inspection</u>: The inspection, sampling or testing is for the purpose of ascertaining the facts and preserving evidence.
    and 3. Inspection is *"in furtherance of the adjustment of any claim or dispute."*

(b) **Third Party Inspections:**
    1. The parties may agree to have a Third Party Inspection or Survey of the goods to determine:
      a) If the goods conform to the contract
      b) The condition of the goods
    2. The parties may agree that all findings by the third party shall be binding upon them in any subsequent litigation or adjustment.

PART 6
BREACH, REPUDIATION, AND EXCUSE

§2-601: Buyer's Rights on Improper Delivery:

1. **Remedies For Imperfect Tender:** If the goods or the tender of delivery *in any way* fail to conform to the contract, then Buyer may:
   - (a) Reject the whole shipment
   - or (b) Accept the whole shipment
   - or (c) Accept any "commercial unit," and reject the rest

2. This rule is subject to
   - a) §2-612 (Breach of Installment Contracts)
   - b) Liquidated Remedy Agreements (under §2-718 and §2-719)

§2-602: Manner and Effect of Rightful Rejection:

(1) **When to Reject:**
   - a) The Buyer must seasonably notify the Seller that it is rejecting the goods.
   - b) Rejection will be ineffective if it is not made within a *reasonable time* after delivery or tender occurs.

(2) **Buyer's Rights and Obligations** (subject to §2-603 and §2-604):
   - (a) After rejection, any "exercise of ownership" over the goods (by the Buyer) is considered *wrongful* against the Seller.
   - and (b) The Buyer will have an obligation to hold the goods with *reasonable care* for a reasonable time *after* rejection (in order to allow the Seller to remove them) if:
       - 1. The Buyer has taken physical possession of the goods before he rejected them
       - and 2. The Buyer does not have a Security Interest in the goods (as per §2-711(3))
   - and (c) The Buyer has no further obligations with regard to rightfully rejected goods (unless he is a Merchant, in which case §2-603 applies).

(3) **Seller's Rights:** The Seller's rights in *wrongfully* rejected goods are governed by §2-703 (Seller's Remedies).

§2-603: Merchant Buyer's Rightful Rejection:

(1) Buyer's Duties Upon Rejection:

    a) After rejection, any <u>Merchant</u> Buyer must follow any *reasonable instruction* received from the Seller, with respect to such goods if:

        1. If Seller has no agent or place of business where goods are rejected

    and 2. After rejection goods are still in the Buyer's possession or control

    b) Upon rejection, the Buyer must make reasonable efforts to sell the goods for the Seller if:

        1. The Seller has no agent or place of business where goods are rejected

    and 2. After rejection goods are still in the Buyer's possession or control

    and 3. The Seller left no other *reasonable instructions*

    and 4. The goods are perishable or threaten to speedily decline in value

    c) Instructions are not reasonable if, on the Buyer's demand, indemnity for expenses is not forthcoming.

    d) This subsection is subject to any S/I in the Buyer (as per §2-711(3)).

(2) Reimbursement to Buyer:

When the Buyer sells goods under §2-603(1), he is entitled to <u>reimbursement</u> from the Seller (or out of the proceeds of the sale) for:

    a. Reasonable selling expenses

    b. Reasonable expenses incurred in caring for the goods

    c. Selling Commissions, if they are:

        1. Not included in expenses

    and 2. *Either:*

          a) Reasonable in the trade/industry

       or b) A Reasonable Sum (if no industry norm), *not to exceed 10% of gross proceeds.*

(3) Buyer's Standard of Good Faith:

    a) The Buyer is held to a standard of *Good Faith.*

    b) Good Faith conduct will not be considered Acceptance, Conversion, or a basis of an action for damages.

§2-604: Buyer's Option to Salvage Rightfully Rejected Goods:

1. **Buyer's Options:** The Buyer has the following options with respect to rightfully rejected goods:
   a. Store the rejected goods for the Seller
   b. Reship the goods back to the Seller
   c. Resell the goods on behalf of the Seller and reimburse him (as per §2-603)

2. The Buyer may only exercise these options if the Seller does not give the Buyer instructions within a reasonable time after notification of rejection.

3. This section is subject to §2-603 (duty to resell) if:
   a) The Buyer is a Merchant
   and b) The goods are perishable

4. These actions will not be considered Acceptance or Conversion.

§2-605: Waiver of Buyer's Right to Reject:

(1) If Buyer does not give specific reasons for rejecting goods, he waives the right to reject them (based on that defect) if:
   i) The defects are ascertainable by reasonable inspection
   and ii) *Either*:
   > (a) The Seller could have fixed the problem seasonably (if the reason was stated)
   > or (b) <u>Between Merchants</u> - the *Merchant* Seller has requested a written statement of defects from the *Merchant* Buyer

(2) **Payment Against Documents:** Recovery of payments for defects apparent on the face of documents will be <u>precluded</u> if payment is made:
   a) Against the documents
   and b) *"Without reservation"*

§2-606: Acceptance Of Goods:

(1) Acceptance of Goods occurs when Buyer:
- (a) Signifies to Seller (after reasonable opportunity to inspect them) that *either*:
    1. The goods conform to the contract
    - or 2. The Buyer will take or retain the goods even though there is a non-conformity
- or (b) Fails to make an effective rejection (as per §2-602(1)) after a reasonable opportunity to inspect
- or (c) Does any act inconsistent with Seller's ownership (i.e. if such an act is wrongful, acceptance is only at the Seller's option)

(2) Acceptance of part of a "commercial unit" is considered acceptance of the whole unit.

§2-607: Effect of Acceptance:

(1) **Price of Accepted Goods:** The Buyer must pay the *contract price* (i.e. the price of the goods as stated in the contract) for any goods accepted.

(2) **Rejection and Revocation:**
- a. Goods cannot be <u>rejected</u> after they have been accepted.
- b. Goods cannot be <u>revoked</u> due to a non-conformity if they were accepted with knowledge of the non-conformity *unless* the Buyer *reasonably assumed* that the Seller would fix the non-conformity.
- c. Acceptance itself does not impair other Article 2 remedies for non-conforming goods.

(3) **Acceptance of Tender:** If tender has been accepted:
- (a) <u>Breach</u>:
    1. The Buyer must notify the Seller of any breach within a reasonable time after discovering such a breach (or a reasonable time after he *should have* discovered it).
    2. If the Buyer does not notify the Seller of such breach within a reasonable time, the Buyer will be barred from any remedy.
- (b) <u>Infringement</u>:
    1. The Buyer must notify the Seller of any litigation against the Buyer if:
        a) The Buyer is sued as a result of the Seller's breach
        and b) The claim is for infringement (or the like (as per §2-312(3))
    2. If the Buyer does not send the Seller such notice within a reasonable time after the Buyer learns of the litigation, the Buyer will not be able to use any remedies against the Seller to recover the liability damages arising out of the litigation.

(4) **Burden of Proof:** The <u>Buyer</u> has the burden of proving a breach with respect to the accepted goods.

(5) **When Buyer is Sued for Seller's Wrong:** When the Buyer is sued for an obligation (ex: breach of warranty) which his Seller may be responsible for:

  (a) The facts determined in the suit against the Buyer will be binding in any similar suit which the Buyer may start against the Seller if:

     1) The Seller is *answerable* to the Buyer for the breach of obligation

    and 2) The Buyer sent the Seller a <u>written</u> notice of the litigation

    and 3) The notice gave the Seller an opportunity to defend himself in the case and described the consequences of not appearing

    and 4) The Seller neglected to defend himself within a reasonable time after he received the notice

  (b) <u>Infringement</u>:

     1) The original Seller may demand that his Buyer give him control of the litigation (including settlement).

     2) The Buyer will not be able to use any remedies against the Seller to recover the liability damages arising out of the litigation if:

       a. The claim was one of infringement (or the like (as per §2-312(3))

      and b. The original Seller demanded control of the litigation

      and c. The Seller's demand was in <u>writing</u>

      and d. The Seller agreed to pay for:

        1. All litigation expenses

       and 2. Any adverse judgment

      and e. The Buyer does not turn the case over to the Seller within a reasonable time after receiving the Seller's demand.

(6) **Applicability:** Subsections (3), (4) and (5) (above) apply to any obligation of a Buyer to hold the Seller harmless against infringement (or the like (as per §2-312(3))).

§2-608: Revocation of Acceptance:

(1) **When Buyer May Revoke:** The Buyer may revoke his acceptance if:
    i) A non-conformity *substantially impairs* the value of the
        goods to the Buyer
and ii) *Either*:
            (a) He has accepted the goods assuming that the Seller would
                cure the non-conformity, but the Seller neglected to
                do so *seasonably*
        or (b) He accepted the goods without knowing of the
                non-conformity either because:
                    1. It was difficult to discover the non-conformity
                        before acceptance
                or 2. The Seller's assurances induced him to accept

(2) **Time of Revocation:**
    a) Revocation of acceptance must occur within a reasonable time:
            1. After the Buyer discovers *or should have discovered* the
                non-conformity
        and 2. Before there is any *substantial change* in the condition of
                the goods (which is not caused by their own defects)
    b) Revocation is not effective until the Buyer notifies the Seller of it.

(3) **Effect of Revocation:** A Buyer who properly revokes has the same
    rights and duties as if he had rejected them.

§2-609: Right to Adequate Assurance of Performance:

(1) **Adequate Assurance:**
    a) A contract for sale creates an obligation in each party to maintain the other party's expectations of due performance.
    b) A party will be excused from performing any contractual obligation if:
        1) The party had *reasonable grounds of insecurity* as to whether the other party will perform according to the contract
       and 2) The party sends a written notice to the other party demanding *adequate assurance* of due performance
       and 3) The other party did not yet respond to the demand
       and 4) It is commercially reasonable to suspend such performance
       and 5) The party did not receive payment (or other return) for the obligations it plans to suspend.
    c) Parties:
        1) *"Repudiating Party"* - The party failing to give adequate assurance of performance
        2) *"Aggrieved Party"* - The party demanding assurance of performance

(2) **Standards:** The following terms shall be construed according to *commercial standards* if the contract is between Merchants:
    a) "Reasonable Grounds for Insecurity"
    b) "Adequacy of assurance"

(3) **Installments:** A party is not precluded from demanding adequate assurance of future obligations even if he accepted an improper delivery or payment of earlier obligations.

(4) **Repudiation:** A party who fails to provide *adequate assurance* (under the circumstances of the case) to a justified demand within a reasonable amount of time (no more than 30 days) will have repudiated the contract.

§2-610: Anticipatory Repudiation:

1. **"Anticipatory Repudiation"** - Anticipatory Repudiation occurs when:
   - a. Either party repudiates the contract (see §2-609)
   - and b. The repudiated portion of the contract is not yet due
   - and c. The loss of such performance will *substantially impair* the value of the contract

2. **Rights of Aggrieved Party upon Anticipatory Repudiation:** The aggrieved party may:
   - (a) <u>Await Performance</u> - from the repudiating party, for a *commercially reasonable time*
   - or (b) <u>Resort to Breach Remedies</u> (as per §2-703 (for Seller) or §2-711 (for Buyer)) - even if he told the repudiating party that he will wait for performance (subsection (a))
   - or (c) <u>Suspend Performance</u> - The aggrieved party may suspend his own performance.
   - or d) <u>Identify and Salvage Goods</u> - The Seller may identify goods to a contract or salvage unfinished goods (as per §2-704).

§2-611: Retraction of Anticipatory Repudiation:

(1) **Time for Retraction:** The repudiating party may retract his repudiation if:
   - a) His next performance is still not yet due
   - and b) The aggrieved party has <u>not</u>:
     - 1. Canceled the contract
     - or 2. Materially changed its position
     - or 3. Otherwise indicated that it considers the repudiation final

(2) **Requirements for Retraction:** A valid retraction of repudiation must:
   - a) *Clearly indicate* to the aggrieved party that the repudiating party <u>intends to perform</u>
   - and b) Include any <u>adequate assurance</u> *justifiably* demanded under §2-609

(3) **Effect of Retraction:**
   - a) The repudiating party's rights under the contract are reinstated
   - and b) The aggrieved party is excused for any delay due to the repudiation.

§2-612: Installment Contract Breaches:

(1) **"Installment Contract"** - a contract which recognizes or authorizes the delivery of goods in <u>separate lots</u> to be <u>separately accepted</u> (even if the contract says that each delivery is considered a separate contract).

(2) **Rejecting Installments:**
    a) The Buyer may reject any installment which is non-conforming if:
        1) The non-conformity *substantially impairs* the value of the installment
     and 2) *Either*:
          a. The defect cannot be cured
        or b. The defect is in the documents and not the goods themselves
    b) The Buyer must accept the goods if the Seller gives adequate assurance that he will fix the defects (subject to §2-612(3)).

(3) **Substantial Non-Conformity:**
    a) A *substantial* non-conformity of one or more installments is considered to be a breach of the *entire* contract.
    b) The Buyer may reinstate an Installment Contract if he:
        1) Accepts a non-conforming installment without seasonably notifying Seller of cancellation
     or 2) Brings an action only against past installments
     or 3) Demands performance as to future installments (not present, non-conforming installment)

§2-613: Casualty to Identified Goods:

(a) **Total Loss:** A contract may be <u>avoided</u> if:

1) The contract requires that the goods be identified when the contract is made

and 2) <u>All</u> of the identified goods suffer from a casualty

and 3) The casualty is not the fault of either party

and 4) *Either*:

a) The risk of loss did not yet pass to the Buyer

or b) The contract was a "No Arrival, No Sale" contract (as per §2-324 (in a proper case))

(b) **Partial Loss or Deteriorated Goods:**

1) The Buyer has the option of <u>avoiding</u> or <u>accepting</u> the contract if:

a) The contract requires that the goods be identified when the contract is made

and b) *Either*:

1. <u>Some</u> of the identified goods suffer from a casualty

or 2. The goods have deteriorated so much that they do not conform to the contract

and c) The casualty is not the fault of either party

and d) *Either*:

1. The risk of loss did not yet pass to the Buyer

or 2. The contract was a "No Arrival, No Sale" contract (as per §2-324)

2) <u>Accepting Goods at a Discount</u>:

a) The Buyer may accept the goods and receive a discount for the deterioration or deficiency in the goods.

b) If the Buyer receives such a discount he will not have any other rights against the Seller.

§2-614: Substituted Performance:

(1) **Substitute Delivery:** Substitute Performance must be Tendered and Accepted if:
    a) *Either*:
        1. The agreed berthing, loading or unloading facilities fail
      or 2. An agreed type of Carrier becomes unavailable
      or 3. The agreed upon manner of delivery otherwise becomes commercially impracticable
  and b) A *commercially reasonable substitute* is available
  and c) Neither party is at fault

(2) **Substitute Payment:**
    a) *Before Delivery Begins*:
      The Seller may Withhold or Stop Delivery if:
        1) The Agreed upon means or manner of payment fails (due to foreign or domestic governmental regulations)
     and 2) The Buyer does not provide a *commercially substantial equivalent* manner of payment
    b) *After Delivery Begins*:
      The Buyer's obligation to pay the Seller will be discharged if:
        1) Payment is made in the manner provided for by the governmental regulations
     and 2) Such regulations are not *discriminatory*, *oppressive*, or *predatory*.

§2-615: Excuse by Failure of Presupposed
Conditions: ("Commercial Impracticability")

(a) Delay In Delivery/Non-Delivery:

The Seller is not considered to have breached its contract if he delays delivery or fails to deliver goods (in whole or in part) if:

1. The Seller had complied with (b) and (c) below

and 2. The agreed upon manner of performance has become *impracticable*, either by

     a. The occurrence a certain event, if the contract was made with the basic assumption that such an event would not occur

or   b. Good Faith compliance with any foreign or domestic governmental regulation or order (whether or not it later proves to be invalid)

(b) Diminished Number of Goods:

1. <u>Allocation of Goods</u>: If the causes in (a) (above) affect only part of the Seller's capacity to perform (by reducing the amount of goods he has to ship) the Seller must allocate production and delivery of the goods among all of his customers.

2. <u>Guidelines for Allocation</u>: The Seller must allocate the goods according to these guidelines (in any manner which is fair and reasonable):

     a) The Seller does not have to allocate the goods only to customers with outstanding orders.

     b) The Seller may allocate goods to "regular customers," even though they do not have outstanding orders for goods.

     c) The Seller may allocate goods for his own requirements or for future manufacture.

(c) Notice to the Buyer:

1. The Seller must *seasonably* notify the Buyer of the delay or non-delivery.

2. If the Seller will be allocating goods (as per (b) above), he must *seasonably* notify the Buyer of the estimated quantity he will be shipping.

d) This Section is subject to §2-614 and to any "greater" obligation which the Seller may assume.

§2-616: Procedure for Notice Claiming Excuse:

(1) Buyer's Rights Upon Seller's Excuse:

i) *Applicability*: This section shall only apply if:

    a) The Buyer receives a notice that *either*

        1. There will be a material or indefinite delay in delivery

    or 2. The Seller will be allocating goods (as per §2-615(b)), and shipping the Buyer a smaller quantity than he originally ordered.

  and b) The deficiency in the amount of goods *substantially impairs* the value of the whole contract (as per §2-612)

  and c) The Buyer sends a <u>written notice</u> of its intentions

ii) *Buyer's Rights*: If the above conditions are fulfilled, the Buyer may choose to *either:*

    (a) <u>Terminate the Whole Contract</u> - and discharge any unexecuted portion of the contract

  or (b) <u>Modify the Contract</u> - by agreeing to take the Seller's available quantity of goods as substitution

(2) The contract will lapse (with respect to any deliveries affected) if:

    a) The Buyer receives such notice of delay or allocation

  and b) The Buyer fails to modify the contract within a reasonable time (no more than <u>30 Days</u>)

(3) The provisions of this section may not be negated by agreement unless the Seller has assumed a greater obligation under §2-615.

PART 7
REMEDIES

§2-701: Remedies for Breach of Collateral Contracts Not Impaired:

Article 2 does not limit remedies for breach of any obligation or promise (collateral or ancillary) to a contract for sale.

§2-702: Buyer's Insolvency; Reclamaton Rights:

(1) **Seller Discovers Buyer's Insolvency Before Delivery:**
If the Seller discovers that the Buyer is insolvent, the Seller may:
a. Refuse to continue delivering unless Buyer promises to
1. Pay Cash on Delivery (C.O.D.)
and 2. Pay for all shipments already delivered under the contract
and b. Stop delivery (as per §2-705)

(2) **Buyer Receives Goods on Credit While Insolvent:**
If the Seller discovers that the Buyer has been receiving goods on credit while he was insolvent, the Seller may <u>Reclaim the goods</u>:
Reclamation Requirements:
1. *10 Day Time Limit* - In order to reclaim the goods, the Seller must:
a) Demand payment or reclamation of the goods
b) Make the *Demand* within <u>10 Days</u> after the Buyer receives the goods
2. *EXCEPTION - Written Misrepresentation of Solvency:*
10 Day limit does not apply if the Buyer made a <u>Misrepresentation of Solvency</u>:
a) In Writing
and b) Within <u>3 Months</u> before Delivery
3. The Seller may not base a right to reclaim the goods based on the Buyer's *Fraudulent* or *Innocent* misrepresentation of <u>Solvency</u> or <u>Intent to pay</u>, except as provided in this subsection (i.e. it must be in writing, within 3 Months before delivery).

(3) **Limitations on the Seller's Rights to Reclaim:**
a. The Seller's rights to reclaim are subject to the rights of:
1. A Buyer In the Ordinary Course (BIOC)
and 2. Any other Good Faith Purchaser (under §2-403)
b. <u>Exclusion of Other Remedies</u>: Successful reclamation of goods *excludes* all other remedies (with respect to the reclaimed goods).

§2-703: Seller's Remedies in General:

1. <u>Seller is entitled to remedies when</u>:
    a. The Buyer wrongfully rejects goods
  or b. The Buyer wrongfully revokes acceptance of goods
  or c. The Buyer repudiates with respect to the whole or a part of the contract
  or d. The Buyer fails to make a payment due on or before delivery;
      Failure to make a payment includes (official comment 3):
        a. The dishonor of a check on due presentment
        b. The nonacceptance of a draft
        c. The failure to furnish an agreed letter of credit

2. <u>The Seller's remedies apply with respect to</u>:
    a. Any goods directly affected
 and b. If the breach is of the whole contract (§2-612), then also with respect to the whole undelivered balance

3. **Remedies Available** - <u>The Seller may</u>:
    (a) Withhold delivery of the goods
  or (b) Stop delivery by any Bailee (as per §2-705)
  or (c) Identify or salvage unfinished or unidentified goods (under §2-704)
  or (d) Resell and recover damages as provided in §2-706
  or (e) Recover damages for non-acceptance (§2-708) or in a proper case the price (§2-709)
  or (f) Cancel the contract

§2-704: Seller's Right to Identify Goods to the Contract Notwithstanding Breach or to Salvage Unfinished Goods:

(1) <u>Rights of Aggrieved Seller under §2-703 may</u>:
    (a) *Conforming Finished Goods:* Identify to the contract goods which have not yet been identified if:
        1. The goods conform to the contract
    and 2. At the time the Seller learned of the breach they are in the Seller's possession or control (the goods are then available for resale under §2-706 (official comment))
    (b) *Unfinished Goods:* Resell goods which have *clearly* been intended for the particular contract (even though those goods are unfinished).

(2) <u>Seller's Remedies Where Goods are Unfinished</u>:
    a. Where the goods are unfinished an aggrieved Seller may *either*:
        1. Complete the manufacture and wholly identify the goods to the contract
    or 2. Cease manufacture and resell them for scrap or salvage value
    or 3. Proceed in any other *reasonable manner*

    b. The Seller must exercise reasonable commercial judgment (the burden is on the Buyer to show otherwise) for the purposes of:
        1. Avoiding loss
    and 2. Effective realization

§2-705: Seller's Stoppage of Delivery in Transit or Otherwise:

(1) <u>Seller's Right To Stop Delivery</u>:

    a. **Insolvency**: The Seller may stop delivery of goods in the possession of a <u>Carrier</u> or <u>other Bailee</u> when he discovers the Buyer to be insolvent (§2-702).

    b. **Other Situations**: The Seller may stop delivery of carload, truckload, planeload or larger shipments of express or freight when:

        1. The Buyer repudiates

    or 2. If for any other reason the Seller has a right to <u>withhold</u> or <u>reclaim</u> the goods

    or 3. The Buyer fails to make a payment due before delivery; Failure to make a payment includes (official comment 3):

        a. The dishonor of a check on due presentment

        b. The nonacceptance of a draft

        c. The failure to furnish an agreed letter of credit

(2) <u>Seller's Time Limit</u>: The Seller may stop delivery until:

    (a) The Buyer receives the goods (this includes receipt by the Buyer's designated representative, the sub-purchaser, when shipment is made direct to him and the Buyer himself never receives the goods (official comment))

    or (b) A Bailee of the goods (except a Carrier) acknowledges to the Buyer that the goods are being held for the Buyer

    or (c) The Carrier acknowledges that the goods are being held for the Buyer, *either*:

        1. By reshipment (this does not include diversion of a shipment when it is merely an incident to the original contract of transportation or does not change the destination (official comment))

        or 2. As a Warehouseman (this requires a contract of a truly different character from the original shipment, a contract not in extension of transit but as a Warehouseman (official comment))

    or (d) Negotiation to the Buyer of any negotiable document of title covering the goods.

(3) <u>Stopping Delivery</u>:

    (a) **Notice:** To stop delivery the Seller must give the Bailee notice in order to enable him to prevent delivery by *reasonable diligence.*

    (b) **Seller's and Bailee's Responsibilities:** After such notification:

        1. The Bailee must hold and deliver the goods according to the directions of the Seller.

        2. The Seller is liable to the Bailee for any ensuing charges or damages.

(c) **Bailee to Stop Delivery:** If a negotiable document of title has been issued for goods the Bailee is not obliged to obey a notification to stop delivery until surrender of the document (a Bailee is under no duty to recognize the stop order of a stranger to the Carrier's contract (official comment)).

(d) **Carrier to Stop Delivery:** A Carrier who has issued a non-negotiable Bill of Lading is not obliged to obey a notification to stop delivery *unless* he is notified by the Consignor (a Bailee is under no duty to recognize the stop order of a stranger to the Carrier's contract (official comment)).

§2-706: Seller's Resale Including Contract For Resale:

(1) <u>Resale By Seller for Buyer's Breach or Insolvency</u>:
    a. Seller's Right: Under the conditions stated in §2-703 (breach or insolvency), the Seller may:
        1. Resell the goods concerned,
    or 2. Resell the undelivered balance of the goods
    b. <u>Seller Damages Recoverable</u>: The Seller may recover:

> **The resale price**
> **- The contract price**
> **+ Any incidental damages** (allowed under §2-710)
> **- Expenses saved in consequence of the Buyer's breach**

    c. <u>Requirements</u>: In order to recover damages, Seller has to resell:
        1. In good faith
    and 2. In a commercially reasonable manner

(2) <u>Method of Resale</u>:
    a. **General Notes**:
        1. Every aspect of the sale including the <u>method</u>, <u>manner</u>, <u>time</u>, <u>place</u> and <u>terms</u> must be *commercially reasonable*.
        2. The resale must be reasonably identified as referring to the broken contract, but it is not necessary for:
            i. The goods to be in existence
        or ii. Any or all of the goods to have been identified to the contract before the breach.
        3. Terms of resale are subject to:
            i. §2-706(3)
        and ii. Agreement otherwise by parties.
    b. **Type of Sale** - Depending on commercial reasonableness, resale may be at:
        1. Public sale (auction)
        or 2. Private sale (ex: solicitation and negotiation conducted either directly or through a broker)
    c. This section includes sale by way of:
        1. One or more contracts to sell
        or 2. Identification to an existing contract of the Seller
    d. **Units of Sale** - Sale may be:
        1. As a unit
        or 2. In parcels
    e. **Time and Place** - Sale may be at any time and place and on any terms.

(3) <u>Private Resale</u> - Where the resale is at private sale the Seller must give the Buyer reasonable notification of his intention to resell (notification of the time and place of this type of sale is not required).

(4) <u>Public Resale</u> - Where the resale is at public sale:
    (a) <u>Type of Goods That Can Be Sold</u>:
        1. Only identified goods can be sold.
        2. Futures Market Exception: Where there is a recognized market for a public sale of futures in goods of the kind.
    (b) <u>Seller's Requirements</u>:
        1. **Place:** The auction must be made at a *usual place or market* for public sale (which prospective bidders may reasonably be expected to attend).
        2. **Notice:**
            a. The Seller must give the Buyer reasonable notice of the time and place so that he may:
                i. Bid
            or ii. Secure the attendance of other bidders
            b. Perishable Goods Exception: In the case of goods *"which are perishable or threaten to decline speedily in value,"* notice is not required.
    (c) <u>Goods Not Present at Sale</u> - If the goods are not to be within the view of those attending the sale:
        1. The notification of sale must <u>state the place</u> where the goods are located
       and 2. The notification must provide for <u>reasonable inspection</u> of the goods by prospective bidders
    (d) The Seller may buy (his own goods) at the sale.

(5) <u>Purchaser's Rights</u>: A purchaser who buys in good faith at a resale takes the goods <u>free of any rights of the original Buyer</u> (even though the Seller fails to comply with one or more of the requirements of this section).

(6) <u>Profits</u>:
    a. The Seller retains profit, if any, made on any resale.
    b. A person in the position of a Seller (as per §2-707) must give any excess (above his "security interest" as defined in §2-711(3)) to the Seller.
    c. A Buyer who has rightfully rejected or justifiably revoked acceptance must also give any "profits" to the Seller (i.e. the difference between the sale price and the Seller's "security interest" in the goods (as defined in §2-711(3)).

§2-707: "Person in the Position of a Seller":

(1) A **"Person In The Position of a Seller"** includes:
- a. An agent who has paid or become responsible for the price of goods on behalf of his principal
- or b. Anyone who otherwise holds a security interest or other right in goods similar to that of a Seller

(2) A person in the position of a Seller may:
- a. Withhold or stop delivery (§2-705)
- and b. Resell (§2-706)
- and c. Recover incidental damages (§2-710)

§2-708: Seller's Damages for Non-acceptance or Repudiation:

(1) <u>Expectation Damages</u>: If the Buyer does not accept or repudiates, the Seller's damages are (subject to 2-708(2) and to §2-723 (proof of market price)):

> **The market price at the time and place for tender**
> - **The unpaid contract price**
> + **Any incidental damages provided in this Article (§2-710)**
> - **Expenses saved in consequence of the Buyer's breach**

(2) <u>Lost Profit</u>: If the measure of damages in subsection (1) is not enough to put the Seller in as good a position as he would have been had the Buyer performed (i.e. the Seller is a "lost volume seller"), then the measure of damages is:

> **The profit** ((including reasonable overhead) which the Seller would have made from full performance by the Buyer)
> + **Any incidental damages provided in this Article** (§2-710)
>   + **Due allowance for costs reasonably incurred**
> + **Due credit for payments or proceeds of resale**

§2-709: Action for the Price:

(1) <u>Buyer Fails to Pay</u>: When the Buyer fails to pay the price as it becomes due, the Seller may recover the following (+ any incidental damages under §2-710):

    (a) **Accepted/Destroyed Goods:**

        1. <u>Accepted Goods</u> - The price of the goods

        2. <u>Destroyed Goods</u> - The price of the goods, if:

           a. The goods were conforming goods,

      and b. The goods were destroyed within a commercially reasonable time after risk of loss has passed to the Buyer

  and (b) **Identified Goods:** The price of goods identified to the contract if:

        1. The Seller is unable after *reasonable effort* to resell the goods at a reasonable price

    or 2. The circumstances reasonably indicate that such effort will be unavailing

(2) <u>Seller's Requirements With Respect to Identified Goods</u>:

    a. Seller must hold goods which have been identified to the contract for the Buyer if:

        1. The Seller is suing the Buyer for their price

    and 2. The goods are still in the Seller's control

    b. <u>Resale</u>: If resale becomes possible, the Seller may resell the goods at any time before the judgment (price) is collected.

    c. <u>Buyer's Rights</u>:

        1. The net proceeds of any such resale must be credited to the Buyer.

        2. Payment of the judgment entitles the Buyer to any goods not resold.

(3) Even if a Seller is not entitled to the price (under §2-709) he may be awarded <u>damages for non-acceptance</u> (under §2-708) if the Buyer:

    a. Wrongfully rejected the goods

  or b. Wrongfully revoked acceptance of the goods

  or c. Has failed to make a payment due

  or d. Has repudiated (as per §2-610)

§2-710: Seller's Incidental Damages:

Incidental damages to an aggrieved Seller include any *commercially reasonable* <u>charges</u>, <u>expenses</u> or <u>commissions</u>:

    1. Incurred in stopping delivery

  or 2. Incurred in the transportation, care and custody of goods <u>after</u> the Buyer's breach

  or 3. Incurred in connection with <u>return</u> or <u>resale</u> of the goods

  or 4. Otherwise resulting from the breach

§2-711: Buyer's Remedies in General; Buyer's Security Interest in Rejected Goods:

Even though the Seller breached, the Buyer may be barred from using these remedies if:
a. The Seller properly tendered goods (as per §2-508)
and b. No delay was involved

(1) <u>Buyer's Remedies Permitting the Recovery of Money Damages</u>:
    a. The Buyer is entitled to §2-711 remedies when:
        1. The Seller fails to make delivery
     or 2. The Seller repudiates
     or 3. The Buyer rightfully rejects
     or 4. The Buyer justifiably revokes acceptance
    b. See §2-714 for remedies available to a Buyer if the goods were finally accepted.
    c. The §2-711 remedies apply with respect to:
        1. Any goods involved
    and 2. The whole contract (if the breach goes to the whole contract (see 2-612))
    d. **Buyer's Remedies** - The Buyer may:
        1. Cancel the contract
    and 2. Recover as much of the price as he has paid (whether or not he has canceled the contract)
    and 3. *Either:*
        (a) *"Cover"* and recover damages under §2-712 as to all the goods affected (whether or not they have been identified to the contract)
      or (b) Recover damages for non-delivery under §2-713.

(2) <u>Additional Remedies Which Permit Reaching the Goods Themselves</u>:
    a. Remedies - The Buyer may:
        (a) Recover the goods under §2-502 if the goods have been identified
     or (b) In a proper case obtain <u>specific performance</u> or <u>replevy</u> the goods as per §2-716
    b. These additional remedies apply when:
        1. The Seller fails to deliver
     or 2. The Seller repudiates

(3) <u>The Buyer's Security Interest In The Goods</u>:
- a. The Buyer has a Security Interest in goods which are *in his possession or control* in the amount of:
  - 1. That part of the price already paid by the Buyer
  - or 2. Any expenses reasonably incurred in **inspection, receipt, transportation, care** and **custody** of the goods
- b. The Buyer may hold and resell (§2-706) such goods.
- c. This subsection applies if:
  - 1. The Buyer <u>rightfully rejected</u> the goods
  - or 2. The Buyer <u>justifiably revoked</u> acceptance of the goods

§2-712: "Cover"; Buyer's Procurement of Substitute Goods:

(1) **"Covering"**:
- a. After a breach (within §2-711) the Buyer may "cover" by:
  - 1. Making any *reasonable purchase* of goods to substitute those due from the Seller
  - or 2. Contracting to purchase such goods
- b. <u>Requirements</u> - "Covering" must be done:
  - 1. In good faith
  - and 2. Without unreasonable delay
- c. <u>Note</u>: It is immaterial that hindsight may later prove that the method of cover used was not the cheapest or most effective.

(2) The Buyer may recover from the Seller the following as damages:

> **The cost of cover**
> - **The contract price**
> + **Any incidental or consequential damages** (as defined in §2-715)
> - **Expenses saved in consequence of the Seller's breach**

(3) Failure of the Buyer to cover within §2-712 does not bar the Buyer from any other remedy. (<u>Note</u>: Cover is not a mandatory remedy for the Buyer. The Buyer is always free to choose between cover and damages for non-delivery under **§2-713**.)

(Note: This subsection must be read in conjunction with §2-715. Moreover, the operation of §2-716 must be considered in this connection for availability of the goods to the particular Buyer for his particular needs is the test for that remedy and inability to cover is made an express condition to the right of the Buyer to replevy the goods.)

§2-713: Buyer's Damages for Non-Delivery or Repudiation:

This section applies only when and to the extent that the Buyer has not covered.

(1) <u>Calculation of Damages</u> (Subject to §2-723) - The measure of damages for non-delivery or repudiation by the Seller is:

> **The market price** (using the **market** in which the Buyer would have obtained cover and the **price** for goods of the same kind and in the same branch of trade) **at the time when the Buyer learned of the breach**
> - **The contract price**
> + **Any incidental or consequential damages** (as defined in §2-715)
> - **Any expenses saved in consequence of the Seller's breach**

(2) "<u>Market Price</u>" - The place where market price is to be determined is:
> a. The place for tender (if the goods never reached their destination)
> b. The place of arrival (if the goods are rejected or their acceptance is revoked after reaching their destination)

§2-714: Buyer's Damages for Breach in Regard to Accepted Goods:

(1) **Remedy:** The Buyer is permitted to recover his loss in *any reasonable manner* if:
- a. There is any non-conformity of tender (not only breaches of warranties but also any failure of the Seller to perform according to his obligations under the contract)
- and b. The loss resulted from the ordinary course of events from the Seller's breach
- and c. The goods have been accepted
- and d. The time for revocation of acceptance has gone by
- and e. The Buyer gave notification (as per §2-607(3))

(2) **Damages for Breach of Warranty:**
- a. <u>Measure</u>: Damages for breach of Warranty equal:

  The value of the goods accepted at the time and place of acceptance

  − The value they would have had if they had been as warranted

- b. <u>Exception</u>: When special circumstances show proximate damages of a different amount.

(3) **Incidental and Consequential Damages:** In a proper case any incidental and consequential damages under §2-715 may also be recovered.

§2-715: Buyer's Incidental and Consequential Damages:

(1) **Incidental Damages:** Reimbursement for the Buyer's incidental damages resulting from the Seller's breach include:
- a. <u>Expenses for Rejected Goods</u>: Expenses reasonably incurred in **inspection, receipt, transportation, care** and **custody** of goods rightfully rejected
- and b. <u>Expenses for Covering</u>: Any commercially reasonable **charges, expenses** or **commissions** in connection with covering
- and c. <u>Expenses for Delay or Breach</u>: Any other reasonable expense incident to the delay or other breach

(2) **Consequential Damages:** Consequential damages resulting from the Seller's breach include:
    (a) <u>Loss</u>: Any loss resulting from "general" or "particular" requirements:
        1. Conditions:
            a. The Seller had reason to know of the need for the requirement at the time of contracting
        and b. The Buyer could not reasonably have prevented such losses by covering or otherwise
        2. Note:
            a. "Particular" needs of the Buyer must generally be made known to the Seller.
            b. "General" needs must rarely be made known to charge the Seller with knowledge.
   and (b) <u>Injury</u>: Injury to person or property proximately resulting from any breach of warranty

§2-716: Buyer's Right to Specific Performance or Replevin:

(1) <u>Availability</u>: Specific performance may be decreed where:
    a. The goods are *unique* (The test is made in terms of the total situation which characterizes the contract, e.g., output and requirement contracts involving a particular or peculiarly available source or market)
  or b. *In other proper circumstances* (<u>Note</u>: Inability to cover is evidence of "other proper circumstances")

(2) <u>Terms of Specific Performance</u>: The decree for specific performance may specify terms and conditions relating to:
    a. Payment of the price
  or b. Payment of damages
  or c. Other relief as the court may deem just

(3) <u>Replevin</u>: The Buyer has a right of replevin in cases in which:
    a. Goods have been identified to the contract
  and b. *Either:*
        1. Cover is not reasonably available
    or 2. The circumstances reasonably indicate that an effort to cover will be unavailing
    or 3. The goods have been shipped under reservation (i.e. the Seller shipped the goods while retaining a Security Interest in them (as per §2-505)) and the Security Interest in the goods has been satisfied or tendered.

§2-717: Deduction of Damages from the Price:

a. The Buyer is permitted to deduct all or any part of the resulting damages from any part of the contract price still due if:
    1. The Seller breaches
  and 2. The Buyer gives notice of his intention to deduct all or part of the price

b. There is no formality of notice, and any language which reasonably indicates the Buyer's reason for holding up his payment is enough.

§2-718: Liquidation or Limitation of Damages; Restitution:

(1) **Liquidated Damages Clauses:**
    a. In an agreement, liquidated damage clauses for breach by either party are allowed.
    b. <u>Requirement</u> - The amount involved has to be reasonable in the light of:
        1. The anticipated or actual harm caused by the breach
      and 2. The difficulties of proof of loss
      and 3. The inconvenience or non-feasibility of adequate compensation with another remedy
    c. A term fixing unreasonably large liquidated damages is considered a *"penalty"* and is void.

(2) **Restitution of Buyer's Payments:** Where the Seller justifiably withholds delivery of goods because of the Buyer's breach, the Buyer may recover restitution in an amount equal to:
    (a) <u>Liquidated Damages</u>:

        Buyer's Payments

        - What the Seller is entitled to (in accordance with subsection (1))

  or (b) If there are no liquidated damages clauses in the agreement for the Seller's damages, *the lower of*:
      1. $500
    or 2. **Buyer's Payments - 20% of the value of the total performance** (for which the Buyer is obligated under the contract)

(3) **Reduction of Buyer's Restitution:** The Buyer's right to recover under subsection (2) may be reduced by the amount the Seller establishes:
    (a) A right to recover damages under Article 2 other than §2-718(1)
    or (b) The amount or value of any benefits the Buyer received by reason of the contract (directly or indirectly)

(4) **"Buyer's Payments":** For purposes of subsection (2), the "Buyer's payments" includes:
    a. The reasonable value of goods received by the Seller as payment (in part performance)
    or b. The proceeds of their resale (provided the Seller does not have notice of the Buyer's breach before reselling the goods; if so, his resale is subject to the conditions in §2-706)

§2-719: Contractual Modification or Limitation of Remedy:

(1) **Contractual Remedy Clauses:** Subject to §2-719(2),(3) and §2-718, the contract may include other remedies:
    (a) <u>These remedies include</u>:
        1. Remedies in addition to Article 2 remedies
        or 2. Remedies in substitution for Article 2 remedies
        or 3. Changes/limitations on the measure of damages recoverable under Article 2, such as limiting the Buyer's remedies to:
            a. Return of the goods and repayment of the price
            b. Repair and replacement of non-conforming goods or parts
    (b) <u>Effect on Other Remedies</u>:
        1. These types of remedy clauses are optional rather than exclusive.
        2. If the parties intend a clause to be the sole contract remedy, this must be clearly expressed.

(2) **Failure of §2-719 Remedies** - The general Article 2 remedies will apply where an exclusive or limited remedy clause *either:*
    a. Fails in its essential purpose because of the circumstances
    or b. Operates to deprive either party of the substantial value of the bargain (see official comment)

(3) Limitation of Consequential Damages:
- a. Consequential damages may be limited or excluded *unless* the limitation or exclusion is unconscionable.
- b. *Consumer Damages:* Limitation of consequential damages for injury to the person in the case of consumer goods is considered *prima facie* unconscionable.
- c. *Commercial Damages:* Limitation of damages where the loss is commercial is not considered *prima facie* unconscionable.

§2-720: Effect of "Cancellation" or "Rescission" on Claims for A Prior Breach:

"Cancellation" or **"Rescission"** of the contract (or similar expressions) shall not be considered a renunciation or discharge of any claim in damages for a prior breach, *unless* the cancellation of the contract expressly declares that it discharges any rights.

§2-721: Remedies for Fraud:

- a. Remedies for Material Misrepresentation or Fraud include all Article 2 remedies available for non-fraudulent breach.
- b. The following do not bar other remedies or damages *unless* the circumstances of the case make the remedies incompatible:
    - 1. Rescission (or a claim for rescission) of the contract for fraud
    - 2. Rejection (or return) of the goods

§2-722: Who Can Sue Third Parties for Injury to Goods:

A third party can be sued if:
1. The third party causes injury to a party to a contract for sale
and 2. The third party was dealing with goods which have been
identified to the contract

(a) <u>Right to Sue Third Party</u>: Either party to the contract for sale has a
   right to sue a third party if it:
   1. Has title to the goods
   or 2. Has a security interest in the goods
   or 3. Has a special property interest
   or 4. Has an insurable interest in the goods
   or 5. *If the goods have been destroyed or converted*, and the party
      Either:
         a. Bore the risk of loss under the contract for sale
      or b. Has assumed the other party's risk since the injury

(b) The party plaintiff acts as a *fiduciary* for the other party of the
   contract in his suit or settlement (subject to his own interest), if:
   1. The party plaintiff did not bear the other party's risk at the
      time of the injury
   and 2. There is no arrangement between them as to dividing the
      recovery

(c) Either party may sue for any other concerned party's benefit if he
   receives consent to do so.

§2-723: Proof of Market Price: Time and Place:

(1) **Trial Before Performance Time:** If an Anticipatory Repudiation case
   comes to trial before the time for performance (with respect to some or
   all of the goods), the market price used for those goods (for purposes
   of §2-708 or §2-713 damages) is the price of those goods <u>at the time
   the aggrieved party learned of the repudiation</u>.

(2) **Market Price Not Readily Available:** When a market price is not readily available, the court may receive evidence of prices current in other comparable markets or at other times comparable to the one in question:

    a. *Substitute for price prevailing at a particular time* - The price prevailing within any reasonable time before or after the time described.

    b. *Substitute for price prevailing at a particular place* - The price prevailing at any other place which in commercial judgment or under usage of trade would as a *reasonable substitute*, accounting for the cost of transporting the goods to or from that place.

(3) **Evidence of Price:**

    a. A party may offer evidence as to a relevant price prevailing at a time or place other than the one described in this Article only if he has given the other party notice (to prevent unfair surprise).

    b. The court uses its discretion to determine whether such evidence is admissible.

§2-724: Admissibility of Market Quotations:

1. **Admissibility:** Market quotations are admissible when the price or value of goods regularly traded in any *established market* is in issue.

2. **Sources of Quotations** - These market quotes may be obtained from:

    a. Reports in official publications or trade journals

  or b. Reports in newspapers or periodicals of general circulation published as market reports

3. **Challenges Against the Quotations:** The circumstances of the preparation of the reports may be shown in order to affect their weight as evidence, but not their admissibility.

§2-725: Statute of Limitations in Contracts for Sale:

(1) **Uniform Statute of Limitations in Contracts for Sale:**
   a. Actions must be commenced within <u>4 years</u> after the cause of action has accrued.
   b. The parties may change the period of limitation in their original contract:
      1. The parties may reduce the period to a minimum of <u>1 year</u>.
      2. The parties may not, however, extend the 4 year period.

(2) **Time of Accrual of Cause of Action:**
   a. A cause of action is considered to have *accrued* <u>when the breach occurs</u> (regardless of whether or not the aggrieved party knew of the breach).
   b. A breach of warranty occurs <u>when tender of delivery is made</u>.
   c. A breach of a warranty of future performance of the goods occurs <u>when the breach is or should have been discovered</u>.

(3) **Saving Provision Allowing an Additional 6 Months for New Actions:**
   a. If an action was commenced within the subsection (1) limitation but is then terminated leaving a remedy still available for the same breach, a new action may be commenced:
      1. After the expiration of the time limited (as per 2-725(1))
      but 2. Within <u>6 months</u> after the termination of the first action
   b. <u>Exception</u> - If the termination resulted from:
      1. Voluntary discontinuance
      or 2. Dismissal for failure or neglect to prosecute

(4) This Section does not:
   a. Alter or modify the law on *tolling* of the Statute of Limitations
   b. Apply to causes of action which accrued before this Act became effective

ARTICLE 5

5-108: Issuer's Rights and Obligations:

a) Issuing Bank's Obligations:

1) **When Issuer Must Honor**: An Issuer Bank shall honor a Presentation only it appears to comply with the terms of the Letter of Credit (as determined by t "Standard Practice" referred to in §5-108(e)).

2) **When Issuer Does Not Have to Honor**:
   i) <u>Fraud Exception</u> The Bank does not have to comply if there is eviden of Fraud (as per §5-109).

3) <u>Non-Compliance</u>: An Issuer shall Dishonor a Presentation that does not comply with the Letter of Credit, *unless*:
   a) The Applicant otherwise directs the Issuer
   b) Otherwise provided where there is a Transfer by Operation of Law (as per §5-113).

b) Time Limits:

1) <u>Time Limit</u>: An Issuer must honor, accept, or notify, by the earlier of
   i) A *Reasonable Time*
   ii) <u>7 Business Days</u> after receiving documents (upon Presentation)

2) <u>Application of Time Limit</u>: The above time limit applies to the following:
   i) *Honoring an L/C*
   ii) *Accepting a Draft*, (or incurring a "deferred obligation") - if the L/C provide for the L/C to be completed more than 7 Business Days after Presentation.
   iii) *Give Notice* to the Presenter - of any discrepancies in the Presentati

c) Failure to Give Notice of Discrepancies - If the Issuer fails to timely notify the Presenter of a discrepancy, the Issuer may not use such discrepancy as a basis Dishonoring the L/C (except as provided in §5-108(d)).

d) Failure to Give Notice of Fraud - Even if the Issuer fails to timely notify the Presenter of a discrepancy (as per §5-108(b)) or that there may be <u>Fraud</u>, <u>Forgery</u>, that the L/C has <u>expired</u>, the Issuer may still assert Expiration or Fraud and Forgery (as per §5-109(a)) as a basis for dishonor.

Issuer's Standard of Practice -
1. <u>Standard of Care</u> - An Issuer shall observe *Standard Practice of Financial Institutions* that regularly issue Letters of Credit.
2. Whether an Issuer has met this standard is an issued to be determined by the court (and not a jury).
3. The court shall allow the parties a reasonable opportunity to present evidence of the "standard practice".

Independent Significance: An Issuer is not responsible for:
(1) <u>The Underlying Contract</u> - the performance or nonperformance of the underlying contract
(2) An act or omission of others
(3) <u>Trade Terms</u> - Observance or knowledge of usage of a particular trade (unless should know under "Standard Practice" as determined in §5-108(e) above)

Nondocumentary Conditions - The Issuer shall <u>ignore</u> any conditions in an Undertaking (constituting an L/C under §5-102(a)(10)) which are <u>Nondocumentary conditions</u> (ex: conditions to payment which are not evidenced by documents to be presented to Issuer

Dishonor - If an Issuer has Dishonored an L/C, it shall do the following:
   1) Return the documents
or 2) *Both*;
         a) Hold the documents (at the disposal of the Presenter)
      and b) Send the Presenter notice that such documents are being held by the Issuer

Issuer's Rights - After appropriately honoring an L/C, the Issuer will have the following rights:
(1) <u>Reimbursement</u> - the Issuer is entitled to Reimbursement by the Applicant n later than the <u>date of Issuer's Payment</u> of the L/C.
(2) <u>Free & Clear Documents</u> - the Issuer takes the documents free any claims from the:
         i) Beneficiary
         ii) Presenter
(3) <u>Limited Right of Recourse</u> - the Issuer may not assert a right of recourse against the Drawer or Indorser of a Draft (under §3-414 or §3-415)

(4) <u>No Restitution for Mistake</u> - the Issuer will be precluded from obtaining restitution for money paid (or value given) by Mistake:
    a) *To the Extent* the Mistake concerns
        i) Discrepancies in the documents (which the Issuer should have spotted)
        ii) Discrepancies in Tender (which was apparent on the face of the documents presented)
    b) Unless otherwise provided for in Warranties (§5-110) or with Subrogation Rights (arising under §5-177).

(5) <u>Discharge</u> - The Issuer will be discharged of its obligations to the Applicant *to the extent* of its performance under the L/C *unless* the Issuer honored a presentation with a forged signature of a Beneficiary required to sign a presented document.

§5-109: Fraud or Forgery:

a) Fraudulent Presentation -
    i) <u>Scope:</u> The following rules apply if
        a) a document that is presented appears to comply, on its face, to the L/C
    and b) *Either*:
        1) A required document is <u>Forged</u> or <u>Materially Fraudulent</u>
        2) Honor of the Presentation would facilitate a Material Fraud by the Beneficiary (hurting the Issuer or Applicant):

    ii) <u>Rules of Honoring with Forged/Fraudulent Documents:</u>
        (1) **Protected Beneficiaries:** The Issuer shall <u>Honor</u> the presentation if Honor is demanded by:
        or (i) A <u>Nominated Person</u> if:
            a. It was given <u>Value</u>
          and b. In <u>Good Faith</u>
          and c. <u>Without Notice</u> of Forgery
        or (ii) A <u>Confirmer</u> - who has honored its confirmation in Good Faith
        or (iii) A <u>Holder in Due Course</u> if:
            1. It is the Holder of a Draft drawn under the L/C
          and 2. The draft was taken *After* Acceptance by the Issuer (or Nominated Party)

or (iv) An <u>Assignee</u> of the Issuer's or Nominated Person's <u>Deferred Obligation</u> (as per §5-108(b)(2)) if:

1. It was taken for <u>Value</u>

and 2. <u>Without Notice</u> of Forgery

and 3. *After* the Obligation was incurred by the Issuer (or Nominated Person)

and (2) **Issuer's Discretion-** the Issuer may honor or dishonor the presentation while acting in <u>Good Faith</u>.

Injunctions:

The court may <u>not</u> temporarily or permanently enjoin the Issuer from Honoring a Presentation (or it may grant similar relief against the Issuer or other persons) <u>unless</u> the court finds that:

(1) <u>Applicable Law Allows Relief</u>: The relief is <u>not prohibited</u> under the law applicable to the Accepted Draft or Deferred Obligation.

and (2) <u>Adequate Protection</u>: The Beneficiary, Issuer, or Nominated Person (who may be adversely affected by the injunction) is *adequately protected* against any loss it may incur as a result of the relief.

and (3) <u>State Law Satisfied</u>: All the requirements for the particular relief under state law have been met.

and (4) <u>Applicant Likely to Succeed</u>:

1. The Applicant is *more likely than not* to succeed under its claim of forgery or material Fraud

and 2. The person demanding honor doesn't qualify for protection under §5-109(a)(1).

and 5) An Applicant claims that a Required Document:

a. Is Forged

or b. Is Materially Forged

or c. Would facilitate a Material Fraud by the Beneficiary (hurting the Issuer or Applicant).

292

ARTICLE 7

§7-303: Diversion; Reconsignment; Change of Instruction:

(1) **Instructions Carrier May Obey:**
    i) The carrier may deliver the goods to a person or destination other than that stated in the Bill of Lading (**"BOL"**) (or may otherwise dispose of the goods) on instructions from *either*:
        (a) The holder of a Negotiable BOL
    or (b) The Consignor (on a Non-negotiable BOL) - regardless of what the Consignee says
    or (c) The Consignee (on a Non-negotiable BOL) *unless*:
        1. The consignor's instructions contradict instructions by the consignee
       or 2. The goods have already arrived at the billed destination
       or 3. The Consignee is in possession of the BOL
    or (d) The Consignee (on a Non-negotiable BOL) - if he is entitled to dispose of the goods against the consignor.
    ii) This section applies unless the BOL otherwise provides

(2) <u>Negotiated Bill:</u> A person to whom a BOL is *duly negotiated*, can hold the bailee according to the <u>original terms</u> of the BOL, unless such instructions are noted in the Negotiable Bill, itself.

§7-309: Carrier's Duty of Care; Contractual Limitation on Carrier's Liability:

(1) **Negligence Standard:**
- a) A Carrier issuing a Bill of Lading must exercise the degree of care that a *reasonably careful man would under like circumstances:*
- b) This subsection doesn't limit a common carrier's liability for damages not caused by negligence, which any other laws may provide for.

(2) **Contractual Limitations on Damages:**
- a) Damages may be limited by a provision indicating the <u>maximum value</u> which the carrier will be liable for, only IF:
    - 1. There is No Set Limitation Filed, but the consignor is advised of an opportunity to declare a higher value (or a value as lawfully provided in the tariff)
    - 2. There is a Set Limitation Filed:
        - a) The Carrier's charge is dependent on the value (ie- the more "insurance" the carrier takes, the more he'll charge the consignor)
        - and b) The Consignor is given an opportunity to declare a higher value (or a value as lawfully provided in the tariff)

- b) A contract may not limit a carrier's liability for <u>Conversion</u> of the goods (for its own use)

(3) **Other Provisions:** The BOL may also contain *Reasonable* provisions indicating the <u>Time</u> and <u>Manner</u> of:
- a) Presenting claims based on the shipment
- or b) Instituting actions based on the shipment

§7-403: Obligations of Warehouseman or Carrier to Deliver:

(1) **Bailor's Defenses:** The <u>Bailee</u> must deliver the goods to the
person *entitled to* them under the Document of Title ("**DOT**") if:
    i) The person entitled to the documents complies with
       sections (2) and (3) (below)
and ii) <u>NO DEFENSES:</u> The Bailee Cannot establish the
       following defenses:
         (a) **Goods Already Delivered**: That the Bailee
            already delivered the goods to a person whose
            receipt was *Rightful* against the claimant
       or (b) **Bailee Not Liable:** That the bailee is not liable
            for any
              a) Damage to the goods
           or b) Delay
           or c) Loss
           or d) Destruction

Note for Some States: <u>Burden of Proof</u>: the person entitled to the Document has the
Burden to prove that the Bailee was <u>Negligent</u> in order to preclude the Bailee's liability
defenses.

       or (c) **Previous Sale or Disposition**: there was a
           previous sale or disposition of the goods,
           either
            1. In lawful enforcement of a lien
          or 2. On the Warehouseman's lawful
            termination of storage

       or (d) **Seller's Right to Stop Delivery:** That the Seller
           exercised his right to stop delivery (as per §2-705)

       or (e) **Disposition:** Pursuant to §7-303 (or a tariff relating to
           such right) there was *either:*
            1. A Diversion
          or 2. A Reconsignment
          or 3. Other Disposition

       or (f) **Personal Defense**: The Bailee had a <u>personal
           defense</u> against the claimant resulting from
           either:
            1. A Release
          or 2. A Satisfaction
          or 3. Any other fact affording a personal
             defense
       or (g) **Any Other Lawful Excuse**

(2) A person claiming goods covered by a DOT ("Claimant")
　　must Satisfy the Bailor's lien if:
　　　　a) The Bailee requests
　　or b) The Bailee is prohibited by law from delivering the
　　　　goods until the charges are paid.

(3) **Receipt of Delivery:**
　　　　a) Upon receipt of the goods, the claimant must surrender
　　　　the Documents of Title (or any other outstanding Negotiable
　　　　Documents covering the goods) so that the Bailee can:
　　　　　　1) *Cancel* the Document - if Complete Delivery is
　　　　　　made
　　　　or 2) *Conspicuously* note the quantity delivered, if
　　　　　　Partial Delivery is made
　　　　b) If the Bailee doesn't do this, he will be liable to whom
　　　　the note is duly negotiated
　　　　c) **Exception:** If the Claimant is a person against whom the
　　　　DOT offers No Right (as per §7-503(1))

(4) **"Person Entitled Under the Document"** - means, *either*
　　　　a) Negotiable Instrument - A HOLDER of a Negotiable
　　　　Instrument
　　or b) Non-Negotiable Instrument - A Person to whom delivery
　　　　is to be made, pursuant to *Written* instructions with a
　　　　Non-Negotiable instrument.

§7-404: Not Liable for Good Faith Delivery:

1) A Bailee is not liable for misdelivering or disposing of goods
　　if he:
　　　　a) Had Good Faith
　　and b) Observed *Reasonable Commercial Standards*
　　and c) Delivered (or otherwise disposed of) goods according to the
　　　　terms of the Document of Title (or pursuant to Article 7)

2) **Scope:** This rule applies even though:
　　　　a) The person who gave the Bailee the goods had no
　　　　authority to *either:*
　　　　　　1. Acquire the Document
　　　　　　or 2. Dispose of the Goods
　　or b) The Person to whom the Bailee delivers the goods had no
　　　　authority to receive them.

§7-501: Due Negotiation:

(1) **Manner of Negotiation:**
    a) <u>Named Person:</u> A *Negotiable* Document of Title
        "running" to the order of a named person, can be
        negotiated *only* if:
        a) <u>Indorsement</u> - The identified person in the
            document Indoreses it
    and b) <u>Delivery</u> - The document is delivered into the
            possession of the holder
    b) <u>Bearer:</u> If the instrument is indorsed in blank (ie "to Bearer"
        or has a "blank indorsement"), it can be negotiated by *delivery*
        alone.

(2) <u>Delivery as Negotiation:</u>
    (a) A Negotiable Document of Title may also negotiated by
        <u>Delivery alone</u> if it "runs" to bearer (by its original terms).
    (b) A Document of Title will be considered as if it had been
        negotiated if it is delivered to the *identified person*.

(3) <u>Special Indorsement:</u> If a negotiable DOT has been indorsed
    to an identified person, the special indorsee must <u>Indorse</u>
    and <u>Deliver</u> it to negotiate it.

(4) **"Due Negotiation":** Requirements for a Negotiable Document
    of Title to be *"duly negotiated"* :
    a) It is Negotiated (in the manner stated above in this section) to a
        Holder (as per §1-201(20))
    and b) The Holder takes by ***Purchase*** (as per §1-201(32))
    and c) It is Purchased:
        1. In **Good Faith** (as per §1-201(19))
        and 2. **Without any Notice** of another person's claims or
            defenses against the document
        and 3. For **Value** (as per §1-201(44))
        and 4. In the *Regular Course of Business or financing* (ie-
            from a merchant)
    and d) It does NOT involve receiving the document in
        settlement or payment of a money obligation.

(5) **Non-Negotiable Documents:** Indorsement of a Non-Negotiable
    Document neither makes it negotiable nor adds to the
    transferee's rights

(6) **Naming Person to Notify upon Arrival:** The naming of a
    person (in a negotiable DOT) to be notified when goods
    (represented by the DOT) arrive <u>does not</u>:
    a) Limit the negotiability of the bill
    nor b) Constitute notice to a purchaser of the bill the named
        person has any interest in the goods.

§7-502: Rights Acquired by Due Negotiation:

(1) **Rights by Due negotiation:** A person acquires the following
   rights if a Negotiable Document has been *Duly Negotiated*
   to him (subject to §7-205 and §2-703):
   - (a) Title to the Documents
   - and (b) Title to the Goods
   - and (c) All rights accruing under the law of agency and
     estoppel (including rights to goods delivered to the bailee after the
     document was issued)
   - and (d) 1. The Direct Obligation of the *Issuer* to <u>Hold</u> or
     <u>Deliver</u> the Goods according to the terms of the
     Document <u>FREE of any defense or claim by the</u>
     <u>issuer</u> (except those arising under the terms of the Document or
     Under Article 7)
     - 2. <u>Delivery Order Cases:</u> The Bailee's Obligation
       accrues only when
       - a) The Bailee accepts its obligation
       - and b) The obligation acquired by the holder is that
         the <u>Issuer</u> (and any indorser) will procure the
         acceptance of the Bailee

(2) **Title and Rights** (subject to §7-503)
   - a) Title and rights acquired by negotiation will not be
     defeated by
     - 1) Any stoppage (of the goods represented by the document)
     - or 2) By surrender of the goods by the Bailee
   - b) Title and rights acquired by negotiation will not be
     impaired, even if
     - 1) Negotiation (or any prior negotiation) constituted a
       breach of duty
     - 2) Any person has been deprived of possession of the
       document by:
       - a) Misrepresentation
       - or b) Fraud
       - or c) Accident
       - or d) Mistake
       - or e) Duress
       - or f) Loss
       - or g) Theft
       - or h) Conversion
     - 3) A Previous sale (or other transfer of the goods or document)
       has made a third person.

§7-503: Defeated Documents of Title:

(1) <u>Interests before Issuance:</u> A DOT confers no right in goods against a person who:

> (a) Didn't delivered or entrust such goods (or DOT covering them) to a merchant (as per §2-403)

and (b) Didn't acquiesce title in the procurement by the Bailor (or his nominee) of any DOT

and (c) Had a legal or perfected S/I in the goods *before* the Document was issued

(2) <u>Unaccepted Delivery Orders:</u>

> a) Title to goods based upon an *unaccepted delivery order* is subject to the rights of anyone to whom a Negotiable warehouse receipt or BOL (covering such goods) has been *Duly Negotiated*.

> b) Such a title may be defeated under §7-504 to the same extent as the rights of the Issuer or a Transferee from the Issuer.

(3) <u>BOL issued to a Freight Forwarder</u>

> a) Title to goods based on a BOL issued to a Freight Forwarder is subject to the rights of anyone to whom a bill issued to the Freight Forwarder is *Duly Negotiated*

> b) Delivery by the carrier (in accordance with Part 4 of Article 7) pursuant to its own BOL, discharges the carrier's obligation to deliver.

GLOSSARY

"Anticipatory Repudiation" (§2-610) - Anticipatory Repudiation occurs when:
    a. Either party repudiates the contract (see §2-609)
  and b. The repudiated portion of the contract is not yet due
  and c. The loss of such performance will *substantially impair* the value of the contract

"Between Merchants" (§2-104(3)) This term refers to any transaction where both parties are deemed to have the *knowledge* and *skill* of merchants.

"Buyer" - a person who buys or contracts to buy goods (§2-103(a))

"Buyer In The Ordinary Course Of Business" (§1-201(9)) - A "Buyer In The Ordinary Course" ("BIOC") is a Person/Organization (not a Pawnbroker) who buys goods:
    a) In Good-Faith (see §1-201(19))
  and b) Without knowledge that purchase is in violation of someone else's other ownership rights or S/I
  and c) From a 'Merchant' - someone in the business of selling *those* goods (except a pawnbroker)
  and d) In the *Ordinary Course*- passing of title *for value* (ie- a <u>SALE</u>) in a typical transaction (ex: inventory, not equipment)
  and e) For **Value**

"Cancellation" (§2-106(4)) - "Cancellation" occurs when a party puts an end to the contract because of the <u>other party's breach</u>.

"C.I.F." (§3-320) - *"Cost, Insurance, Freight"* - means that the Price includes:
    1. The cost of the Goods
  and 2. The Insurance
  and 3. The Freight (to the named destination)

"C. & F." (§3-320) - *"Cost & Freight"* - means that the Price includes:
    1. The cost of the Goods
  and 2. The Freight (to the named destination)

"Commercial Unit" (§2-105(6)) - Something is considered a "Commercial Unit" if:
>1. It is a unit of goods which, by commercial usage, is a single whole (for purposes of sale)
>and 2. Division of such a unit would *materially impair* the character or value on the market or in use

"Confirmed Credit" (§3-325(3)) - means that the credit carries the direct obligation of a financing agency which does business in the Seller's financial market.

"Conforming to Contract" (§2-106(2)) Goods or conduct (including any part of performance) will be deemed to ***"conform to the contract"*** when they are in accordance with the obligations under the contract.

"Contract for Sale" (§2-106(1) includes both:
>1. A <u>Present Sale</u> of goods
>and 2. A contract to sell goods at a <u>Future Time</u>.

"Covering": (§2-712(1)) - A Buyer may "cover," and mitigate damages by buying substitute goods. After repudiation or breach (within §2-711) the Buyer may "cover" by:
>1. Making any *reasonable purchase* of goods to substitute those due from the Seller.
>or 2. Contracting to purchase such goods.

"EX-SHIP" (§3-322) means (unless otherwise agreed):
>a. That goods need not be delivered on a particular ship
>and b. Delivery will be made from a ship which has reached a place at the named port of destination (where goods of that kind are usually discharged).

"F.A.S. (vessel)" (§2-319(2)) - *"Free alongside"* - unless otherwise agreed, the term F.A.S. implies that the Seller has the following responsibilities:
>(a) Pay for and bear the risk of *either:*
>>1) Delivering the goods alongside the vessel (in the manner usual in that port)
>>or 2) Delivering the goods on a dock designated and provided by Buyer
>and (b) Obtain and Tender a receipt for the goods, in which the Carrier promises to issue a BOL

"Future Goods" (§2-105) - goods which are NOT *both* <u>Existing</u> and <u>Identified</u>
- a) Goods must be *both* **Existing** and **Identified** before any interest in them can pass.
- b) An alleged *"present sale"* of Future Goods (or any interest in them) is considered a contract To Sell.

"Financing Agency" (§2-104(2)) A Bank, Finance Company or other person who *either*:
- a. Makes advances against goods or documents of title, in the *Ordinary Course of Business*
- or b. Intervenes in the Ordinary Course (by arrangement with either the Seller or Buyer) to make or collect payment due or claimed under a contract for sale as by:
  - 1) Purchasing or paying the Seller's draft
  - or 2) Making advances against the Seller's draft
  - or 3) Taking the Seller's draft for collection (whether or not documents of title accompany the draft)
- or c. Similarly intervenes between Sellers and Buyers with respect to the goods (as per §2-707)

"Firm Offer" (§2-205) - an offer which:
- a. Is made by a <u>Merchant</u>
- and b. Is evidenced by a <u>Signed</u> Writing
- and c. By its terms, gives assurance that the offer will be held open
- and d. Is <u>not revocable</u> for lack of consideration.

"F.O.B." (§2-319(1)) - *"Free on Board"* the term F.O.B. implies the following :
- (a) <u>F.O.B.</u>(Place of Shipment):
  - The Seller has the following responsibilities:
    - 1. Deliver goods to their specified place of shipment (i.e. to the Carrier's possession) (as per §2-504)
    - and 2. Pay for the shipment
    - and 3. Bear the risk of putting the goods into the Carrier's possession
- (b) <u>F.O.B.</u>(Place of Destination):
  - The Seller has the following responsibilities:
    - 1. Pay for the transport of the goods to the specified place of destination
    - and 2. Bear the risk of transporting the goods to their specified destination
    - and 3. Tender delivery of the goods to the Buyer (as per §2-503)

(c) **F.O.B.**(Vessel, car, other vehicle) (either under (a) or (b)):
    1. <u>Seller's Responsibility</u>: The Seller has the following *additional* responsibilities:
        a. Pay for loading the goods on board
        b. Bear the risk of loading the goods on board
        c. Comply with §2-323 (regarding the form of the Bill of Lading)

"Goods" (§2-105) - all things which are *movable at the time they are identified to a contract.*

"Good Faith" (§1-201(19))
    a) "Good Faith" means <u>Honesty in Fact</u> in the Conduct or Transaction Concerned. (§1-201(19))
    b) *For a Merchant* - requires both (§2-103(b)):
        1. Honesty in fact
    and 2. The observance of *reasonable commercial standards* of fair dealing in the trade

"Installment Contract" (§2-612) - a contract which recognizes or authorizes the delivery of goods in <u>separate lots</u> to be <u>separately accepted</u> (even if the contract says that each delivery is considered a separate contract).

"Lot" (§2-105(5)) - a parcel or single article which is the subject matter of a separate sale or delivery (*whether or not it is sufficient to perform the contract*).

"Letter of Credit" (§3-325(3)) (or "banker's credit") - means (unless otherwise agreed) an irrevocable credit issued by a financing agency of good repute.

"Market Price" (§2-713(2)) - The place where market price is to be determined is:
        a. The place for tender (if the goods never reached their destination)
        b. The place of arrival (if the goods are rejected or their acceptance is revoked after reaching their destination)

"Merchant" (§2-104(1)) A person is considered a "Merchant" if he is *either:*
    a) <u>Dealer</u>: A person who *deals* with goods of the kind
  or b) <u>Expert</u>: A person who *either:*
        1) Holds himself out as having <u>*knowledge or skill*</u> peculiar to the type of goods involved in the transaction
      or 2) Employs an Agent, Broker, or other Intermediary who holds himself out as having such *knowledge* or *skill*

"Overseas" (§3-323)- an "overseas" contract or shipment is one:
    a) Involving shipment by <u>water</u> or <u>air</u>
  and b) That is subject to commercial, financial, or shipping practices characteristic of *international deep water commerce,* either by Usage of Trade or Agreement.

"Output Term" (§2-306(1)) a term which measures the quantity of the contract by the Seller's output (ie "Total Production" contract).

A **"Person in the position of a Seller"** (§2-707) includes:
    a. An agent who has paid or become responsible for the price of goods on behalf of his principal,
  or b. Anyone who otherwise holds a security interest or other right in goods similar to that of a Seller.

"Present Sale" (§2-106(1)) a sale which is accomplished by the making of the contact.

"Purchase" (§1-201(32)): A **"Purchase"** is any <u>*Voluntary Transaction*</u> creating an interest in property,
  <u>including a:</u>
    1. Sale (ie- involving a Buyer and Seller)
  or 2. Discount
  or 3. Negotiation
  or 4. Mortgage
  or 5. Pledge (ex: a Secured party)
  or 6. Lien (ex: a Secured party)
  or 7. Issue or Re-issue
  or 8. Gift (donee)

"Purchaser" (§1-201(33)) is a Person" who takes by *purchase"*
(ex: a buyer, a Security Interest holder,etc... (as per §1-201(32))

"Receipt" [of goods] - means taking <u>*Physical Possession*</u> (§2-103(c))

"Requirement Term" (§2-306(1)) a term which measures the quantity of the contract by the requirements of the Buyer (ie "Total Needs" contrcat).

"Sale" (§2-106(1)) a sale consists of the passing of title from the Seller to the Buyer for a price (as per §2-401).

"Signed" (§1-201(39)) - includes any Symbol executed or adopted by someone **intending** to *authenticate* a writing.

"Seller" - a person who sells or contracts to sell goods (§2-103(d))

"Termination" (§2-106(3)) - "Termination" occurs when either party puts an end to the contract - pursuant to a power created by the terms of the contract or an applicable law (ie - not because of a party's breach).

"Value" (§1-201(44))
1) A Person is deemed to give **"Value"** if he acquires his rights *either*:
   (a) In return for either:
      1. A Binding Commitment to **Extend Credit** (ex: L/C)
     or 2. An Extension of **Immediately Available Credit**
  or (b) A Security for total or partial **Satisfaction** of a pre-existing claim
   or (c) By accepting delivery pursuant to a pre-existing contract for purchase
   or (d) In return for any "sufficient" consideration

INDEX

(See also Shipping Terms)

FORMATION OF CONTRACT,
§2-204
(See also Contract)

FRUSTRATION OF PURPOSE,
§2-618
(See also Failure of
Presupposed Conditions)

GOOD FAITH
definition,
generally, §1-201(19)
merchant standard,
§2-103(1)(b)
implied in all contracts, §1-203

GOOD FAITH PURCHASER
from seller with voidable title,
§2-403(1)
of goods in transit, §2-403(2);
§7-502(2)
of negotiable bill, §7-502
precluding seller's right of
stoppage
in transit, §2-403(2); §7-502(2)

GOODS
acceptance of, (See Acceptance
of Goods)
as means of payment,
§2-304(1)
attached realty, §2-107
casualty to, §2-613
conforming to description or
sample, §2-313(1)(b),(c)
damaged, §2-613(b)
definition, §2-105(1)
disputed, §2-515
identification of, (See
Identification of Goods)
identified, §2-105(2)
insurable interest in, §2-501
nonconforming, (See
Nonconforming Goods)
nonexistent, §2-613(a);
§2-105(2)
price payable in, §2-304(1)
"receipt of" defined,
§2-103(1)(c)

rejection of, (See Rejection of
Goods)
security interest in, §2-501(2);
§2-711(3)
severed from realty, §2-107
shipment of to form contract,
§2-206(1)(b)
sold, secured creditor's rights
against, §2-702
special interest in, §2-501
substitute, §2-712(1)
suit against third party for
damage to, §2-722
unborn young of animals,
§2-105(1)

IDENTIFICATION OF GOODS
buyer's repudiation after,
§2-501(3)
definition, §2-501
method of, §2-501(1)
passing title, §2-401
prerequisite to capture,
§2-502(1); §2-711(2)(a)
requirement of, §2-105(2)
seller's interest pursuant to,
§2-501(2)
seller's repudiation after,
§2-711(2)(a)
seller's right of upon buyer's
breach, §2-704(1)(a)
substitution after, §2-501(2)
unfinished goods, §2-704(1)(b)

IMPLIED WARRANTY
(See Warranty, seller's)

IMPOSSIBILITY OF
PERFORMANCE
(See Failure of Presupposed
Conditions)

IMPROPER TENDER, CURE
OF
(See Cure)

INCIDENTAL DAMAGES
(See Damages)

INCONSISTENT TERMS,
§2-207

317